JUST
MINISTRY

PROFESSIONAL ETHICS FOR PASTORAL MINISTERS

RICHARD M. GULA, SS

Paulist Press
New York/Mahwah, NJ

Excerpts from Praesidium Inc. in chapter 6 are used with permission of Dr. Dangel, CEO, Praesidium Inc. (2007)

Cover and book design by Lynn Else

Library of Congress Cataloging-in-Publication Data

Gula, Richard M.
   Just ministry : professional ethics for pastoral ministers / Richard M. Gula.
      p. cm.
   Includes bibliographical references (p.   ) and index.
   ISBN 978-0-8091-4631-4 (alk. paper)
      1. Clergy—Professional ethics. 2. Catholic Church—Clergy—Professional ethics.
3. Pastoral care. 4. Pastoral theology—Catholic Church. I. Title.
      BV4011.5.G855 2010
      241′.641—dc22

                                                                    2009037241

Published by Paulist Press
997 Macarthur Boulevard
Mahwah, New Jersey 07430

www.paulistpress.com

Printed and bound in the
United States of America

CONTENTS

CONTENTS

Contents

CONTENTS

INTRODUCTION

This book on professional ethics is intended to serve as a resource for those already involved in ministry and for those in ministry training programs. I hope it will stimulate a new attitude among ministers to view themselves as professionals and to take seriously the responsibilities that come with this identity.

My first book on this topic was published in 1996 under the title *Ethics in Pastoral Ministry*. Since that time, signs of further interest in the topic are emerging. For example, seminaries and schools of theology have begun to incorporate a segment on professional ethics in the curriculum for training both clerical and lay ministers. Some dioceses have shown some interest in adopting codes of ethics for ministers. Moreover, the sexual abuse crisis has brought the professional ethics of ministers under closer scrutiny than ever before, and the public disclosure of ministerial misconduct has increased everyone's interest in professional ethics for all ministers, not just for priests and bishops. For some time I have wanted to take into account the many insights and new questions that I have garnered from the workshops and classes I have given around the country on this subject to nudge ministers closer to assuming a professional identity. This book attempts to serve that need.

Professional ethics in general enjoins common traits of character and standards of conduct, such as compassion, justice, and fidelity, as well as respect for the rights of others—their privacy, their property, their life—that bind everyone to form a stable society. However, professional ethics further specifies the traits that correspond to a particular role serving a human need and to the relationship formed in providing a service. So, for example, the priest is bound to confidentiality in the confessional but not in social relationships. Norms that prohibit sexual contact in a professional relationship do not apply in a marital relationship. Professional ethics has to do with the moral character of the one assuming a professional role and the sum of obligations that pertain to the practice of the profession.

The particular interest of this book is the professional ethics of the pastoral minister, whether ordained or lay. Pastoral ministers are professionals because we serve a basic human need—the need for salvation—that requires the exercise of expert knowledge and skill and good moral character. One requirement of being professional, often lacking in pastoral ministers, is the practice of accountability. Perhaps this reflection on professional ethics will stimulate more critical thinking on criteria for everyone in ministry and how to implement these ideas creatively. The sudden rise in interest in a "code of ethics" for ministers is a step in that direction, but more needs to be done.

In this book, I revisit the topics of my first book that have stimulated the most interest and have seemed to address many pastoral needs. But this book is new and stands on its own. While preserving the central themes of the first book, this one develops some of them further, recasts a few in a new context, and adds new material that ministerial groups have found useful for understanding better their professional identity and responsibilities.

My primary objective in this book is to offer a theological-ethical framework for reflecting on the moral responsibilities of pastoral ministers. I begin by looking at ministry as both a vocation and a profession. I use the same structure in chapters 1 and 2 in order to show that having a vocation and being professional are compatible; they need not be contrasted with one another. Chapters 3 and 4 are devoted to moral character. Chapter 3 draws upon insights from virtue ethics to describe the nature and importance of character; chapter 4 sketches the profile of a virtuous minister. Chapter 5 addresses the dynamics of power in pastoral ministry, since the right use of power is one of the most significant challenges of being a professional person. This chapter explores some of the more neuralgic issues about personal and social power in pastoral ministry. Chapters 6 through 8 examine particular moral issues: sexuality, confidentiality, and pastoral care. I close the book with an appendix featuring two "Statements of Ministerial Commitment" written by two of my students to fulfill an assignment in our course on professional ethics. These are not codes of ethics in a

Introduction

formal sense, though they are analogous to one. I offer them as a summary of the themes of this book and as a stimulus for others in pastoral ministry to develop their own statements.

I owe a great debt of thanks to many people in pastoral ministry who have helped me to focus and refine the position presented here. I am grateful to my students at the Franciscan School of Theology in the Graduate Theological Union in Berkeley, California, and to the many participants of my workshops in ministerial ethics who tested this approach and provided questions and examples that bring this material closer to home in the ministry. I am indebted to the Franciscan School of Theology for a sabbatical semester to complete this book and for my Sulpician community that supported me during this time. I am grateful to those who took the time to read parts of this manuscript along the way and made suggestions for its improvement. I especially want to single out two: my Sulpician colleague, Fr. Philip S. Keane, SS, and my friend Fr. Stephen C. Rowan, dean of the School of Arts and Sciences of the University of Portland, who read the completed work and offered many good suggestions to make the book clearer. The roll call of people whom I can thank for helping me bring this book to fruition can go on. They are more than I can name and they know who they are. Thanks to you all. This book could not be what it is without so much help.

1

MINISTRY AS VOCATION

Mary Jane has been working in the corporate world as director of human resources for the past ten years. Anyone who knows her would say with confidence that she has been successful. Her income is more than she needs; she is well received at all levels in the company; she received public recognition for outstanding service in managing delicate personnel issues during the company's recent merger. Her coworkers enjoy working with her since she has such an ease with sharing responsibilities and finding just the right task to match each person's talents. Many who work in the company say that they do not want the day to go by without having their paths cross, for Mary Jane is like a calm oasis in the midst of so much frenetic activity.

As Mary Jane continued to work for human resources and to be involved in her parish social outreach programs, she felt a growing sense of wholeness about herself as she was bringing her life into line with the drift of her deep desires. Her pastor commended her for her initiative and creative responses to local needs.

Working for the parish opened Mary Jane to a desire to learn more about the Catholic social justice tradition and to the possibility of assuming a full-time justice-oriented ministry. She had been doing some reading on her own and attended the occasional workshop sponsored by the diocese. She was an open and eager learner and began to put together her spiritual practices with her commitment to the social concerns of her company and of the church. Everything was coming together in a holistic way.

From her prayer life, together with the encouragement of her friends, Mary Jane began to feel a call to ministry in the church. The parish team has suggested to her that she consider combining her corporate skills in human resources with her ecclesial interest and become trained as a pastoral associate for one of the priestless parishes in the diocese. They think she has a vocation to such a ministry, but Mary Jane still wonders if it is right for her.

She didn't know if leaving her position with the company was a good idea right now, but the call to ministry was strong enough to free her to step into the unknown and begin a program in pastoral ministry at the nearby school of theology. Her dreams of marrying her best friend and serving as a minister in the church were beginning to grow together.

What can the story of Mary Jane tell us about "having a vocation"? Her story is a familiar one these days, as more and more talented laity are taking the initiative to be trained in theology and in pastoral skills so as to be of service to the church as lay ecclesial ministers. They are also bringing a "professional" style of serving from their positions in business, education, health care, and other service-oriented professions. This development fits well with the trend in the church to be more explicit about the professional aspects of ministry so as to improve the quality of our ministerial service.

However, some attempts to professionalize ministry have met with opposition. Sociological opposition comes from pastoral ministers who lack the necessary structures of accountability that foster oversight, characteristically symbolized in a code of ethics that represents the values and standards to which all are committed and that enforces self-regulation.[1] The theological opposition comes from the status of ministry as a vocation that resists structures and procedures of accountability.[2] As a "vocation," so the objection goes, pastoral ministry is such a unique kind of Christian life that it cannot be compared to other professions and so ought not to be subject to the same standards and expectations. To "professionalize" ministry would not only reduce it to style and function but also ignore its spiritual, transcendent dimension.

However, if we were to cut ministry loose from professional requirements, we would easily breed a sense of isolation, superiority, and, even worse, entitlement. Neglecting the professional aspects of ministry can open the way to all sorts of special pleading and of making excuses for substandard performance by saying, "I have a vocation from God; therefore, the expectations, standards, and responsibilities that belong to professionals do not apply to me." But we must resist the temptation to hide behind the status of a "religious vocation" to avoid fulfilling the sometimes heavy demands of moral character, duties, and responsibilities of the pastoral relationship that brings a professional dimension to our vocation. This chapter and the next presuppose that the status and function of ministers should not be in opposition to each other. The new relationship to Christ and the community that comes through ordination or ministerial installation or commissioning must be seen as one with a concomitant spirituality of putting on the mind of Christ to empty oneself in service and pastoral charity.

The practice of ministry has professional aspects that need not detract from our religious vocation. In fact, professionalizing the ministry can enhance it as a vocation. My goal for chapters 1 and 2 is to show that having a vocation is compatible with being professional. This chapter focuses on four traits of ministry as a vocation: to be called, to be gifted, to be of service, and to be chosen by the community.[3] Chapter 2 examines the professional aspects that correlate with each of these.

VOCATION

"What do you want to be when you grow up?" That question generally starts a conversation about seeking a vocation. In secular terms, we understand a vocation as a purpose in life that uses our gifts to serve a human need. Those of us in religious circles, however, know vocation from a spiritual perspective as "being called by God" for a special role in the church. The term *vocation* derives from the Latin *vocare* meaning "to call." This meaning helps us distinguish vocation from a job and a career. A job is the work we do to earn money to pay our bills and to enjoy the times when we are not working. A job defines us by economic success and security. A career turns a job into an occupation. For many, a career becomes the primary source of identity, self-esteem, and means of social recognition. A vocation, by contrast, is something we do out of an experience that God has blessed us with particular gifts. We often speak of this experience of blessing as an invitation, or calling, to serve in a particular way.

In the Catholic imagination, "Do you think you might have a vocation?" generally invites a response primarily in terms of the priesthood or religious life, even though marriage is also a vocation. But associating vocation with only these states in life is changing. *Lumen Gentium* (nos. 39, 40) of the Second Vatican Council has broadened our understanding of vocation to mean that everybody, in their own way, hears the call of Jesus to holiness, wholeness, fulfillment, and mission. Everyone has a vocation. That is, everyone is called to discipleship of Jesus and to participate in and to mediate the creative Spirit of God to bring about a better world. Since the Second Vatican Council, the United States Conference of Catholic Bishops (USCCB) has published three documents on lay ministry that reiterate this broader vision of vocation: *Called and Gifted* (1980),[4] *Called and Gifted for the Third Millennium* (1995),[5] and *Co-workers in the Vineyard of the Lord* (2005).[6]

This chapter focuses on the specific way of living out our call to discipleship as a minister in the church. I am using *ministry* here more inclusively than the call to the priesthood or to the religious life. This inclusive view of ministerial vocation has come about in large measure because of the emphasis given to the church as the whole people of God and not just the hierarchy, to the universal call to holiness, to the priority of the sacraments of initiation as the sacramental basis for having a responsible share in the threefold mission of Christ to teach, sanctify, and guide the community, and to the generally positive valuation of the role of the laity in the church. The church today has awakened to the Pauline vision of many gifts and different ways of serving the common good within the body of Christ (1 Cor 12:4–7).

We are experiencing today an unprecedented response from the laity, like Mary Jane in the opening scenario, to the call of their baptism and confirmation to serve the mission of the church to promote the reign of God in the world in ways other than as a cleric. Thus, we have many apostolates today that do not require ordination. Laypeople (canonically, anyone not in holy orders) are now being commissioned by the bishop or his delegate to serve on behalf of the diocese or parish as pastoral associates, parish life directors, heads of marriage tribunals, directors of religious education, directors of liturgy, directors of pastoral music, youth ministry leaders, school principals, presidents of colleges, chief executive officers (CEOs) of hospitals and charitable organizations, chaplains in hospitals, prisons, and on campuses. These services, now called "lay ecclesial ministries," involve commitments for which people are prepared by theological training, field supervision, apprenticeships, and other forms of instruction appropriate to the level of responsibility of the ministry assigned to them that make these ministries quite different from being an usher, a choir member, or an extraordinary minister of the Eucharist.[7] The qualifier *ecclesial* underscores their sharing in the mission of the church while being subject to the discernment, authorization, and supervision of the hierarchy. These are ministries because they participate in the threefold mission of Jesus to teach, sanctify, and guide the community.

In summary then, just as we no longer restrict "ministry" to the ordained, so we no longer restrict the meaning of having a "vocation" to ministry to the call to holy orders. Rather, we mean that one is responding to a gift of the Spirit in baptism and confirmation to share in the threefold mission of Jesus by serving the ecclesial community as one who has discerned and whose discernment has been affirmed by the community through the bishop or his delegates, who alone can authorize someone to function in the name of the church as an ecclesial minister. The 1999 report of the subcommittee on lay ministry for the National Conference of Catholic Bishops puts it this way:

> Some, whom we are naming lay ecclesial ministers, are called to a ministry within the Church as a further specification and application of what all laity are called and equipped to do. This group of laity can be distinguished from the general body of all the lay faithful, not by reason of merit or rank, but by reason of a call to service made possible by certain gifts of the Holy Spirit, by the generous response of the person, and by an act of authorizing and sending by the proper ecclesiastical authority (cf. Luke 10:1).[8]

This statement provides the minimal requirements for recognizing a vocation to ministry: one is called, gifted, commissioned to service, and authorized by the community. I explore each of these as pertaining to having a vocation to pastoral ministry.

CALLED

"I feel called to do this" is a common testimony of those aspiring to ministry. "What am I attracted to?" and "What draws me in a certain direction over time?" are foundational questions of vocational discernment. God invites us by evoking desires within us, but we still need to discern whether these desires are rooted in God. Feeling called is a start. It is a necessary but not a sufficient basis for a vocation to ministry in the church.

Having a sense of call or a strong feeling for ministry as Mary Jane does, for example, may prompt a process of discerning our particular call to ministry. This initial attraction shows how vocation is radically personal: God calls me. However, this aspiration alone is no guarantee of having a vocation to ministry. No one ought to be chosen for a ministerial role simply on the basis of his or her attraction to, desire for, or feeling the emotional tug of ministry. It takes time to sift through these attractions, desires, and feelings in order to get to the roots of our motivation and to the proper fit of ourselves with the ministerial role.

We can ground our understanding of vocation as "call" in the very way we understand what it means to be human, to be called to discipleship, and to live under the providence of God's love.

To Be Human

About what it means to be human, the Book of Genesis says that, in the beginning, God's animating breath or spirit has given us life. To be enlivened with the Divine Spirit is the fundamental gift of God's call. So in the most generic of senses, this spiritual dimension of being human is our capacity for vocation. With our human spirit imprinted with the Divine Spirit, we have a readymade inclination toward God. This makes us spiritual or transcendent at our very roots. God is calling us to live in response to the gift of divine love already stirring in our hearts.

The human spirit's inclination toward union with God is the divine invitation, or calling, to move beyond ourselves by reaching out to others in love. From the perspective of faith, then, all the roles we assume and the work we do, even as a director of human resources as Mary Jane was, bear a transcendent, religious dimension. Our whole life is marked by a response pointing beyond ourselves to the deeper mystery calling us to share in God's creative activity. So we fulfill our basic vocation as human persons by responding to God's love for us by loving God and loving our neighbor as we love ourselves.

To Be a Disciple

In light of this vocation to love and serve, we speak in faith of the distinctive vocation of the Christian as the call to be a disciple of Jesus signified by our baptism. We make our way of discipleship specific by discerning the path that appears to be God's personal call to us. The moral responsibilities of being a pastoral minister arise ultimately from the call of God to love in ways that reflect what being a disciple of Jesus demands of us in the practice of ministry. The call to ministry must be situated within this distinctively Christian vocation to follow Jesus as a disciple. The vocation to discipleship is primary and pervasive as long as one is a Christian. The call to ministry is secondary to discipleship as a specific expression of it. But the call to ministry should not be seen as coextensive with living out the call to discipleship. After all, some ministers retire from ministry and so no longer serve in that capacity but remain committed to discipleship; others serve as ministers for a limited period of time and then take on a different form of expressing their discipleship. The call to discipleship for a Christian is forever; the call to ministry may not be.

We can follow Jesus as a disciple only by virtue of God's loving us through the Spirit: "God's love has been poured into our hearts through the Holy Spirit that has been given to us" (Rom 5:5). Authentic discipleship reflects the freedom to accept God's offer of love but not to be enslaved by it. We can say "Yes" or "No." God creates us free. We can be loving or selfish. We can hand ourselves over to grace or to sin. To follow Jesus as a disciple in pastoral ministry presumes that we have said "Yes" to God's offer of love. We now seek to incarnate God's grace through our ministry.

To enter the way of discipleship is to respond to Jesus' invitation, "Come, follow me" (Matt 19:21). We commonly speak of following Jesus as the imitation of Christ. But we must be careful not to confuse imitation with mimicry. Mimicry replicates external behavior. It asks, "What would Jesus do?" in the twenty-first century, as if this could easily be inferred from what he said and did in the first century. Although well intentioned, this is the wrong question to open the way to authentic imitation. It too easily leads to another form of fundamentalism by wanting to copy Jesus point for point. It ignores the historically conditioned nature of Jesus and of the biblical texts that reveal him to us.

The way of discipleship cannot mean simply accepting literally every command of Jesus, nor can it mean reproducing the externals of his life and work as if he were a blueprint for our life today, or as if we were being invited to exercise nostalgia. Just as we would not want to say that authentic imitation requires that we be a carpenter, Jewish, male, and itinerant preacher, so we do not want to say that we must die at the hands of political and religious leaders because Jesus did, or that we ought to have no dealings with money because Jesus drove money changers from the Temple, or that we ought to relate to others without regard for appropriate boundaries because Jesus was not afraid to touch or to be touched by people like lepers, sinners, children, or women. Trying to transport the practices of Jesus into our own day is anachronistic and reductive. It opens the way to misplaced and inappropriate behaviors. Mimicry is the death of faithful, creative discipleship.

The way of discipleship today is to make Jesus' way of life our own, not point for point as a mimic would, but to live in his spirit by means of the Spirit. So rather than asking, "What would Jesus do?" we ought to ask, "How can we be as free and as faithful to God in our day as Jesus was in his?" This question does not lead to deducing by strict logic faithful behavior from a command or deed of Jesus. Rather, we can let our imaginations be stirred by his story and the demands of our own ministry so that our character and actions might harmonize with his by analogy in the new situation of ministry today.

A collage of gospel stories gives us a picture of what the spirit of Jesus is like and who we might become in imitation of him. One poignant story for ministers, for example, is the scene in Matthew's Gospel in which Jesus instructs his disciples to avoid all known techniques that would secure positions of superiority in their religious and social community. They were not to use religious dress (to broaden their phylacteries or to lengthen their tassels) in order to attract attention. Nor were they to take the reserved seats in religious assemblies that symbolized superior roles in the community. They were not to use titles, such as "rabbi," "father," or "master," that require others to recognize a superior status (Matt 23:5–10). In short, they were not to dominate in the name of service. The way of Jesus is the way of "servant leadership"—leading without lording it over others, and inviting people to change without forcing them to think the way he did. He did not have to abuse his power to influence change. Rather, he knew that whatever power he had was rooted in God. He expressed this power of divine love through his life of inclusive love.

Authentic discipleship is living in the spirit of Jesus, sharing in his free and loving obedience to the Father. In short, it is living with "the mind of Christ" (1 Cor 2:16). That is, we are to have the dispositions and values of Jesus so that we can remain faithful to him while being creatively responsive to the needs of our day. Being faithful yet creative looks for ways that harmonize with the life he exemplified. A faithful pastoral ministry informed by the spirit and vision of Jesus is one that is inclusive of all, that deals with others as persons and not as customers, and that exercises a nurturing and liberating power in imitation of God's ways with us. In imitation of his Father's love, Jesus made inclusiveness the basic value for anyone who would be identified with him and his mission. From the way Jesus received others, we learn that the criterion for discipleship is to be able to make room in one's heart for everyone, and especially to be ready to stand on the side of those who are the weakest and lowliest in society. Authentic discipleship is to manifest in our ministry what Jesus manifested in his: a life centered on God, inclusive of all people, and standing in right relationships with everyone.

God's Providence

To believe that the providence of God's love governs our vocation (what some call "God's will") means that we believe that God is always and everywhere redemptively present to us, calling us through our experiences to a deeper life of faithfulness and love. But God's care for us does not translate simply into some preconceived plan or blueprint fixed from the beginning in every detail. If that were so, then human freedom would be a charade. It would reduce us to playing some mind game with God, like "Guess what number I'm thinking." Such a view of providence creates undue anxiety about missing our chance to heed God's call. If we fail to guess what's on God's mind, then we have grounds to say, "I missed my vocation."

God's providence or love for us is like a compass. It gives a general orientation to our lives to be open and inclusive. However, the street map, or the specific path our love will take, is left to us. We heed God's call fundamentally in the way we allow God's love to flow through us in the ways we love others. The way we express our love in our vocation taps into our deeper values to express what we believe is important about life, and it stamps our life with personal meaning. This makes living out our particular vocation more than holding down a job that pays the bills and more than pursuing a career that enhances our self-esteem or gives us social recognition.

Some of the vocation stories in the Bible—especially the calls of Moses, Mary, and Paul, for example—can too easily give the impression that God so overwhelms us that we have little to say in the matter, or they lead us to believe that the call is so clear that we can't miss it. However, it generally doesn't happen that way. It certainly is not happening that way for Mary Jane, whom we met in the opening scenario. Normally the specific call of God for each of us does not come as a burning bush, the message of an angel, or as bright light and a heavenly voice that gives an unmistakable word of direction. Nor are we born into the world stamped with a Post-It note from God that has the directions for what we are to make of our lives.

As a general rule, hearing the call of God is more like the experience of Samuel in the Old Testament when "the word of the Lord was rare" (1 Sam 3:1). Samuel was being raised by Eli at the shrine of Shiloh. Presumably, Samuel was familiar with the voice of Eli but not with God's, since we are told, "Samuel did not yet know the Lord, and the word of the Lord had not yet been revealed to him" (1 Sam 3:7). While sleeping one night, he heard his name called. Since Eli's voice was familiar to him, three times Samuel went to Eli and said, "Here I am, for you called me." It was Eli who realized that Samuel could not distinguish the voice of the Lord from his. So Eli instructed Samuel to say, if he heard the voice again, "Speak Lord, for your servant is listening" (1 Sam 3:9). When Samuel heard his name again, he responded as Eli had instructed; he assumed the ministry of the prophet and mediated God's word to the people.[9]

As it was for Samuel, so it is for us. The call of God comes through ordinary human experiences and people and is open to diverse interpretations. If we believe that all of life is related to God, then we can be open to God's presence and providence working through very ordinary means, such as our talents or gifts, immediate needs and opportunities to serve, and the various influences of the communities in which we live that surround us with people to inspire us, to invite us into ministry, to guide us, and to confirm us in our way of participating in the life of the community. Insofar as the call of God is mediated through other persons and personal experience, it is always a little obscure, a little ambiguous. That is why Mary Jane from the opening scenario is still wondering whether a vocation as pastoral associate is right for her. We need to discern it by paying attention not only to the external signs of confirmation from the community but also to the internal, affective responses evoked in us by these mediators of God. Through the community's affirmation or rejection, and by heeding our emotional resonance of harmony and peace or the dissonance of anxiety and confusion, we come closer to discovering God's call for us.

The pastoral ministry is a way of specifying our basic vocation to the discipleship of Jesus by assuming a religious, ecclesial role within society. The pastoral minister focuses the call to discipleship on all that pertains to being a representative of the church committed to sharing in God's mission of bringing all peoples and the whole of creation into harmony under God's reign.

GIFTED

"What do you have to work with?" is the question of discernment that enables us to express the call of vocation in a particular way. Normally, God works in and through our natural abilities, not against them. To hear a call from God is to discover our gifts and through them to discern a deeper orientation of our lives. So, how well do you know yourself? It is rare that someone's ineptness for a task does not hinder their service. Among pastoral ministers, for example, we need to be careful how we use the Pauline notion of God choosing the simple to confound the wise (1 Cor 1:27). We cannot let this become the biblical justification for not having to do critical discernment to determine whether we have the capacities most relevant to the ministry in question.

Discerning Gifts

Receiving and giving are the fundamental dynamics of the spirituality of vocation. It is captured well in the Johannine version of the Great Commandment: "Just as I have loved you, you also should love one another" (John 13:34). We are first loved through the blessings of God that are our gifts, and then we are to love by living out of these blessings in gratitude for the love we have received. So discerning giftedness is an indispensable part of any genuine vocation, for a vocation corresponds to one's capacities for the task. Just as the tone deaf are unlikely candidates for a musical vocation, and those who lack nimble finger dexterity are not good candidates to be surgeons, so those who do not have the gift to feel the rhythm of God moving amid the wonders and agonies of life are not good candidates for the pastoral ministries of counseling, spiritual direction, or preaching.

Naming our gifts is a fundamental requirement for discerning whether we have a vocation to pastoral ministry at all and to what kind of ministry in particular. Our gifts are the ways God's Spirit is at work blessing us so that we can, in turn, bless another. Some common questions for discerning our gifts are these:[10]

> What comes naturally to you?
> What are you good at?
> What enthuses and energizes you?
> What are your passions?
> What enables you to keep moving ahead?
> What gives you a sense of joy and fulfillment so that you want
> to say, "This is a good way to live, and it really fits me!"?
> What have others recognized in you and asked you to con-
> tribute to them?

A vocation is a matter of living the self one already possesses. Parker Palmer, well known for his writing on vocation, is a staunch advocate for connecting the call of vocation with claiming one's authentic selfhood. He is critical of any understanding of vocation that is rooted in some voice external to ourselves. When we are uncertain about who we are and what our gifts are, then we easily let other voices determine what we should do—family expectations, opinions of peers, or even the demands of the market can become the controlling force dictating the shape our life will take. According to Palmer, a true vocation would not ask us to become someone we are not capable of becoming. About his own attempts to seek ordination, for example, he says, "God spoke to me—in the form of mediocre grades and massive misery—and informed me that under no condition was I to become an ordained leader in His or Her church."[11]

Palmer's connecting vocation with personal identity puts us squarely in the realm of the kind of knowledge and freedom we need to discover our vocation and express it. We discover our vocation through ordinary means that affirm or deny our gifts. Whatever we can do to become more keenly aware of the ways God has gifted us would be an asset in discovering the ways we are experiencing the call of God. Time-honored practices of prayer and meditation can be ways that we awaken to our true self. From a spiritual perspective, these practices done in faith can be opportunities to hear God naming our blessings and to accept them as the ways God loves us. Friends can be a big help, too. Good friends can be a mirror to our own lives. They help us see ourselves in ways that we may want to deny. Experience is another resource. Experience of success as well as of failure can teach us both our gifts and our limits. They make us ask ourselves whether we have the skills and personality for this way of living. Psychological tests are another means. They help us discover our potential, our preferences, or whether we have any character disorders. We should be open to using whatever means are available to us to come to a greater understanding of ourselves.

Recognizing our gifts, or claiming our original blessings, includes identifying both our capacity for practical skills (public speaking, organizing groups, listening) as well as for virtue (being trustworthy, compassionate, generous). We need to recognize whether we have the skills that fit the ministry and whether we have the moral dispositions that will support ministry. For example, since the pastoral ministry is primarily a matter of relating to others in ways that mediate God's presence, we ought to have the skills and dispositions that foster faithful, life-giving relationships with those we are called to serve. This means that we are not fit for ministry if we cannot relate—that is, if we show no signs of having sustained friendships, are careless about boundaries, are arrogant or quarrelsome, or if our style of relating is to control, intimidate, exploit, manipulate, demean, or shame. Nor should anyone be a candidate for ministry who is ideologically or emotionally rigid, aloof, passive, defensive, argumentative, authoritarian, selfish, dismissive, or resistant to learning.

Rather, we ought to manifest a fundamental openness to people and ideas, be hospitable and affable, nondefensive, flexible, capable of collaborating, compassionate, desiring justice, and able to move beyond our own interests in order to be ready to serve others. From my years of experience in seminary formation, I have concluded that seminarians come to the seminary with their relational habits well in place. The seminary cannot do much to get seminarians to acquire the habits needed to have life-giving, satisfying, supportive relationships. Consequently, the diocese should not accept candidates who have not already manifested a history of healthy relationships.

Freedom for Ministry

The gift dimension of having a vocation means not only that we have a critical self-understanding of our abilities for ministry, but that we also have a keen sense of our own freedom. The freedom at stake is not limited to choosing one form of service over another. Nor is it simply freedom from coercion of family, culture, or peer pressures to follow a particular path. The freedom at stake is the freedom of self-possession. This is the freedom of a paschal spirituality. It enables us to subordinate our self-interests in order to give a greater degree of preference to serving the needs of others over our own. Servants take their cues from the people they serve, not from their own needs. To be free enough to do so enables us to share our gifts by opening ourselves to the world and making ourselves available to others.

This freedom of self-possession is possible because of God's absolute acceptance of us that is mediated by the liberating love of others. Accepting God's love for us in and through the love of others can free us from the need to be self-protective so that we can be available to others without the need to dominate or to attract attention to ourselves. We can dispose of ourselves without losing ourselves. This is the kind of freedom that makes our gifts instruments of God's love.

Moreover, those who are fit and free for ministry may not be suited for every kind of ministry. For example, no one should preach who lacks skills for public speaking or a commitment to the gospel, and no one ought to strive for a ministry that has the prophetic dimension of confronting social sin who lacks courage and the competence to understand the complexity of public issues and political strategies. Then there are those who have characters more fitting a monastic lifestyle; others, as Mary Jane seems to be, are more suited to be social activists. The highly extroverted would probably have a very difficult time ministering in remote areas of isolation but would be well suited for an active urban ministry. Being aware of our basic skills and personality traits is an important aspect of discovering whether, how, and where God is calling us. In pastoral ministry, we should not expect every minister to have all the gifts the church needs for its mission. Saint Paul instructed the Corinthian community about the diversity of gifts that the Spirit had given to them. They were to respect these differences and use the diverse gifts for the common good (1 Cor 12:4–11). We ought to do likewise.

In discerning our vocation through our gifts, we have Jesus as a model of the free and faithful response to God, and we have the Spirit to empower us to make such a response. But ultimately, the governing virtues for responding to our vocation are the humility to accept the ways God has gifted us, trust in God's Spirit to empower us to use them, and heartfelt gratitude in using these gifts for serving God and neighbor through them. Hoarding our gifts by refusing to develop or to use them can seem to be mocking God. In the Gospels, Matthew sums up life in the Spirit in four words, roughly translated as "freely receiving, freely giving" (Matt 10:8). What we have received through the Spirit must be given in the Spirit for the sake of the good of all. In an authentic vocation, God calls us for others.

The judgment parable that Jesus told of the talents given to the three servants in Matthew 25:14–30 is a powerful indictment of what happens when we withdraw into ourselves, hoard our gifts, and cut off the dynamic of receiving and giving love. In this parable, the master distributes his possessions to his three servants before going off on a journey. Each is given according to his ability. The first is given five talents, the second is given two, and the third is given one talent. The first two servants invest what they were given and earn more. The third servant, however, stuffs his in a sock for safekeeping. When the master returns, those who invested their money are praised. However, the better-safe-than-sorry servant is called wicked and slothful, his talent is taken from him, and he is cast outside.

The parable warns us not to become complacent with what we have been given but to take care to increase it. The parable encourages the attitude of taking a risk on the abundance of our blessings and overcoming the fearfulness that paralyzes us from taking on the responsibilities that we should assume. No one of us is a virtuoso of every talent, but that does not mean that we do not have some gifts to offer. The parable reminds us that, regardless of the little we may think

15

we have, how we play the hand we have been dealt is what our vocation is all about. Our sense of being called, then, is shaped by our awareness of the way God lives within us through our gifts, talents, or blessings. Developing our gifts and using them for the sake of others is our way of giving thanks to God for what we have received while also giving glory to God and life to God's people by manifesting these divine blessings within us.

SERVICE

The subjective aspects of feelings, attractions, desires, and gifts are only part of the story of having a vocation. "What does the world need?" is the question of discernment that opens us to the other part. Authentic vocation must go beyond the subjective dimensions that can too easily make self-fulfillment the end of having a vocation. An authentic vocation as a calling from God, however, is not only about the self. It is also about "us." Vocation demands that we consider not only what contributes to personal fulfillment but also what is good for the world. In an authentic vocation, the needs and sufferings of the world touch us, and we in turn give to the world what we can in response.

By sharing our gifts for the sake of serving the world, we are participating in the commission Jesus gave his apostles before sending them out on mission. Translated freely, it reads, "What you have received as gift, give as gift" (Matt 10:8). The understanding that our gifts are for giving opens us to put our gifts in service of the world's needs. Our vocation emerges when what we have to work with intersects with what the world needs. Mary Jane, of the opening scenario, used her gifts to serve the needs of a corporation to care for its employees in ways worthy of their human dignity. Now she is wondering whether her gifts might be directed to needs of the church lacking sufficient priests to lead the parishes.

Parker Palmer likes to quote Frederich Buechner on a true vocation as "the place where your deep gladness meets the world's deep need."[12] This understanding of vocation combines the internal, subjective aspects of what lies in one's heart (feelings, desire, and gifts) with the external, objective aspect of human need. To include service to human need in our understanding of vocation roots an authentic vocation in a commitment to justice that seeks to align our gifts with what will serve the common good. God speaks to us through both gift and need. The convergence of gift and need is where the Spirit of God invites us along a path that is our unique calling. We make specific our basic vocation to be loving by tailoring our gifts to serve a particular human need. For example, the need for health is served by the vocation to medicine; the need for knowledge is served by the vocation to teaching. The vocation to pastoral ministry serves the need for salvation through advancing the mission of the church.

The primary energy of the Spirit in calling us to the vocation of pastoral ministry is to take us out of ourselves and into the world by participating in the mission of the church through ministry. According to *Lumen Gentium* (no. 1) of the Second Vatican Council, the mission of the church is both spiritual and social: the church is to be both a sign and an instrument of our union with God and of the unity of all humankind. Pastoral ministers, in different ways, play a special part in this mission through our ministries of preaching, teaching, celebrating, organizing, and providing individual pastoral care, as well as through living a life of discipleship that witnesses to the gospel.

COMMUNITY

"Does anyone want you to do it?" is the question of discernment that evokes the communal dimension of a vocation. We experience the call to ministry within the life of the community, which is an agent of God's call; our vocation is to serve the community; and the community sustains us in our vocation. The service orientation of ministerial vocation is revealed in the fact that we are not called into ministry primarily for our own benefit, but for the sake of the mission of the church. A vocation is communal through and through.

Called from the Community

God calls us through the church. While we may be accustomed to interpreting *church* narrowly as the hierarchy that officially sanctions our call to ministry, we need to think more communally of the church as the whole people of God sharing in this role of calling forth ministers to serve the mission of the church. This more holistic understanding of the church fits with our understanding of God's Spirit working through the experiences we have of and with other people who help us become aware of our gifts and the world's needs. We live out of the relationships that make up our lives, especially relationships with those who are significant in our lives. This begins with the crucial influence of our parents and family and continues as a permanent dimension of our life. In other words, there are many agents of God's call to ministry beyond the hierarchy. God uses other people to call us to a particular way of life.[13] The people we admire most, those who have captured our imaginations to influence what we think of ourselves and what we aspire to be like, are mediators of God's call. This is the sacramental way of the incarnation. God calls us through us.

When talking with a group of priests about what drew us to the priesthood, the importance of community and good models to inspire us came home to me clearly. For all of us, it was not any idea about priesthood but a real living flesh-and-blood priest who inspired us. We could each name someone in our lives who lived with an energy that was infectious in its attractiveness. They ministered with a confident competence that nurtured a desire to want to be like them. They were our heroes who inspired hope and modeled a way of life that we wanted to follow and imitate. The experience of someone whom we wanted to be like, together with a personal invitation from a priest and the encouragement from others to give it a chance, were at the roots of following a vocation to the priesthood.

That is one way that the community calls forth vocations to ministry. But the vocation to lay ecclesial ministry also comes from within the community. As Edward Hahnenberg affirms:

This ecclesial call can be heard in the words of the Second Vatican Council affirming the baptismal dignity of the people of God; it can be heard in the lives of individuals responding to needs and seeking out ways to participate; it can be heard in colleges and schools developing programs for lay ministry formation; it can be heard in pastors and other leaders inviting and encouraging new roles [for] the parish staff; it can be heard in parishioners and whole communities welcoming lay ecclesial ministers into their midst;

and it can be heard in the affirming words and the modest proposals of *Co-Workers in the Vineyard of the Lord*.[14]

Serve the Community

All programs of ministerial formation these days have some component of pastoral involvement that comes with supervision and ultimately some evaluation by those who represent the community served. This is a concrete way to show how the community is involved in calling forth vocations and affirming or reserving their support for someone seeking a ministerial role. The community's input into the formation and ongoing evaluation of ministers can be a check against self-deception that easily creeps into the ministerial role without appropriate oversight. The community's role in discernment can take a variety of forms. It can be through peer support groups, a mentor, a supervisor, a spiritual director, or other conversation partners who help those in ministry to stay focused on their mission, competent for their tasks, and accountable to those they serve.

Sustained by the Community

Communities sustain vocations, too. The call to pray for vocations stands out as the spiritual support to those who are living out their vocations and as an invitation to those who are discerning their vocations. However, this call to prayer cannot stop with our petitions and intercessions. Our prayer must also have hands and feet. We must extend our prayers of determination to sustain vocations by noticing and calling forth those who both feel drawn to ministry and have gifts for it, as Mary Jane's community is doing for her. We must also actively affirm and support those in ministry who serve well. Our prayer can take action in the form of creating a culture in the church along with structures of accountability that would, on the one hand, reward good performance and, on the other hand, challenge, correct, and even dismiss those who are not really suited for ministry but continue to play the role.

In the end, we judge the authenticity of a vocation to ministry by the community's reception of it. Not all of those who have been called to ministry *de jure* through ordination, profession, installation, or commissioned appointment are *de facto* ministers with a vocation to ministry because the community has not received them as such. These ministers may be tolerated or, even worse, endured. However, they have not been affirmed in the call to ministry because the community is not calling them forth to serve. The community does not invite them into its life to celebrate its joys and sorrows, nor does the community heed their words as inspired by the Spirit.

The official way that the community plays a role in discerning vocations to ministry is to give external authorization to our internal sense of call by means of some juridical intervention by ecclesial leadership. Yet this way of authenticating a call to ministry stands in tension with the growing experience within the church of people saying that it would be good if married men were allowed to be ordained, that priests who married could return to active ministry, and that women be ordained. In other words, the call to ministry as a gift of the Spirit might be given to more people than the official structures of the church presently recognize.

Yet the church is not a liberal democratic polity that will make its decisions on who will serve in its name based on polls and majority opinion. The challenge before us as a spiritual communion is to cultivate an ecclesial process of discernment in which everyone will be able to contribute their sense of what the gospel is demanding of us today. This process will acknowledge the role of the Magisterium as the unique guardian of the apostolic faith while also remaining open to the prophetic voices emerging outside the established institutional structures. We have precedent for God's call to cut against the grain of the rule of established leaders in the call of the prophets, especially Amos and Jeremiah. The unresolved issue for us today is how our official church leaders and the *de jure* "vocations" to ministry could better reflect the *de facto* calls to ministry. The presence of unauthorized ministers and ministries in the church that are being accepted by various local communities may very well be the seeds for change. Yet, they still require the discernment of the whole community to test them as the work of the Spirit.

As a vocation, then, pastoral ministry is a free response to our experience of God in and through the community. Through the ministry, we live a life of service that promotes the mission of the church to bring everyone into fuller communion with God. To see that having a vocation and being professional need not be at odds with each other, we turn next to what it means to be professional.

2

MINISTRY AS PROFESSION

Fr. Jim has been ordained for four years and is beginning to settle into a routine that is losing its professional edge. When he got ordained, Fr. Jim made a commitment to himself that he would not become a priest who was careless about presiding, preaching, or pastoral care. He promised that he would continue with the spiritual disciplines that he developed while in the seminary, and that he would keep up with reading at least in his areas of greatest interest, scripture and systematic theology.

This weekend he overheard a few comments made by parishioners about his liturgical style and availability around the parish. This caught him a bit by surprise, but it was enough to make him realize how easy it had become for him to let his having a vocation to the priesthood replace his lack of professionalism. Now that he has been awakened from his complacent slumber, he wants to revive his commitment to professional excellence.

Since the diocese has no formal process of evaluation, Fr. Jim approaches his pastor and the parish council with a request to help him develop some structures of accountability in his ministry. He begins by asking the pastor of a neighboring parish to serve as his supervisor so as to avoid any conflict of interest with his own pastor. Then he establishes a spiritual direction relationship with a member of the staff at the nearby retreat house. In the parish, he works with the parish council to develop an instrument of evaluation for his pastoral ministry, and he works with the liturgy committee to develop one for his liturgical ministries. He asks the president of the parish council to oversee this evaluation process.

Fr. Jim knows that these steps may be overly ambitious, but he is committed to enhancing the professional aspects of his vocation to the priesthood.

In chapter 1, we considered ministry as a vocation. We saw that pastoral ministry as a vocation is a free response to the call of God that we experience in and through our own gifts and the affirmation of the community to live a life of service that participates in the mission of the church to bring everyone into fuller communion with one another and with God. This chapter correlates professional demands with the four aspects of vocation to pastoral ministry. While there are ecclesial differences in the vocations of the ordained and lay ecclesial ministers, there are common professional aspects across all forms of ministry.

ON BEING PROFESSIONAL

Any effort to elaborate a professional ethics for ministers can be successful to the extent that we can be described as professionals and identify ourselves as such. Ministry has long been included among the learned professions. *To profess* means "to testify on behalf of" or "to stand for" something that defines one's identity and commitment to the community. Without this commitment, a practitioner is an opportunist or careerist. In the history of the development of the professions, the oldest use of the term *profession* carried fundamentally the religious meaning of "a calling." Having a religious vocation and being professional were of a piece with each other. The source of what today we call the "professions" grew out of the religious setting of monks and nuns making a religious profession of their faith in God by taking the vows of poverty, celibacy, and obedience. With the established church well in control of society, and with the monasteries as the center of culture, the professed religious became the dominant "professional" group. They reached out to respond to the immediate needs of people for education, legal rights, health care, and salvation. By the late Middle Ages, through a process of secularization and the organization of commercial groups into guilds, nonreligious institutions began to serve those functions once provided by the professed religious. Even though the term *professional* no longer applied only to religious, it continued to carry the connotation of being motivated by love to commit oneself to acquiring expert knowledge and skill in order to serve human needs with good moral character.[1]

This classical sense of being professional is lost on many today, but Fr. Jim, from the opening scenario, wants to retrieve it for himself. In classes and workshops on professional ethics, I have found that some aspirants to pastoral ministry resist the idea that to be a minister is to be a professional. The resistance comes largely from negative connotations associated with being professional. For example, some think that being "professional" means being interested in making big money rather than rendering a service. For others, it means privilege, the prestige of social status, or being "one-up" on another. It also suggests applying technical competence, but in a cold, insensitive, detached, and uninterested manner. If this is what being professional means, then no wonder some pastoral ministers resist identifying with the term. These characteristics run counter to all that pastoral ministry is about.

Canonist John Beal has discussed the issue of regarding ministry as a profession more extensively. Positively, he identifies certain attitudes that support identifying ministers as professionals by saying, "They generally have a strong sense of calling to their field of endeavor and are deeply dedicated to service to those who entrust themselves or are entrusted to their care."[2] But on the other hand, he identifies some features of being professional that do not apply to ministry: "The use of a professional organization as a primary reference point, self-regulation, and professional autonomy, which are the hallmarks of other professions, are notably lacking."[3]

Beal then gives a more sophisticated account of obstacles within canon law and the theology that underlies it for regarding ministers as professionals. He concludes that we do not yet have sufficient development in our official theology and canon law to recognize the professional character of ministry. He identifies three tensions that obstruct appreciating ministers as professionals. One is that an overemphasis on ministry as vocation privileges the status of being ordained over the function of providing service and makes it difficult to enforce professional standards of behavior in order to have any public accountability for one's ministerial performance. Fr. Jim, from the opening scenario, recognized his susceptibility to this view. The second tension is between the public and private life of the minister. We must be able to determine when we are acting in our ministerial capacity and when as a private person in order to apply professional ethics. The inability to distinguish our public and private life blurs the boundaries of appropriate professional behavior. The third tension is between bureaucracy and professionalism. The predominantly bureaucratic organization of our life and work in the church, such as being subject to centralized leadership and fixed procedures, often conflict with the professional call to respect leadership based on expertise and to adapt one's response to individual circumstances. The prevalence of these three tensions within the church in its theology and canon law undermine accepting the professional character of its ministers.[4]

This chapter focuses on the tension between vocation and profession. Chapter 5 deals with aspects of the second two tensions. This chapter, like chapter 1, presupposes that our status and function should not be seen as antithetical to one or other but as complementary: not either/or, but both-and. When taken together with the spirituality of putting on the mind of Christ to empty oneself in service and pastoral charity, ministry is enhanced by being professional—that is, by being committed to theological and pastoral competence, by being a person of good moral character, by providing selfless dedication to service, and by being accountable to the community and to others in ministry. These characteristic marks of a professional can inform and guide our practice of ministry so that it enhances our being signs and agents of God's love.

To show how having a vocation to pastoral ministry and being professional are compatible, this chapter correlates what it means to be professional in ministry with the characteristics of vocation explored in chapter 1: to be called, to be gifted, to be of service, and to be chosen by the community.

CALLED

The dimension of being called correlates with two professional aspects of ministry: the covenantal model governing pastoral practice and the minister as symbolic representative of the holy.

Covenantal Model of Pastoral Ministry

When we disagree among ourselves about our professional obligations, we are often disagreeing over different models of the professional relationship, even if we do not name our disagreement this way.

Some of us assume a covenantal model and require more flexibility and generosity from ministers. Others favor a contractual model and draw clear lines around whom they will serve, at what time, for how long, and at what price.

The contract model is a close cousin to the covenant. Both include agreement and exchange between parties. Both include obligations that protect human dignity and block the tendency of one to take advantage of the other. But they differ in significant ways, especially in spirit.[5] From the perspective of being "called" to ministry as a vocation, I favor covenant over contract as the primary metaphorical frame for interpreting ministry as a profession. Covenant defines ministry responsively. Ministerial service (such as preaching, prayer leadership, organizing, and individual pastoral care) ultimately derives from and responds to a calling. Covenant clearly keeps God at the source and center of this call, and it opens us to seeing all actions as responses to God and governed by what we can know about what God is calling us to do. Contracts have no necessary relationship to God.

Contracts work well if the necessary services and fees can be clearly spelled out in advance. They acknowledge the limits of what a person can do and clearly distinguish rights and duties within those limits so that there is no ambiguity about what is expected from each party in the contract. The contract spells out the least we have to do within very specific limits. Nevertheless, these features make the contract model inadequate for ministerial relationships that are not predictable enough to spell out their demands in advance.

Ministers need to be flexible. Ministry must allow for spontaneity. When we act according to a covenantal commitment, we look beyond the minimum. A covenantal relationship accepts the unexpected; it makes room for the gratuitous, not just the gratuities. Partners in a covenant are willing to go the extra mile to make things work out. Covenantal thinking wants to know what we can do in grateful response for what we have received.

It is true that the covenantal model in ministry creates some problems that the contract model would resolve. For example, the covenantal model does not acknowledge human limitations as explicitly as the contract model does, and it may more easily encourage unprofessional behavior, such as offering a service that is inappropriate or that cannot be done well. The contract model acknowledges the human limitations of the contracting parties, since it clearly distinguishes rights and duties. It circumscribes the kind and amount of service being sought and offered. It leaves little or no room for the ambiguity that is inevitable with the covenantal model.

While covenants also have stipulations that draw boundaries, these are interpreted according to what loving faithfulness would demand. In the Gospel of Matthew, Jesus, who is the New Covenant, teaches that the whole Law of Moses and the teachings of the prophets can be summarized in the Great Commandment of love (Matt 22:37–40). However, to know what love demands and where to draw the line that separates loving from unloving behavior in ministerial relationships requires the demanding task of moral discernment and the vision and sensitivity of a virtuous person. Contracts are easier to interpret and to enforce because they spell out the least that we have to do in very specific terms. Even with these limitations, I still find the covenantal model for pastoral relationships to be more appropriate than the contract for establishing the context within which to explore moral responsibility.

The biblical witness highlights three features of the covenantal relationship that can mark pastoral ministry: motivated by love, respectful of freedom, and held together by trust.[6]

MOTIVATED BY LOVE

The basic feature of the covenant is the very way it is formed: namely, grace is the first move. In love, God calls. We respond. We are not so much searchers as the ones searched for. Israel recognized that the covenant is a gift, an honor bestowed on them out of love (Exod 6:7; 19:4–5; Lev 26:9–12; Jer 32:38–41). Our image of the church as the people of God is linked with God's initiative to call a people into a covenantal relationship (2 Cor 6:16; Heb 8:10; Rev 21:3).

Covenant helps us to appreciate that the pastoral minister links the one seeking a pastoral service not only with God but also with the whole community. One way to keep the focus on God in the pastoral ministry is to avoid fostering a cult of personality in pastoral ministers. A covenantal ministry is primarily about responding to God. So we must decrease while God increases as the object of attention, devotion, and respect.

In relation to the whole community, pastoral ministers can imitate God's making the first move by being the "searchers" who reach out to others, including those who are alienated from the church and society, and create for them a place of welcome. This may take the form of a monthly dinner for the homeless or a formal program of "homecoming" that reorients those who have been away from the church. Covenantal ministry is also responsive to different cultural needs and forms of spirituality by providing opportunities for different religious expressions, from traditional devotions (such as novenas) to a more contemporary form of Taizé prayer around the cross.

RESPECTFUL OF FREEDOM

The covenant also respects freedom, not only God's freedom to love us but also our freedom to accept or reject that love. The divine love that calls us into covenantal relationship does not destroy our freedom but awaits our response. Entering into covenant is voluntary. God makes an offer we *can* refuse. However, once we accept the invitation to covenant, then we commit ourselves to being faithful to what the covenant requires. In pastoral relationships, we respect covenantal freedom when we encourage others to seek enlightenment from Christian wisdom and the teaching authority of the church and then honor their own moral agency in taking responsible action. We promote a kind of moral infantilism if we encourage dependency on ecclesial officials and give the impression that pastoral ministers of every sort are such experts that they can give a solution to every problem, no matter how complicated.

HELD TOGETHER BY TRUST

Fidelity is the virtue that weaves the fabric of the covenant together. The action of a covenantal relationship is entrusting and accepting trust. In a covenant, we place into another's hands something of value to ourselves. In God's covenant with us, for example, God has entrusted to us divine love, most fully expressed in the person of Jesus. In pastoral ministry, those seeking pastoral service entrust to the minister their secrets, sins, fears, and need for salvation. This act of trust is risky business. When we entrust something of ourselves to another, we give the other power over us. We trust that we will not be betrayed and that this power will not be abused. To accept another's trust is to commit oneself to the fiduciary duty of being trustworthy with what has been entrusted to us. Betraying this sacred trust by exploiting the other's vulnerability violates the covenantal commitment by a breach of fidelity.

In some relationships, like marriage or friendships, the act of entrusting and accepting trust goes equally in both directions, so that the relationship is reciprocal and the covenantal partners share equally the obligations of the covenantal commitment. However, the pastoral relationship is different. It is one directional. In ministry, the act of entrusting comes from the one seeking the ministerial service. For this reason, professional ministerial relationships are not mutually reciprocal. The minister does not entrust matters of personal concern to parishioners, students, directees, or patients and so is less vulnerable and at less risk. Yet the demand of fidelity to be trustworthy in these relationships is all the more important, since the minister can easily take advantage of the other by abusing what has been entrusted.

The Bible also witnesses to the qualities of God in the covenant that ought to inform the character and actions of ministerial covenants. One characteristic is God's holiness; the other is God's steadfast love or faithfulness.[7]

HOLINESS

Holiness makes clear that God and Israel are not equal. The moral implication of this fundamental inequality between covenantal partners is that the one with greater power must not take advantage of the other's vulnerability through any form of manipulation or exploitation, but must show a special protection and advocacy for their concerns. In the Old Testament, this aspect of holiness is expressed through the works of God's justice. The biblical measure of justice is the treatment of the powerless (orphan, widow, poor, and stranger) who, though lacking power to access social goods, still have a rightful claim to share in the common good (Exod 22:21–26; Deut 10:17–19; Isa 1:17). In the New Testament, Jesus insisted that God will judge us by how we treat the least among us (Matt 25). In professional ministry, we are to protect those who seek ministerial services by not taking

28

advantage of the inequality of the relationship where we have power over those seeking our pastoral care.

STEADFAST LOVE, OR FAITHFULNESS

The other quality of God's holiness is steadfast love, or fidelity. In the promissory covenant with Noah (Gen 9:8–17), with Abraham (Gen 15 and 17), and with David (2 Sam 7), the promise of fidelity is in one direction. In the Sinai covenant, by contrast, the emphasis is less on God's fidelity and more on the demands of Israel to be faithful to the covenant. In pastoral ministry, we reflect this fidelity in the way we strive to be faithful representatives of the church and the way we strive to be faithful to those who have entrusted themselves to us.

Covenant in the Bible also has its prophets. When the people of Israel started blowing kisses at calves and flirting with gods that they did not know, the prophets rose up to denounce what was happening. They had to remind Israel whose they were and how they were to live as partners in covenant. The prophets continued to declare God's faithfulness while interpreting the covenantal demands on the people to be a return to fidelity (Hos 6:6). The prophets show that God continues to be faithful by supporting the covenant even in the face of infidelity. In Hosea, for example, God is faithful in spite of Israel's flirting with other gods (Hos 11). Amos is notorious for giving unqualified insistence to fidelity. He had no room for indulging special favors of privileged entitlement. To be in covenant is to be held accountable to its demands. In the New Testament, God's promise of loyalty is in Jesus, whose very title, *Christ*, witnesses to his being the promised one of God, the Messiah, who fulfills all the hopes of the covenant. But who will play the prophet for us today? We can show that we honor the place of the prophet in the way we include structures of accountability for our ministerial service and create an environment in which others feel confident to offer criticism without the fear of reprisal.

In sum, to use covenant as the primary metaphorical frame for interpreting the professional aspect of a ministerial relationship is to commit ourselves to being faithful to God, to others, and to the church. The act of entrusting and accepting trust makes the ministerial relationship one of unequal power. The primary obligation of the minister in such a "power over" relationship is to be ready to sacrifice one's own interest in order to serve the best interest of the other. The covenantal commitment of a pastoral relationship resists an easy accommodation to self-interest, privileged entitlement, and greed. It favors service, self-discipline, and generosity. So the biblical experience of covenant gives us the basic structure of the pastoral relationship:

Motivated by love
Respectful of freedom
Held together by fidelity

Symbolic Representative of the Holy

As a specific way of responding to God's call, pastoral ministry as a vocation means that our life and service bear a symbolic significance in the community of faith. We are like everyone else in so many ways, but there is always something different about us. The difference is that we bring something more to ministry than just ourselves. The "something more" that we bring is expressed succinctly as being a "symbolic representative of the holy." This means that we represent for others the church, a religious tradition, a way of life, and yes, even God. Some people feel that to talk with us is to talk with God, or to be accepted or rejected by us is to be accepted or rejected by God. Being a symbolic representative gives added significance or a "sacred weight" to what we say and do. For this reason, it gives us significant power over others that we must manage well. I revisit this notion of being a symbolic representative in chapter 5, where I explain further its professional dimension as a source of power. For now, I identify it as a corollary to being called to ministry.

GIFTED

The gift dimension of vocation correlates with two professional aspects of ministry: our capacity for specialized knowledge and skills and our character. Since I devote chapter 3 to the character of the pastoral minister, I comment here on the gift of specialized knowledge and skill appropriate for pastoral ministry.

30

Specialized Knowledge and Skill

Professionals are commonly defined as experts who have mastered, over an extended period of formal education, a specialized area of knowledge and skills. Becoming an expert in a certain area helps to clarify the professional's identity and to specify the service that he or she can contribute to the community. Such clarity and specificity pave the way for a tighter job description, for ways to focus recruitment, for programs of initial training and ongoing education, and for standards of performance and peer review.

Pastoral ministry is marked by many specializations. There are the special ministries of spiritual director, chaplain, youth minister, catechist, director of liturgy, school principal, pastor, preacher, and more. Each particular ministry has its own specialized skill set and corresponding knowledge. As a result, to speak of the specialized knowledge and skills of pastoral ministry in general is difficult.

For many, pastoral ministry is a hodgepodge of tasks requiring a wide range of knowledge and skills, such as the mediator of meaning through preaching and teaching, the leader of worship, the chief administrator, the financial manager, a counselor, the staff advisor, and a social worker, to name a few. As generalists, some ministers do not feel expert at anything. Being a generalist, expected to fulfill many interrelated roles but not feeling especially competent in any of them, and lacking any universally agreed-upon set of standards of competence or skillful practice, can easily undermine our sense of being professional. The National Association for Lay Ministry, the National Federation for Catholic Youth Ministry, and the National Conference for Catechetical Leadership have taken a giant step forward toward professionalizing lay ministry by collaborating on a project that produced *National Certification Standards for Lay Ecclesial Ministers*, a common set of competency-based standards for pastoral associates, parish life coordinators, parish catechetical leaders, and youth ministry leaders.[8]

Theological Reflection

The cohering theme of these standards that identifies the specialized knowledge and skills for pastoral ministry is that each of us in our own ministries is to be a theological resource for the people we serve.

One does not have to be in pastoral ministry very long before hearing the cry of the people who want to deepen their spiritual life. While what they mean by this is not always clear, one aspect that it does seem to include is the desire to make their commitment of faith more than a matter of going to church on Sunday. They want to be able to touch the holy in the everyday events of life. As pastoral ministers, we profess to be able to respond to this religious need, for we are called to be the theological resource for the believing community.

Pastoral ministry, in whatever expression it takes, bears the distinctive identity and purpose in society of being the profession people turn to in order to see the sacred dimensions of everyday life. While we share many of the helping skills of other professions, we are unique in bringing a theological understanding to human experience that ought to influence the way these skills are used to serve the mission of the church and to express what it means to be a Christian believer. No one else in church or society is trained in matters pertaining to the Christian tradition so as to provide theological reflection on human experience. This means that we ought to be able to draw upon the stories, symbols, rituals, and traditions of the Christian faith in order to help believers understand and respond to what is happening in their lives from the perspective of faith and so reclaim, preserve, and strengthen their identity in Christ. This does not mean that everyone in pastoral ministry must become an accomplished academic theologian. But it does mean that, in the midst of the many functions that we are to perform, we ought to have only one focus: God's Word in Jesus Christ; and we ought to serve primarily one purpose: to bring the Word of God to bear on concrete situations in the life of those we serve.

Theological reflection seeks to interpret life's experiences in light of God's purposes in Jesus, and it seeks to understand the Christian story about God in light of what we experience day to day. In other words, it holds in dialectical tension the relation of faith and experience in order to make faith-sense of experience and experience-sense of faith. As individuals and as communities, people face hopes (childbirth), fears (death, church closures), life changes (marriage, retirement), moral dilemmas (labor strikes, appropriate care of the dying, where to invest money), tragedies (unemployment, accidental death), and disasters (earthquakes, floods, airplane crashes, war) that call for interpretation and that challenge us with questions of meaning. The way faithful

32

people understand and respond to such experiences can and ought to be informed by their religious beliefs. The pastoral task is to stand with individuals and communities in these experiences and to help reflect on them, find meaning in them, and respond to them in ways that make sense and express our Christian identity. Without theological reflection, the commitment of faith in the people can get so far removed from human experience that the faith itself becomes irrelevant.

It is one thing to have right knowledge about the Christian tradition and its theological concepts (God, grace, sin, salvation, and so on), but it is a special skill to use this knowledge to help people find meaning and value in their experiences from the perspective of faith. Incarnational theology affirms that "earth is crammed with heaven" so that every experience, if given a chance, can speak to us of God. In so much of pastoral ministry—especially the ministries of preaching, teaching, celebrating, organizing, and pastoral care—we are like poets or interpreters of obscure texts. By using the stories, images, and symbols of our religious tradition, we try to name grace. That is to say, we try to help others see life as touched by God and to notice what needs specific attention as a Christian believer. We help people to see life in the light of faith. However, to provide such theological reflection for the community requires that we have the knowledge and skill for discerning the presence and action of God. This is what the competence of theological reflection demands, and it is what we profess to be able to do as a theological resource to the community of faith.

As pastoral ministers, we share with other professionals many skills (counseling, organizing, teaching, active listening, and so on) that are not unique to ministry, but we do not have to be therapists, sociologists, or accountants. Competence also means knowing one's limitations. One of my professors identified this as the virtue of humility, which he defined as "being down to earth about oneself." Being humble about our competence means that we have appropriate self-knowledge and do not try to provide services in areas where we lack the competence. We must be ready to refer our people to other professionals when they need help that we are not trained to give.

From the perspective of the covenantal model of pastoral ministry, maintaining our theological competence by developing the habit of reading, study, and reflection is more than a moral requirement. It is a spiritual discipline as well. Maintaining our competence ought to be an integral part of our spiritual life. It is our way of responding to the call and gifts that God has given us for ministry. As we develop these gifts in order to serve the community better, we are giving as gift what we have received as gift. A friend of mine gave me as a gift an ink drawing of a woman holding a small bird in her hand. It comes with an inscription taken from Matthew's account of Jesus' instruction to his apostles before sending them on their first missionary journey. It reads, "The gift you have been given, give as gift" (Matt 10:8). This image and this inscription continue to remind me to cherish the gifts that are mine, to develop them, and then to share them. In this way, we are expressing more clearly what it means to be made in the image of a God who is self-giving in relationships. The time and effort that we put into initial training, ongoing formation, and education through study leaves and sabbaticals can be likened to a form of prayer that binds us to God and to the community we are called to serve.

SERVICE

The service dimension of vocation correlates with the professional commitment to serve human need. The need that the professions serve defines the purpose of the profession and in turn helps to identify the kind of behavior appropriate in professional practice. Those who enter a profession promise to meet the fundamental need for which the profession exists and to conduct themselves in ways that further the purpose of their specialized role.

Mission of the Church

Pastoral ministry serves the need for salvation through advancing the mission of the church; the theological task for understanding the service of pastoral ministry is to identify that mission. When we lose touch with the church's mission as the defining reality for our pastoral service, we mistake the sorts of skills and tasks that are required of us.

According to *Lumen Gentium* (no. 1) of the Second Vatican Council, the mission of the church is both spiritual and social: the church is to be both a sign and an instrument of our union with God, and of the unity of all humankind. Pastoral ministers, in different ways, play a special part in the church being what it is and practicing what it preaches. As the whole people of God, the community of all the baptized, the church is moving through history sharing in Christ's saving mission to proclaim, embody, and serve the coming of the reign of God in its fullness. Pastoral ministers contribute to this mission through:

Proclaiming the word
Celebrating the sacraments
Organizing and administrating the community
Witnessing to the gospel through a life of discipleship
Providing service to those in need

Officer of the Church

Our professional commitment entails the duty to represent the church in faithful and loving ways through various ministries. When serving as a minister of the church, we do not act simply as private individuals. We are official representatives of the church. Some ministers react defensively to this professional obligation to be an "officer of the church." They do so because they interpret it in an overly restrictive way, as if they were a puppet of the Magisterium with no personal freedom, or an ecclesial robot whose words and actions are so programmed into them that they cannot think for themselves. Certainly being an officer of the church does limit personal autonomy. For no matter how charismatic or prophetic we might be, we must represent more than ourselves. Yet being an officer of the church does not deny us pastoral discretion in the way we represent the church and promulgate its teaching. Prudence is always welcome. However, as officers of the church, we must consider how our actions affect the overall well-being of the community.

Even though the tradition of church law does not hold lay ecclesial ministers accountable as officers of the church to the same degree as its does ordained ministers, we are all still responsible to witness on behalf of the church. This means that the public can rightfully expect that we will provide witness, worship, preaching, teaching, direction, and pastoral care in accord with the church's doctrinal, moral, liturgical, and spiritual traditions. The church, in effect, is expressing its vision, values, and beliefs through us.

Fiduciary Duty

The commitment to provide service as an officer of the church includes the commitment to the other's best interest. This entails fulfilling our fiduciary duty of subordinating self-interest so as to give a greater preference to the needs of the other over our own, even when this comes as a personal inconvenience and demands some personal sacrifice. In a biblical idiom, this mark of professionalism means that we are willing to "go the extra mile." Such a commitment falls squarely within the covenantal model of pastoral ministry in which we are like good neighbors to each other—self-sacrificing and interested in the welfare of others. Permanent deacons and other married ministers find this fiduciary duty especially challenging because they have to discern carefully how to negotiate their commitment to family, work, and ministry. By fulfilling our fiduciary duty, we participate in the spirit and mission of the servant leadership of Jesus (compare Mark 10:45).

Being committed to the other's best interest also means that our practice of ministry can be assessed morally and not just technically. We may be highly skilled as preachers, teachers, or administrators, but we can still fall short morally by lacking in virtue—by not making ourselves accessible, by refusing to answer the door, the mail, or the phone, or by looking out primarily for ourselves, by avoiding any meeting with people where we might not be in control, by discriminating between people and serving only a select group, or by showing little interest that justice is being done in the community. However, when we give a greater degree of preference to the interest of others over our own, we imitate Jesus in the way he had a special feeling for those who hurt, and in the way that he was inclusive in spirit and in deed. The covenantal model of ministry further supports this commitment to the other by not allowing ministerial obligations to get reduced only to what is agreed upon to meet minimum requirements of time and money. Remember, covenantal relationships have room for the gratuitous and the unexpected, not just the gratuities that we have come to take for granted as an entitlement.

While it is true that everyone is under a moral obligation to help others, people expect this even more of a professional minister. This may be due to the nature of our covenantal commitment to the people and to our being symbolic representatives of the unconditional, inclusive love of God. Recall from the opening scenario that Fr. Jim was criticized by some parishioners for failing to realize how he is "on call" in the way others are not. In some of my workshops with ministers, I have heard some complain of their peers being more committed to their time at the gym than they are to their pastoral duties. As ministers, we are expected to be available to others, and we are probably more susceptible than other professionals are to the criticism of showing undue concern for self. This criticism only highlights the ever-present challenge to meet our fiduciary duty to serve while also attending to personal needs and to family for those who are married.

Our professional commitment to service is really incomplete without attending to appropriate self-care, the flip side of meeting the needs of others. We rightly speak of ministry being other directed. However, we will never have the energy to give if we do not first get what we need for ourselves outside the pastoral relationship. We must respect our own needs to maintain our physical, emotional, social, and spiritual health. This means giving time for exercise, leisure, days off, vacations, friends, family, retreats, spiritual direction, and therapy as needed. We must guard against the misuse of alcohol and drugs, and we ought to be aware of the warning signs in behavior and mood swings that indicate conditions detrimental to good health.

If we can honor the obligation to supply what we need for ourselves, then we may have the energy to transfer that same regard to others. Here is the crucial part: as professionals, we must be careful that we are supplying what we need for ourselves outside our professional relationships. Otherwise, we too easily turn these relationships in toward ourselves instead of using them to serve the best interest of those seeking our service.

COMMUNITY

The communal dimension of vocation correlates with structures of accountability in professional life. Accountability is a way of doing justice to the community. It recognizes the ties that bind us to one another and that we are responsible to others for what we have been given to assume our professional role in the community. Fr. Jim, from the opening scenario, is awakening to this moral dimension of his ministry.

Accountability

While ministry has traditionally been numbered among the learned professions, along with law and medicine, we cannot say that ministry satisfies all the requirements that we often associate with being professional. For example, noticeably absent are the standard structures of accountability, namely, a code of ethics and the structures and processes of review and discipline. However, ministry is not totally lacking in some structures and requirements for admission and performance. For example, we are bound to the teaching of the church and to canon law. We also have the U.S. Bishops' *Program of Priestly Formation*, their *Permanent Deacons in the United States: Guidelines on Their Formation and Ministry*, and the *National Certification Standards for Lay Ecclesial Ministers* that set forth some requirements for admission and performance. But the absence of a shared code of ethics, a professional organization as a primary reference point, professional autonomy, structures for peer review, and the disciplinary procedures and sanctions for controlling deviant behavior all stand in the way of appreciating ministers as professionals in the fullest sense.

While many of us may have high personal standards, these are often not reinforced by the corporate practice of ongoing review and evaluation. A priest's ministry, for example, is largely free of supervision or formal scrutiny by colleagues. This is what makes Fr. Jim's proposal at the end of the opening scenario so outstanding. One priest told me that he was in his first pastorate for eighteen months. During that time, no one from any level of the diocese ever checked in on him to see how he was doing. Since he did not draw any public attention to himself, he was left alone. I have since learned that this is a typical experience of many in ministry. Since maintaining skills in the ministry is left to the individual for the most part, communities can be misled about our competence, especially if there is no ongoing review of performance measured against shared standards.

Developing standards for accountability does not mean turning a covenantal commitment into a mere contract with the community. Covenants, too, have expectations. The most famous, perhaps, are the Ten Commandments given through Moses and the Great Commandment of Jesus. The covenantal obligations we undertake as ministers warrant holding us accountable in order to protect others from being harmed. William F. May writes incisively, "In professional ethics today, the test of moral seriousness may depend not simply upon personal compliance with moral principles but upon the courage to hold others accountable."[9] But even before we have the courage, we need commonly shared criteria for measuring professional performance.

Code of Ethics

These commonly shared criteria can make up a code of ethics. In recent years, there has been an increased interest in developing a code of ethics for ministers. In fact, codes of ethics for ministers are emerging all over the world. It is hard to keep up with the trend.[10] A code of ethics is one way to bring some accountability to ministry, but we need to be critical about what a code can offer and we ought to proceed with caution when developing and implementing these codes. My conviction is that a code of ethics properly developed, personally appropriated, structurally supported, responsibly implemented, and justly enforced can strengthen a just ministry. It may also contribute in a modest way to restoring trust in the church by setting standards for high quality and accountable ministerial service.

At this point in the life of the Catholic Church in the United States, the question is not whether we should have a code of ethics. The professional character of ministry requires one. The Dallas Charter (Article 12) can be interpreted as requiring each diocese to develop one, and this means something more than a policy on sexual misconduct. I suggest in the following paragraphs some aspects of a code of ethics that we need to consider in this process of developing a code of ethics for ministers, since some diocese or ministerial communities already have one or are in the process of developing one.[11]

The primary purpose of a code of ethics is to foster authentic ministry. This means that a code can make explicit both the primary values that should govern personal growth in our professional identity as a minister and the basic moral obligations that mark professional responsibilities in the exercise of ministry. Part of being professionally responsible is to be open to public accountability for our performance. A code of ethics makes explicit the commonly shared criteria for making this assessment.

Codes also aim at assuring the public of the trustworthiness of those accepted into the profession. Codes can engender trust in two ways. One is by serving as a set of criteria for screening candidates for ministry. The careful screening of candidates to protect the church from those unfit to serve as its ministers can be one way to assure the faithful that we already manifest the character and conduct befitting the ministry. Second, codes can also engender trust by providing the public with an explicit expression of the core values and standards of practice that define our commitment to the community and, if followed, could serve as a check on our blindness to the misuse of power that violates trust and causes harm.

Codes also provide a set of standards that help to define, interpret, and measure responsible pastoral practice. We are often the victims of many unrealistic expectations. The clarity of a code can support, protect, and liberate us from the social pressure to be and do more than our professional role requires of us. A code that sets a clear baseline for the morally appropriate exercise of ministry can also be an effective tool in our initial formation and education as well as provide a point of reference for ongoing formation, education, and evaluation.

The content of the code seeks to establish expectations of good character and right conduct in the exercise of the ministerial role. The content focuses primarily on one-to-one pastoral responsibilities along with obligations for personal and professional development. This common content gets elaborated in more or less detail through a variety of literary forms. A code instructs as well as inspires; it supports as well as challenges. The great challenge in giving content to a code is to distinguish statements of theological vision from prescriptive rules on the one hand and from ideals of aspiration on the other. Therefore, making the appropriate distinctions in semantic forms will be important for the proper interpretation, application, and enforcement of a code of ethics.

Whether a code of ethics will be effective in achieving its purposes will depend on who is responsible for putting it together. Its credibility depends on it. Most codes are written by members of the profession whose behavior the code is to govern. This approach gives a great deal of autonomy to the professional group, but it lacks public accountability by including no one from outside the closed professional circle to check or challenge the group's definition of what it means to act in a professional way. The danger in this mode of authorship is that it can lead to in-house protectionism, since a committee of self-appointed professionals may privilege their own interests and be blind to the interest of those they are to serve. If ministerial codes were developed by a single clerical author, or even a committee, and then imposed from on high, it may weaken the code's authority, since it is the product of the experience and vision of only a few.

My contention is that there may be greater hope for restoring trust in the ministry and achieving accountability from ministers if the code is developed from the ground up by a collaboration of those in different types of ministry as well as of the laity. Since the reason for a code in the first place lies in the need to define the kind of attitudes and relationships we ought to have with other ministers and with the community of the faithful, and since we are called from the community, sustained by the community, and entrusted to serve the community, then the whole community (not only those in ministry) should be an integral part of the process of defining the ethical standards, shaping the structures of accountability, and supervising the enforcement of the code. This means that the code would not be the product of one author, or a committee, or of some risk management firm. The code would emerge as the product of consulting the community by engaging a broad base of collaboration and deliberation. We already have precedent for such a consultative and deliberative process from the bishops' pastoral letters on peace and nuclear weapons (1983) and the economy (1986).

However, no matter how broad the base of consultation for developing a code, it will still have some limitations. One is that having a code does not guarantee compliance. The code will not solve the problem of virtue, discipline, and discernment that we need in order to evaluate and respond appropriately in ambiguous pastoral situations. So we must remain modest in what we think a code will be able to do to change or direct our behavior.

Another limitation is that a code will not prevent lawsuits. In fact, in this highly litigious climate, having a code may even prompt more lawsuits by making public clearly defined standards of practice. The code could be used in litigation against a minister even if the breach is not criminal behavior.

One of the greatest limitations of a code is the lack of a culture and structures that support enforcing accountability in order to make the code credible and effective as an instrument of a just ministry. My experience working with ministers of all sorts is that, long before the sexual abuse crisis, ministers tended to resist standards and procedures that would make them publicly accountable for their ministerial performance, especially when diocesan administration had a hand in it. Without a culture that supports rewarding good performance, on the one hand, and reporting professional misconduct on the other, the code as an instrument of accountability is an empty promise. For any code to be effective, it has to be accompanied by, if not preceded by, a change in the culture of the church that would make it more receptive to the evaluation of ministerial performance. It also needs a regulatory body that can oversee the implementation of the code and provide structures and procedures that will support reporting violations and applying sanctions.

Another limitation is that codes tend to focus almost exclusively on attitudes and practices of the individual minister to the exclusion of the social structures that influence them. However, ministers always work within structures (office structures, living arrangements, procedures for compensation and promotion, and so on) that influence for good or ill how ministry is shaped, maintained, and exercised.

A perennial limitation of a code is its proper interpretation. Codes are not self-interpreting. This has a great deal to do with the semantic forms used to express the code. Whereas inspirational ideals may be too vague to provide guidance in a pastoral situation, a prescriptive rule may be too specific to be applicable to changing circumstances. The assumption that practical decisions can rest on a code of rules attracts and perhaps encourages a legalistic and minimalist interpretation. Legalists can reduce the code to an oppressive means of control; minimalists can cite the code to defend self-interest by claiming that what is not forbidden must be permitted. Both an excessive scrupulosity and a slipshod laxity threaten the sound enforcement of a code.

Furthermore, the code will never be able to take us more than partway to an appropriate pastoral practice. The morally relevant features of the situation in which we act must be considered in determining what to do. Too many specific rules put the burden on the code and not on the individual minister, who must decide in the midst of many contingent factors. The responsible use of the code calls for moral sensibilities, perceptiveness, and the artful discrimination of the weight given to a standard and its prudential application in ambiguous pastoral situations. These can never be supplied by rules. The ambiguity that fills the pastoral ministry is too great for any code to be a definitive summary of what an ethical ministry should be so that we only need to consult the code to know what to do.

Moreover, codes cannot be expected to solve every ministerial problem or guarantee the safe negotiation of a pastoral conflict without fear of false accusation. Codes will have to be subject to ongoing analysis of their implications with the nuance that any moral statement requires, and they will have to be subject to ongoing revision as new ministerial challenges and conflicts emerge.

In the end, we need to be modest in our expectations of what a code of ethics can do to ensure a just ministry. While we need a code of ethics for ministers, we ought to go slowly in developing it. The process of developing the code ought to be as inclusive as possible. This means collaborating with grassroots groups representing the diversity that makes up the church. This process should be kept as public as possible with plenty of opportunity for feedback and revision. The process of developing the code, with the mutual learning fostered along the way, may well be more important than the product itself to foster a just ministry.

These first two chapters have tried to show that being professional does not undermine having a vocation to pastoral ministry. In fact, it can enhance it. Table 1 presents a summary of the four aspects of vocation correlating with professional demands.

TABLE 1. VOCATIONAL AND PROFESSIONAL IDENTITIES				
Vocational Identity	Called	Gifted	Service	Community
Professional Identity	Covenantal relationship; Symbolic representative of the holy	Specialized knowledge and skills for theological reflection; Fiduciary duty	Committed to serve the mission of the church as an officer of the church	Accountability

Adhering to the professional demands of each aspect of vocation can make pastoral ministers clearer sacraments of God's loving care for all people and can help nurture a just ministry that will restore trust in the church and its ministers.

3

THE MINISTER'S
CHARACTER

An intelligent, conscientious, and socially engaging woman (let's call her Amy) grew up nurtured in the faith by her loving family and closely knit, small-town parish of St. Bart's. All through high school, Amy practiced her faith regularly and enjoyed many of the social activities of the youth group, as there was no Catholic high school in her area. When she went off to college, Amy gradually drifted away from the church. She didn't find much support for practicing her faith among her college peers. But she never lost her keen social consciousness and hard-working spirit. She majored in business and psychology to prepare for a career in the corporate world.

After graduation, she got a job in the human resources department of a small company that manufactured and distributed environmentally safe household products. At work, she quickly made very positive impressions on her supervisors and coworkers. Amy was a highly responsible woman whom you could count on to follow through on her commitments, to share tasks easily, and to do it all with good humor.

Working for this company brought her into contact with many coworkers who shared her social concerns. Some were practicing Catholics, and their fidelity inspired Amy to return to the church and to get involved in its social outreach programs. The people she met at the parish, along with her core group of friends from work, were a strong motivation for Amy to share more in their religious values and social commitments. What was important to her friends, especially her very best friend Mike, became important to her, too. Through her friendships, she came to understand herself better. Mike in particular was like a moral mirror to her. Through him, she learned to own the virtues that were already well developed in her, such as her sense of justice, her fidelity to friends, her trustworthiness, and her solidarity with those *who cared for the Earth. Mike was instrumental in helping her acquire the virtue of self-care, as she learned to recognize more clearly her vices, especially her tendency to overwork or to be overly ambitious.*

Too often ethics is presented as if its only concern is to find a resolution to a troublesome situation. To determine what is right or wrong, some like to draw upon principles that help us recognize our duty in some instance; others look to the consequences a possible action will produce; still others use a combination of principles and consequences along with other forms of moral analysis. Amy's story, however, proposes a different perspective on ethics.

As important as it is to be able to decide the right action to take, there are other questions just as important and that ought to be asked first: Who am I? What sort of person do I want to become? How am I going to get there?[1] These are the primary concerns of virtue ethics, a mode of ethics that is more interested in the moral agent's character than in isolated actions, that is, more attentive to the agent's motives, intention, disposition, and perspective than in a model of decision making. By focusing on the moral person, virtue ethics provides moral guidance by developing what biblical anthropology calls the "heart," that is, those inner realities of the moral agent that give personal meaning to what we do. So rather than giving primary attention to rules for action, or even to the action itself, virtue ethics focuses on what it means to be a good person and the character traits that make up such a person. Right and wrong are derived from that.

As chapters 1 and 2 on the meaning of having a vocation and being professional have shown, ministry is both a religious and a moral enterprise. Everyone who serves in a ministerial role is bound by a common purpose to share in the mission of the church to serve the religious needs of the people. In carrying out our mission, we are guided by some shared morality—some fundamental rules and character traits that describe the moral life that is consistent with the purpose of ministry. This chapter draws upon the contributions of virtue ethics to sketch the characteristics of the pastoral minister. After a brief rationale for turning to virtue ethics, this chapter examines the various aspects of moral character, discusses the formation of character, and finally offers some implications for forming candidates for just ministry. Chapter 4 sketches a profile of the virtuous minister by examining specifically some virtues we ought to have.

THE VIRTUE OF VIRTUE ETHICS

Why turn to virtue ethics for an ethical reflection on ministry? First, because virtue ethics is a mode of ethical reflection that brings together who we are with what we do. It emphasizes the connection between what ministry needs to do to promote the reign of God and the personal strengths we need in order to pursue it. If there is any profession in which the medium and the message are so closely tied together, it is the ministry. We judge the effectiveness of ministers not only on the basis of their pastoral skills but also on the basis of their integrity, on whether their personal lives are congruent with their message. In the idiom of traditional Catholic moral theology, *actio sequitur esse*: Who we are shapes what we do. Then there is the dialectical return: What we do in turn shapes who we are. Or, in the folk wisdom of Forrest Gump's mother, "Stupid is as stupid does." More than any other approach to the moral life, virtue ethics focuses on the integral relation of character to action. Whether we have a problem to face, what we think the problem is, and how we respond to it depends a great deal on the kind of person we are. In the pastoral ministry, what we bring to a situation by way of personal character will influence a great deal the way we see, judge, and act.

Second, if the crisis of sexual abuse committed by members of the Catholic clergy and the response by some bishops to the crisis taught us anything, it is that being in ministry and being virtuous do not always go together. One does not have to be in ministry long to realize that it is too late to prevent us from doing harm if we wait until we come face to face with a moral challenge, such as the seduction of a sexual relationship or the lure of easy access to a great deal of other people's money. Virtue ethics recognizes that the paradigm of ethical decisions is not the occasional tough choice that we have to make in a difficult time of crisis. Rather, for virtue ethics, the small, daily efforts count. Virtue ethics recognizes that most of the hard work of making decisions lies in the way we live before we are morally tempted.

Virtue ethics jolts us out of the taken-for-granted attitude that morality has only to do with rules, critical incidents, or extraordinary events, like those that make the headlines. In virtue ethics, the ordinary is the realm of the moral. Virtue ethics is concerned with how we live, especially how we live day by day and not just in those times

46

when we have to make a tough choice. How we live between those extraordinary moments of big decisions will have a great influence on what we choose when things are really ambiguous. The daily cultivation of habits through the seemingly insignificant acts of gratitude, generosity, compassion, humility, courage, and so forth are what count toward making the big decisions. When the critical moment comes, our response to it is the result of the habits we have already formed by acting appropriately when the stakes were not so high and the situation not so tense or ambiguous. For example, the pastoral minister who takes a stand for her convictions in staff discussions is more likely to be the one who has the courage to speak up to the bishop at a deanery meeting to support the role of women in the church than is a staff member who is too mild-mannered to stand up for himself in less intimidating settings.

Third, virtue ethics is particularly helpful for cultivating ministerial character that inclines us to do what is fitting in situations of great ambiguity. A rule-oriented approach to morality, by contrast, rushes to a code of conduct to keep ministers on the right path. Granted, these codes will have some clear rules, such as those regulating sexual contact with parishioners or maintaining confidentiality. However, ministry is too ambiguous for codes of ethics to cover all circumstances, and there is no guarantee that we will appropriate the rules and policies of the code. In the thick of pastoral ministry, what counts most in relationships filled with ambiguity and the unexpected is our emotional responsiveness and keen moral sense of what would be "reasonable" or "appropriate" in the situation. Such a judgment requires practical wisdom, or prudence. A code of ethics may be helpful in defining our role and in prescribing general responsibilities. But we ultimately must rely on our practical wisdom to navigate the ambiguities of pastoral care. The requirements of virtue vary from one situation to another and look different for different people because of their strengths, habits, and circumstances. So if we hope to be the kind of people who are inclined to do what is right, especially when it is difficult to do so, then we must begin far ahead of the pastoral problems and look to the character formation of candidates. Virtue ethics helps us do that in its concern not only with who we are but also with how we get to become that way.

Fourth, in this process of moral and ministerial formation, we need a model to serve as our point of reference for determining good character and identifying what counts as virtue. In natural law ethics, reason discovers the moral intentions of God in human nature and names these as fundamental rights, absolute rules, or basic goods. In virtue ethics, we turn to the character of a moral exemplar as the ultimate court of appeal for what constitutes the good life, or the life of a fully flourishing person. Christians know something about what it means to be human, to be good, and to live the good life because we have seen it in Jesus. Christian morality regards the life of discipleship, or being conformed in the image of Christ, to be the best life for us to live. The long tradition of following Christ (*imitatio Christi*) echoes this feature of virtue ethics. In Christian virtue ethics, we turn to Jesus to see whom we are called to be, to know what constitutes good character, what counts as virtuous behavior, and what the good life looks like. However, imitating Christ is not mimicry. We do not set out to repeat slavishly what Jesus literally did. We turn to Jesus as our model, not our blueprint. Like all Christians, we learn best how to be virtuous by striving to make his wisdom, his spirit, and his disposition toward life shape our own. Our life is a faithful variation of his when we can detect the consonance between the Gospels that witness to Jesus and the moral demands of the moment. Faithful attention to the character of Jesus and creative openness to what is at hand are the challenges we face in trying to follow Jesus today.

So for at least these four reasons—the focus on the integral relation of character and action, the paradigm of practicing everyday virtues, the importance of virtues over rules in negotiating complex ambiguities in ministry, and the centrality of Jesus Christ as our exemplary model of character, virtue, and the good life—we need to draw upon virtue ethics if we are to practice a just ministry. But what is this "character" that is front and center in virtue ethics?

CHARACTER

Character, in short, refers to our moral identity. Character is who we are behind all our roles and actions. It is the result of how we have chosen and what we have done, since we are all the sum total of our actions. Character expresses in action the moral identity of one's self, composed of several inner realities. Four of these give us a good sense of what we mean by character in virtue ethics: intention, emotions, imagination, and virtues. While these work together in expressing our moral identity, I separate them here for closer analysis of what each contributes to the whole character.

INTENTION

Every action that we do knowingly and freely has a mission to accomplish. It is directed toward a target. That is, we act with a purpose, or with a goal or end in mind. The discipline of ethics has a name for that. We call this purpose, goal, end, mission, or target our "intention." This intention does not have to be a mission impossible, like finding a cure for cancer. It can be performable and within reach, like eating to be nourished. But whether momentous or mundane, we become identified with what we do intentionally.

When we act intentionally, we do more than get something done. What we do stays with us to become part of who we are. In other words, as a result of repeating actions over and over again purposefully, we begin to look like what we do. When we do something often enough, we take on the quality of that action. Whereas one random act of kindness does not make us kind, a pattern of intentionally kind actions does. Kindness becomes characteristic of our personal identity and style of life. It is how we recognize a person's distinctive quality. In the opening scenario to this chapter, for example, we can say of Amy that she is a trustworthy woman because she has shown herself to be that way over time.

When we try to determine a person's character, we size them up by paying attention to their patterns of action and not just to one isolated act. We try to catch their way of being among us. It is like looking at their home movies, not just at their graduation picture. In order to get closer to their core moral identity (something that we will never know absolutely clearly or totally), we draw from their style of life the basic intention that gives coherence and consistency to their life. This is what gives them a moral identity. For example, we see that Dorothy Day's intention was to create a world in which everyone would be kind to everyone else and make room in their lives for the differences in each other. Her moral identity was her commitment to hospitality. Gandhi's basic intention was to bring people together and to overcome the sufferings of injustice through nonviolent means. His moral identity was his commitment to harmony through nonviolence.

More immediate to our interests in ministerial character and formation are our attempts to capture a person's moral identity in the assessments we make whenever we write a letter of recommendation or an evaluation of readiness for ministry. In these portraits, we identify personal traits and paint a word picture of the style of life that makes this person stand out from everyone else and fitting for the ministry in question. So we might say in reference to Amy of the opening case, "Amy is a self-disciplined person. She sets goals for herself, keeps her focus, and then works persistently toward her goal. She is gracious and inclusive of differences and so enjoys a broad base of rapport among her coworkers. She is a person of convictions committed to justice. She can stand behind even unpopular positions when the integrity of her convictions is at stake." By drawing upon her behavioral patterns, we get a glimpse of her "intentionality," or the kind of person she is becoming: one committed to the dignity of persons, to justice in the community, and to loving others as she loves herself. By seeing what she most loves (self-respect and justice), we are able to name the basic intention of her life—namely, to be loving. Only then can we begin to understand her specific actions as expressions of her core moral identity. This fundamental intentionality is who she is, her true moral character.

EMOTIONS

Emotions have fared poorly in some Roman Catholic natural law approaches to the moral life. Reason alone has ruled. Austin Fagothey's widely used and recently reprinted *Right and Reason* is representative.[2] For him, right reason is the proximate norm of morality, and logic teaches when reason is right. From a perspective like this, emotions get disparaged as the font of fallacy and so are dangerous to right moral living. Under the influence of an Enlightenment interpretation of moral reasoning, reason must reign as the wellspring of wisdom, and nothing clouds the mind quite like the emotions. To be objective is to be dispassionate, neutral, and detached. "Don't be emotional" means "Don't be stupid." If we get emotional, the rationalists fear, we will not be able to act freely or grasp the truth of a situation and act reasonably.

While the capacity to reason is characteristic of being human, and the rational is indeed an important aspect of the moral life, rational reflection is not the sole arbiter of our moral response. Emotions give us a window on the world that is not always transparent to reason. The noble and necessary role of the emotions holds an honorable place in the Catholic spiritual and moral tradition. In spirituality, Ignatius of Loyola talked about the affective experiences of consolation and desolation as reliable ways of discerning God's movement in our lives. The tradition of discernment of spirits has shown that emotions awaken insight that conceptual knowledge can miss. Just as a mother's love for her child alerts her to slight changes in the child that detached observation would miss, so the affective movements of one trying to live in union with God can tell us whether one is in tune with God or not in ways that logic never could. In the tradition of discernment, murmurings of the heart are messages of God because emotions bring us into a closer bond with what we value than conceptual knowledge does.

In morality, the tradition has distinguished two ways of knowing moral values. One way is to acquire information about moral values but to remain detached from them. This is conceptual or head knowledge. The other way is to know moral values through personal encounter that affords a felt appreciation of their significance. This is evaluative or heart knowledge. The emotional connection to values makes it possible to be sensitive to those aspects of a situation that are relevant to deciding how to act in ways that fit the values. Without the affective feel for the situation, our moral assessment is incomplete and can be misleading. Knowing moral values by ways of the head and the heart underscore moral living as an alliance of feeling as well as reasoning about what is right or wrong.

Today the cooperative efforts of psychologists and neuroscientists are helping us understand that reasoning cannot be thoroughly detached from emotion. Neurologist Antonio Damasio's research shows that decision making is filled with bodily and emotional content. Since the person is an integrated whole, decisions come as a mix of bodily, emotional, and rational processes.[3] Daniel Goleman's

Emotional Intelligence[4] is a more popular primer on the science of emotions. He reports that we are born with a predisposition to a favored range of emotions. For example, some of us are genetically endowed to be shy, others to be bold. However, Goleman insists that biology is not destiny. The environment, especially the crucible of family life, plays a major role in how our emotional predispositions get expressed as life unfolds.

The emotional lessons we learn as children from our parents, especially mothers, play a major role in whether a temperamentally timid child grows bolder or continues to shy away from challenge. Emotional skills are honed with friends over the years, but the family environment remains the major social setting in which we learn to think about emotions and the choices we have in expressing them. Parents do much to impart the basics of emotional learning—recognizing, managing, and expressing emotions—through what they say and do to their children as well as through the way they model the handling of feelings between themselves. As Goleman summarizes, "All the small exchanges between parent and child have an emotional subtext, and in the repetition of these messages over the years children form the core of their emotional outlook and capabilities."[5] The emotional lessons we learn at home and at school during childhood and into the teenage years sculpt the neural pathways that shape the emotional patterns that govern our lives. "Habits acquired in childhood become set in the basic synaptic wiring of neural architecture, and are harder to change later in life."[6] However, we are not fated by these emotional habits. Since emotional learning is lifelong, the emotional lessons we learned as children can be reshaped. This is often the primary work of psychotherapy. Because the brain continues to develop, though at a slower rate as we age, we continue to grow. We can change.

Virtue ethics, with assistance from developments in psychology,[7] honors emotion as an important aspect of character greatly influencing not only what we do but also the quality of our perception and actions. Emotions connect character to action both as a way of knowing moral values and as a source of motivation. A word on each.

Along with Aristotle, Aquinas, Ignatius of Loyola, and modern psychology, we can say that, as a way of knowing, emotions are not blind feelings or neutral outbursts, but value-laden ways of understanding our world.[8] Emotions are immediate and initial evaluations we make of a person or situation. As Daniel Maguire has argued, we enter the moral enterprise of reflection, argument, and responsible living through an affective grasp of the value of persons and the web of relationships we have with others and the environment.[9] Emotional reactions tell us that, in moral matters, we feel and intuit, immediately and without argument, an evaluative estimate of the world that strikes us. We read situations affectively: we are delighted *in*, in love *with*, sad *about*, afraid *of*, angry *at* someone or something. Our emotional connection to the situation influences our interpretation of it, what we regard as its morally relevant features, and our initial evaluative attitude that inclines us to respond in a certain way. This affective way of knowing calls for completion in practical reasoning. The moral awareness that leads to action, then, is a marriage of head and heart, conceptual and affective knowledge working together.

Perhaps a handy way of grasping how emotions are a way of knowing moral values is to think of our emotional reaction as a kind of diagnostic tool, a primitive "ethics attack" of attraction to what is good and of repulsion to what is evil. Experiencing the feelings appropriate to the morally salient features of a situation is a mark of virtuous character. Our emotions reveal the kind of person we are by showing up in the types of things that elicit feelings of pleasure and those that pain us. Our attraction to something that seems right and good to us is love. We move toward what we love out of desire to behold it, and we feel joy when we are in its presence. By contrast, if something strikes us as wrong or evil, we feel aversion toward it and we move away from it, and feel sad and sorrowful if we cannot escape it. We are driven to get straight our practical reasoning on what to do because we feel deeply about the values that have struck us. Wisdom grows out of not only our cognitive but also our affective engagement with what strikes us because an adequate interpretation of our situation is only possible when we have a certain emotional connection to it. Genuine bonds of affection already involve us in a preliminary, precritical appraisal of the ethically salient features of the situation and of what our moral responsibility ought to be.

While the process of acquiring character involves training the emotions and learning to trust them as interpretively reliable, we also need a healthy sense of distrust. Just as we do not want to put a heartless head in charge of the moral life, neither do we want a headless heart directing our moral affairs. Moral living is an alliance of head and heart. This requires maintaining a tension between trusting and distrusting our emotions. After all, are not bigots, racists, and fanatics leading with the heart, too? Such undisciplined emotion, however, can lead to social chaos or crimes of passion. So, while emotions are inevitably involved in an evaluative process, some emotional conditions can impede or disrupt it. Extreme depression, rage, hate, and scorn, for example, can impair thinking and appropriate action. Intemperate emotions require therapy or, perhaps, sedation before they can be trusted.

We only need to recall those who move in and out of manic states. No one wants to trust such individuals' judgment. And for good reason. The things they say they ought to do at those times really are unwise. Manic highs and lows are unreliable states for reading reality rightly. These intense moods misperceive what is going on and impair judgment. In fact, these are the kinds of emotional conditions that can ruin emotion's reputation as having any moral value. Out-of-control emotional states are not reliable grounds for moral judgment. Our spiritual tradition of discerning spirits that honors emotions as a source of truth recognizes the same. In times of desolation, so says spiritual wisdom, we ought to resist making a significant decision or reversing the direction of a formerly well-made decision. However, extremes of distorted emotions should not prejudice us against all emotional influences on our behavior. Psychologist Sidney Callahan argues that reasonable moral agents can critically assess emotional reactions by applying rational criteria, such as whether the emotions are based on the correct evidence or are proportionate to the stimuli.[10]

Emotions also connect character to action by being a source of motivation. Emotions (from the Latin *ex + movere*) literally move us out of ourselves. As Sidney Callahan puts it, "We do things because we emotionally care about them and are personally invested; when we stop being moved, we stop moving."[11] We need emotions to empower us, such as hope that gives us the energy to pursue what is difficult, courage to face our fears, and anger to protect what we love.[12] The successful persistence in the process of becoming a virtuous minister requires substantial motivation that grows out of our emotional attachment to the goal of ministry to participate in the mission of the church. Just as a good scientist acts out of love for truth, and physicians perse-

vere with difficult patients because they value well-being, so good ministers cultivate a love for the reign of God and do not have to struggle
with inner conflicts about whether or not to pursue it.

Besides, naked reason is not enough to move us to act. Reasoning
helps, but only if informed by a feeling for values. Not until we feel the
touch of the values that strike us are we moved to respond. The source
of moral paralysis is in the heart, not the head. Prize-winning brilliance
that does not have roots in the heart is sterile, static, and peripheral to
moral action. Philosopher Nancy Sherman underlines the role of emotions by saying that "without emotions, we do not fully register the
facts or record them with the sort of resonance and importance that
only emotional involvement can sustain."[13] In other words, simply to
note a moral wrong (or right) but not feel moral indignation (or admiration) is a failure to understand the full moral significance of the act.
Dazzling rational accounts of homelessness and migrant workers, for
example, will count for little toward effective moral action if our feeling for the preciousness of these people does not move us. Men who
are not angry at the exclusion and oppression of women in church and
society, humans who are not outraged over the abuse of nonhuman
creation, and heterosexuals who are not offended by the demeaning of
homosexuals show signs of affective numbness, lacking care for persons and the environment.

When we are not angry in the face of injustice, then we care
about justice too little. Our emotional reaction of indignation in the
presence of injustice highlights how deeply we care about seeing that
justice be done. We can easily miss the morally salient features of an
unjust situation if we are cool, calm, and collected. Other moral emotions, such as disgust, guilt, remorse, worry, regret, and shame, function similarly. Empathy, compassion, and care belong to this list, too.
One of the greatest threats to becoming a good person is not that we
do not know what is right, but that we are too lazy to care. The theological word for this is *sin*. Without a commitment of the heart, we will
not seek to be good or to do what is right. This is what led Sidney
Callahan to warn that we should "be especially aware that graver moral
danger arises from a deficit of moral emotion than from emotional
excess."[14]

The close relationship of emotions to moral reason and action
suggests how important the proper formation of our emotional life is

for the character of a minister. Becoming a good minister, no less than a good person, hinges on cultivating emotional awareness. We not only need to learn how to trust the interpretive reliability of emotions, but we must also learn what emotions are appropriate to the situation. For example, feeling pleasure in the face of another's misfortune is inappropriate. As Aristotle might put it, we have to have the right feelings, at the right time, toward the right values, and in the right way in order to make the right choice.[15] We need an aptitude for being attracted to what promotes human flourishing, such as being treated fairly, enjoying equal respect as a man or woman, or enjoying the freedom to develop one's gifts for the sake of the common good. In addition, we need an emotional aptitude for abhorring and avoiding what undermines becoming fully human, such as treating another cruelly, manipulating another's freedom, or exploiting their dependency on us. To be good ministers, we need emotional intelligence aligned with reason in order to be sensitive to what is valuable and to be empowered to act in favor of it.

IMAGINATION

The imagination is closely related to the emotions. Reflections on the moral life since Aristotle have acknowledged how our moral responses are governed by what we see going on.[16] According to philosopher Iris Murdoch, seeing is prior to choosing;[17] and as H. Richard Niebuhr once put it, "We respond as we interpret the meaning of actions upon us."[18] In other words, we respond to what we see. It is as simple as that. The way we interpret the world determines the way we relate to it. While the emotions move us, the imagination helps us "see."

If we regard the imagination as our private mental entertainment center, or equate it with the preserve of those who like to make things up so that it is a gift of creativity that some people have and others do not, then we can easily dismiss its moral significance. The imagination is integral to character and to the moral life. It is formed in us out of the language, images, and role models offered to us by the company we keep and the communities we live in. It houses the metaphors, or frames of reference, through which we perceive the world, make sense of it, enter another's world, and create our future. Because of our imagination, certain aspects of a situation stand out, others recede into the background, and still others do not appear at all. In short, whatever we do finds its direction in the imagination. That is why a Chinese proverb can say, "Ninety percent of what we see lies behind our eyes."

Moral problems, like poverty, racism, sexism, and clericalism, do not come with Post-It notes announcing themselves as problems. They become such when we see them that way. What we see sets the direction and limits of what we do; it generates certain options rather than others; and it disposes us to respond in one way rather than another. People with different frames of reference will notice different features of a situation as morally relevant. What is an option for one may never occur to another, for they simply don't see the situation the same way. We respond differently because we come from different places emotionally and imaginatively. The way we see what is happening shapes what we do as much as or more than how we reason. One of the sources of impasse in public discussions on moral issues is often not just a matter of our reasoning but of the differences in our underlying vision of the human good, or the metaphors we use to interpret what is going on. We see details of a situation against the background of our understanding of what the human good ought to be. If we are confused about that, then our perception of what is morally relevant will be clouded.

We "see" by means of the imagination not just by taking a look but by interpreting what we see. The imagination affects the way we describe and evaluate a situation. The interpretive imagination asks, "What is going on?" The kind of response we make is governed more by what we see going on than by a conscious rational choice. For example, if I see you as friendly, I will respond openly. If I see you as a threat, I will respond defensively. In ministry, if clergy look on lay colleagues as competitors, they refuse to cooperate with them. The good Samaritan saw the beaten man in the ditch as a fellow human being and stopped to help him. The priest and Levite saw him as a source of defilement and passed by on the other side of the street. Each perceived from a different frame of reference in their imaginations.

Since we "see" by means of images that influence our interpretation and evaluation of what is going on, the images that form our moral frame of reference are of primary importance in setting the direction and the limits of what we do, in generating certain options rather than others, and in disposing us to respond one way rather than another. Alice Walker's novel *The Color Purple*[19] is a powerful story of the liberation that can come about through a change in one's frame of reference. Celie, a depressed and battered woman, falls in love with Shug Avery, a self-possessed woman who lives a free style of life. Through Shug, Celie is introduced to a new way of seeing herself and her oppressive situation. Celie liberates herself from male domination only after she no longer lets the images of patriarchy and sexism rule her imagination and distort her vision. Celie's liberation shows that if we see one way rather than another, our behavior will reflect the difference.

One of our goals as ministers is to form a "pastoral imagination," which Craig Dykstra describes as "'a way of seeing into and interpreting the world' that, in turn, 'shapes everything the pastor thinks and does.'"[20] The core images that shape such an imagination ought to come from our beliefs about God and what God has done for us in Christ. Charles E. Curran has proposed that, when taken together, the five Christian mysteries of creation, sin, incarnation, redemption, and resurrection-destiny form the proper moral perspective for understanding and living the Christian moral life.[21] The challenge for us is not just to give assent to these beliefs as the basis of morality but to see the world by means of them and to bring our lives in line with their practical significance. It is not enough, for example, simply to profess that God is our Creator and that we are creatures made in God's image. We must also be able to see ourselves as ultimately dependent on God so that we find life meaningful even though we do not have absolute control over how things will turn out.

Interacting with the interpretive function of the imagination is the affective function of the empathic imagination. It asks, "How does it feel?" The affective imagination has deep roots in the emotions, especially our capacity for empathy. Research on empathy shows how important our emotional capacity is in the development of character.[22] Empathy is an affective and imaginative capacity to cross over into another's experience, identify with the pains and pleasures of the other, and then return to one's self. When empathy is born, care is born, and with it morality. Empathy's moral strategy is the Golden Rule. Our empathy and compassion are engaged when we feel happy for those rescued from a natural disaster but feel revulsion by another story of domestic violence. That we are moved and how deeply we are moved register the response of the self in the depths of our moral identity.

Good moral character is endangered by the great enemy of empathy—apathy—the root of all evil. The apathetic don't care. They are without pity, unmoved by any feeling for doing the right thing or becoming a good person. A foundational biblical text puts it this way: "For I was hungry and you gave me no food, I was thirsty and you gave me nothing to drink, I was a stranger and you did not welcome me, naked and you did not give me clothing, sick and in prison and you did not visit me" (Matt 25:42–44). When the evening news covers a mugging incident that leaves an elderly woman near death, the reporter's story is not about cruel muggers but about those who did not respond to the beaten woman. The priest and Levite are faulted because they saw the victim but "passed by on the other side." The hero of the story, the Samaritan, was "moved with pity" and responded with caring generosity (Luke 10:29–37). Compassion is at the center of moral character. Complacency is its sinful shadow. It is hard to imagine ministerial character apart from the capacity to feel compassion for those who suffer or to feel anger at injustices done against those who are vulnerable. We must learn to feel our emotions and to tutor them so that we learn to love the right things in the right way and at the right time.

Along with the interpretive and empathic functions of the imagination is the creative role the imagination plays to move us into the future to create our world. It is our muscle for change by envisioning something new. The creative imagination asks, "What else is possible?" We will not be able to act differently if we cannot imagine what it would be like to be someone else. Only if we can imagine a new way of life can we ever make it real for us. The bumper sticker, "Imagine Peace," is on to something. If we cannot imagine a peaceful world, we will not be able to bring it about. Growing morally is a matter of seeing what does not yet exist but ought to, and then working to bring that vision into being.

An example of the creative imagination at work in shaping the face of ministry today is how we are enjoying the benefits of developing the potential of the image of a "discipleship of equals." This image has opened the church to avenues for honoring the place of women in ecclesial ministry. We would not be likely to act differently toward women in the church today than we did in the past if we had not imagined what it would be like, through baptism, to be equal partners with them in ministry. The role of the creative imagination is to expand the possibilities of what our faith demands. A moral character fit for ministry has an openness to the "not yet" and the freedom to take risks on something new.

VIRTUES

While emotion and imagination contribute to one's distinctive identity, virtue is what we most frequently associate with character. How do we understand virtue?

First of all, the Greeks used the word *virtue* (*arête*) to express "excellence." For them, everything has a purpose or end (a *telos*) that expresses the most complete form its nature can take. So anything could have the quality of *arête*—a knife, an arrow, a farmer, an olive— when it is a good example of its kind. A knife, for example, has "virtue" when it cuts well. When "virtue" is used of a person, it means that the person is good or has the skills and qualities of character to be what a person is meant to be. For Aristotle this would be to reason well and act accordingly. He called living this way "happiness." For Augustine, Aquinas, and the larger Christian tradition, this is living in communion with God.

Moreover, while we recognize virtue in behavior (and so talk of virtuous thoughts, feelings, or acts), virtues are primarily qualities or strengths of character (such as skills, habits, tendencies, inclinations, or dispositions—all terms often used interchangeably in virtue ethics). Virtues are conducive to developing our potential. So virtues lead to actions that express us at our best. It makes no sense, then, to speak of "virtuous" thoughts or feelings that are unaccompanied by behaviors that lead to full human flourishing. To feel generous but not to follow through with a generous act is not enough to qualify as a "virtuous" person. Virtues connect the person to actions.

However, virtues reflect, in their primary sense, not the good that we do (the action) but the goodness of the actor (the morally good person). They are rooted deeply within us where our desires, commitments, feelings, attitudes, and intention lie. These are all matters of the "heart" (in the biblical sense) that infuse our actions with personal meaning. We can do the right thing or even fulfill an obligation but not be virtuous because we lack the right intention or motivation. So we cannot claim that a person is virtuous simply by observing their actions. For example, the act of giving alms may seem to reflect virtue (generosity), but we still need to know the action's intent to know its true moral quality: Am I acting out of self-interest or out of concern for justice? From obedience to duty, or out of love?

For the purposes of shorthand, then, I like to think of virtues metaphorically as "habits of the heart." "Of the heart" says that virtues are rooted someplace inside us and are ultimately a matter of love. John Shea has an anecdote that says it best:

> There is a story about a busy man who one day hurriedly headed out the door for work. In his path was his three-year-old son playing with blocks. The man patted the boy on the head, stepped over him, opened the door, and went outside. Halfway down the walk a guilt bomb exploded inside him.
>
> "What am I doing?" he thought to himself. "I am ignoring my son. I never play with him. He'll be old before I know it."…
>
> He returned to the house and sat down with his son and began to build blocks. After two minutes, the boy said, "Daddy why are you mad at me?"[23]

Shea goes on to show that the quality and effectiveness of our actions is affected not only by what we do but also by the inner source of our actions. This story also illustrates one of the key insights of virtue ethics over duty and utilitarian ethics. The virtuous person must be moved to act out of an inner, emotional commitment to the good rather than being pushed from the outside by the force of obligation or utility. Just doing the right thing is not enough to be virtuous. As Shea says, "Playing blocks out of guilt is not the same as playing blocks out of love, and the difference is quickly spotted."[24] Doing the right thing for the wrong reason is not a virtue and does not make the agent virtuous.

In summary, virtues (or vices) are stable dispositions that enable us to be (or not) all that we can be and to realize the best kind of life we ought to live. These dispositions are deeply rooted in our identity, have affective and cognitive dimensions to them, and, while not readily visible to the observer, determine the moral quality of ourselves as agents and are the pathways to our actions. As Aristotle would have it, virtuous dispositions make persons good and also their actions.[25]

"Habit" is a common way of talking about virtue. This designation both hinders and helps our understanding of virtue. Habit hinders our understanding of virtue when we associate it with a stimulus-response or unthinking reflex action, like having a cigarette with a cup of coffee or punctuating our speech with "ah" or, even worse, with "like" or "you know what I'm saying?" But virtue as habit is not an unthinking Pavlovian-like reaction. When we use *habit* in this sense, we make virtue seem action specific and done without thinking. However, virtues do not denote a specific action. One can display courage by facing death on the battlefield, and, on another occasion, by retreating to safety. Moreover, virtues are not mindless. We act virtuously when we know what we are doing and choose to do it.

Habit helps our understanding of virtue by suggesting that we act virtuously by inclination, or habituation. To act by inclination means that doing what is right comes easier to us and it feels more natural because the habit (virtue) is so deeply part of us or, more exactly, characteristic of us. Acting by inclination is possible because virtue as habit connects head, heart, and hands so that acting from virtue is neither mindlessly blind nor emotionally numb. Acting virtuously dynamically unifies the whole self—reason, will, emotions, and the body work together to respond correctly to a situation.

Honed by reflected experience, emotional development, and committed practice, virtue gives us an intuitive ability to see in the blink of an eye the salient moral features relevant to deciding what to do, the way a skilled artist can distinguish in an instant a fake from the real masterpiece.[26] Once acquired, virtue gives us the power to act spontaneously and fittingly without having to stop and think about what to do every time we do it. We rely on the patterns of habituation that intuitively and spontaneously lead us to action. Sometimes we catch this ancient insight into virtue by saying that the virtuous person has an "affinity for," a "nose," or a "taste" for the fitting action in situations of great ambiguity. The Thomistic moral tradition speaks of this kind of moral awareness proper to virtue as "connatural knowledge," a rapid, penetrating, intuitive ability to know without thinking.[27]

Connatural knowledge reminds us that, while we might reach a correct judgment through rational deliberation, there is another way. It is the way of a felt and reasonable resonance between one's own being and the act to be done. Aristotle means much the same thing when he urges us to pay attention to the opinions of people with practical wisdom acquired by experience deepened by reflection and practice, "because they have an insight from their experience which enables them to see correctly."[28] Since it takes a lot of experience to acquire keen moral sensibility and judgment, we should not expect young people to have such practical wisdom, even though they may be whiz kids at computers, math, or science. The practical wisdom required for moral judgments is a different skill. It comes from years of experience of navigating life's complexities. Having experience, reflecting on it, and learning from it are essential to practical wisdom.

Habit also helps us understand virtue as an attribute acquired by practice. The ancients were much impressed with the long years of sheer practice (habituation) necessary to become a thoroughly good person. Aristotle saw that the way we develop in virtue is akin to becoming a great artist. We learn by practicing our craft.

> But the virtues we do acquire by first exercising them, just as happens in the arts. Anything that we have to learn to do we learn by the actual doing of it: people become builders by building and instrumentalists by playing instruments. Similarly we become just by performing just acts, temperate by performing temperate ones, brave by performing brave ones.[29]

Once acquired, acting according to virtue becomes second nature to us. However, the practice we do to acquire the virtue should not be confused with merely repeating behavior that externally conforms to that of a virtuous person. We only become virtuous by doing virtuous deeds the way a virtuoso does them. A habit moves toward a virtue when it is done attentively and with the right intention. Repeating these interior actions, not just the external action, puts us on the way to virtue.[30]

Consider the example of becoming grateful, a virtue we would expect to find in a minister. A predisposition to be grateful gets drawn out when our parents affirm us for saying "Thank you" and punish us when we don't. At this point, being grateful is still largely a superego function. We repeat the external action of saying "Thanks," but this is not expressing a virtuous disposition, even though our gratitude may appear to be virtuous. If we continue to repeat the behavior of saying "Thanks," we may learn to appreciate the value of being grateful as part of what it means to live a good life, whether we get praised for it or not. Eventually, by repeating the internal action of desiring to be grateful and by purposefully saying "Thank you," we gradually become disposed to being grateful, whether our parents are watching us or not. We don't stop and ask, "What good is it to be grateful here?" We just do it. This is a sign that the habit of gratitude is taking on the form of a virtuous disposition.

In becoming grateful, what began as rote behavior, an unreflective pattern of going along with parental pressure, gradually became a stable practice. It is not surprising to realize that what we now recognize as virtuous behavior in ourselves first began as rote behavior reinforced by others we admired and tried to imitate. However, to remain virtuous, we must continue to practice, reflect on our practice, and strive to be our best. Virtues orient us toward excellence, toward being "all that we can be," to borrow the one-time Army recruiting slogan. Minimalism and mediocrity have no place among the virtuous. They are the first steps toward the deterioration of virtue. Not to exercise a virtue is to weaken it as a skill for being good. Growth and development are key features of virtue ethics. We are always on the way of becoming virtuous. Acquiring virtue requires the whole course of a person's life, and not just "a day in the life of" a person.

Another salient feature of the habitual nature of virtue is that it gives stability to character and momentum to moral living that does not go in reverse easily. When we do something often enough, we take on the quality of that action. What we do in every moment and in each circumstance contributes to the growth of virtue or not because purposeful behavior has an effect not only on the world but also on the kind of person we are becoming. We become what we do. By habitually having the intention to tell the truth, for example, and expressing that intention in action, we gradually shape ourselves into truthful persons who can be trusted to be honest. Honesty is a virtuous disposition that we have nurtured through practice. Once acquired, the virtue gives us stability as a person characterized as being honest, and it gives us momentum to be honest in the future.

On the basis of the stability and momentum of virtue, we wouldn't expect a liar suddenly to tell the truth, a slanderer to break forth in paeans of praise, or a domineering and controlling pastor to have a fit of collaboration with the lay staff. How we behave in crucial moments of great significance is born out of the habits we form from the way we behave in the day-to-day course of our lives. Telling the truth now in this difficult situation makes it easier to tell the truth the next time. If we treat our friends with respect, chances are we will become respectful and treat even the stranger respectfully in turn. But if we treat our friends in a condescending way, then we will likely become arrogant and patronizing and so treat others in a condescending manner as well. Making a nonviolent response in the face of unfair attacks will make it easier to live gently all the time. The way we act now will affect the way we act later.

So the kinds of habits we form prior to entering ministry, as well as those we acquire in ministry, influence a great deal the kind of ministers we become and the style our ministry takes. Our early religious education and relationships with religious people—whether parents, teachers, or pastors—form attitudes and habits that affect our capacity to integrate new practices and information later on. Aristotle is instructive here. He points out that it is a matter of real importance whether our early education confirms us in one set of habits or another, for our habits make all the difference in the moral quality of our life.[31] As the Maples-Schuth study, "Character and Assessment of Learning for Religious Vocation," shows, those raised with rigid or authoritarian views of the faith carried this mind-set into adulthood and resisted ideas and approaches that did not fit their framework.[32] The wisdom of Aristotle and the empirical study of Maples and Schuth can help us to be more realistic about just how much influence formation personnel and programs really have on the character of ministerial candidates.

Given that consistency and stable patterns of behavior reflect character, one can appreciate the objections some raised against the zero-tolerance policy promulgated during the sexual abuse scandals. The policy is to remove from ministry anyone who has had even one isolated incident of sexual misconduct. If the insight of virtue ethics is true that we live more out of habits than out of consciously calculated reflection, and that character gives stability to moral identity and a fair degree of consistency to our behavior over the long haul, then it would be quite understandable, right, and just to remove from ministry someone who has established a pattern of sexual exploitation as a sexual predator, not someone for whom such misconduct is an isolated incident. This is also why so many were scandalized when serial predators were merely reassigned and not removed from ministry. While religious authorities may have seen them as acting "out of character," these predators were actually "in character." While character is not separate from our actions and the inner realities that feed them, character is not totally expressed by any one of them either. So we must be careful about judging a person's character simply on the basis of a single action. We may get a glimpse of character through an action, but patterns of action shaped over time (for example, predatory behavior) are better indicators of character, since character is our tendency to see, feel, think, and act with a certain degree of consistency.

In general, virtuous dispositions incline us to live the good life— a life worthy of Christian discipleship or of being human in the way Jesus was human—whether or not an obligation is prescribed by duties or principles, and whether or not anyone is watching to supervise us. "One test of character and virtue," William F. May once said, "is what a person does when no one is watching."[33] We reveal our true moral character in those spontaneous situations in which our deeper inclinations become transparent because we have to act without time to deliberate or to get supervision.

In ministry, virtuous dispositions help us to express the purpose of ministry in all situations, but especially in the complex and ambiguous ones that do not fall neatly under a moral rule or that are private so that no one is watching to correct us if we go astray. At these times, we need to be virtuous if we are to strike a balance between serving self-interest or the interest of others, or between acting at the extreme of "always" and "never." Take the issue of the use of physical touch as an expression of pastoral care, for example. I have heard many discussions about the wisdom of whether, when, where, and how to touch another as an expression of care. Some never want to touch anyone. Others hug everyone quite readily, no matter who he or she is or what his or her condition. The virtuous minister would seem to strike a balance between "always" and "never" touching.

To behave moderately toward each person at the right time and in the right way is not easy. Our original blessing that disposes us to goodness is impaired by a powerful opposing tendency, called by theologians "original sin." By it, they mean that there seems to be in all of us a diminished capacity to work for genuine well-being. However, when grace and virtue work together, we can overcome the tendencies to the corrupting behaviors we know as vices.

Even though I am putting so much emphasis on virtue, I am not abandoning the normative morality of duty and principles, or the value that codes of ethics can have for guiding pastoral ministry. Principles can be the eyes of virtue. They can help us notice aspects of a situation we might otherwise miss, and they can point us in the direction we ought to go. For example, the principle that says, "The one with the greater power bears the greater responsibility to maintain boundaries," helps us recognize the power gap in a pastoral relationship and it points us in the direction of what fidelity in that relationship requires.

Virtue also makes it possible to fulfill duty, or what the principle prescribes, as a true expression of one's self. Without virtue, duty is empty. We would simply go through the motions because we have been commanded to do so, or because we are under the watchful eye of someone in authority. Acting out of a virtuous disposition entails a difference in kind and quality from acting out of duty and principles. If we act simply out of duty, our moral backbone is outside us, and our actions are superego functions. Virtuous dispositions are interior principles of action, not ornaments of the self. They express an internally, self-directing commitment to what promotes human flourishing. They reveal the kind of person we are from the level of our moral identity. Moreover, the virtuous are committed to acting as excellently as possible in achieving their ends. Virtuous dispositions link us to action by leaning us toward what discipleship and human well-being demands, whether or not an obligation is prescribed by duties or principles. For the virtuous, living morally is more than doing one's duty or following a rule. It is striving for excellence. Minimalism and mediocrity have no place among the virtuous.

Given this understanding of character and four of its salient aspects, we always have to admit that the complete character of anyone eludes our grasp. Consider how many biographies get written about the same person to explore just who they are. Or how often we are surprised by the unexpected actions of someone whom we thought we knew well. Given their early lives, who would have thought Thomas Merton would ever become a revered contemplative, or that Dorothy Day would become a devout Catholic committed to the homeless poor? Our character is never completely defined; it is always forming and unfolding. Our character, while stable, is not fixed in stone. Character traits get shaped and reshaped by our actions, by our experiences, and by our reflection on what they mean to us. We are all works in progress. No one is finished. Conversion is always possible. Nevertheless, the arc of changing character is long, not short. It does not come easily and without intention. We must be intentional about changing our intention, emotions, perspective, and habits if we want to refashion our character.

So much for this extended treatment of these inner realities of the self that make up our moral identity, or character—the central concern of virtue ethics. The stability and interaction of these aspects of the self express the quality of our moral lives. But how is character formed in the first place?

FORMING CHARACTER

As human beings, we are oriented to the good. Yet virtuous character is not given to us from the beginning as something innate so that we have nothing to say about what we become. Our natural disposition toward goodness is the raw material for developing virtuous character. But this disposition for good must be nurtured and developed into a skill, or stable quality of being and doing. Virtues perfect our capacity for goodness. While we may have an innate capacity for the virtues, how each of us grows in virtue will be very personal. It depends a great deal on our personalities, on the people we meet, on the experiences we have, on the effort we put into it, and even on a certain amount of luck.

My favorite metaphor of forming virtuous character comes from my mother—learning to cook. We learn to be virtuous the way we learn to cook: we watch; we imitate someone who is good at it; we are encouraged to try it ourselves; and then we practice it repeatedly until it becomes second nature to us. This is the embodiment of Aristotle's insight that we learn by doing, and we first learn to do by observing.[34] Or, in the idiom of Yogi Berra, "You can see a lot by observing."

"Watch so you'll learn" was my mother's singular instruction. Standing at the head of her pasta board where she would mix, roll, and cut her pasta and bread dough, we watched. From time to time, we touched in order to get the feel of the dough as it progressed through its various phases from flour, eggs, salt, and water to its silky finish. Watch so you'll learn. Then came her second instruction, "Now you do it." Doing it yourself, over and over, makes the mixing, kneading, and rolling become second nature. Only through practice do we catch the nuances of feeling for the dough, a feeling that lives in our fingers and not in the recipe. In time, after much practice, we no longer need the recipe, or our model. We are now good at it and become an example for the next generation, who will also have to watch so as to learn. Then practice. And so it goes.

Character formed by observation, imitation, and practice is largely a matter of living from day to day doing things over and over with the intention to embody values that make us good, to think and to act in the way a virtuous person does, and to counteract contrary desires. Gradually these thoughts and actions become second nature to us from doing them over and over. We become compassionate by intentionally making ourselves available to the needs of others and then purposefully responding to them in an appropriate way. We become generous by purposefully curbing our tendencies to selfishness and then offering ourselves in reasonable ways to others. In deciding to act compassionately or generously, we are also deciding to be that sort of person.

What we do influences who we become, and who we become in turn influences what we do. A moral feedback loop functions here. We acquire a virtuous character through the hard work of making the right choice repeatedly. The habit of making the right choice makes it easier to do it again because we have acquired the virtue that trains us to exercise our freedom rightly the next time we have a chance. As we deliberately choose the good, aware that we could choose otherwise, we grow in virtue. If we want to be a better person, then we need to recognize and to take the opportunities we have to do better. Just as one swallow does not make a summer, one random act of kindness does not make us genuinely kind. However, it is a start, for the practice of kindness will habituate us or form in us a settled disposition to acting kindly. So, if we want to become more loving, peaceful, generous, sincere, and friendly, then we have to act in those ways when we have the chance. In time we identify with these virtues as they become characteristic of us.

From the perspective of forming character through practice, every day matters. The moral life is going on continually. We draw upon our character all the time, and not just for the occasional hard choice. As stated at the beginning of the chapter when introducing virtue ethics as a framework for thinking about ministers, the real work of making big decisions happens in the quality of how we live our everyday lives leading up to bigger decisions. If we want to be able to make a virtuous decision in the hard, ambiguous times, then we need to develop the habit of virtue in daily affairs. We are influencing the development or decay of our character all the time.

Nevertheless, forming good character, the character for ministry befitting a disciple today, by training the emotions, forming the imagination, and practicing good habits, does not happen in a vacuum. Character not only forms cumulatively by doing things over and over; character forms relationally through observation and response to the company we keep. We form character under the influence of the communities in which we live by observing and imitating people within those communities who have captured our imaginations.

To form good character, we need to have people of good character in our lives who can model for us what being good looks like. Over the years, as I have studied how we acquire character, one important lesson stands out: We do not acquire character on our own. Forming character is a cooperative adventure. I have vivid memories of growing up with our extended family meeting frequently for backyard fun at various family homes. I remember Mom or Dad announcing, as the last car pulled into the driveway, "The gang's all here!" Surrounded by the "gang" I learned about generosity and stinginess, hospitality and alienation, fair play and cheating. While no one member of the family embodied any one or all of these traits fully, collectively the family portrayed the kind of person I wanted to be or not, and I knew that I was in the company of people who could help me get there.

Social scientists tell us that, as we grow, the character we acquire is in part the result of internalizing the beliefs and values, causes and loyalties of the communities that make up our environment. Family, school, and church have long played a primary role in such a formative community. Today we should not forget to add the arts and the media (including the Internet). The styles of life and systems of values that are communicated to us through the arts and the media are quickly usurping, if they have not already overtaken, the role of family, church, and school in shaping character. Since we live in multiple communities that overlap and often compete with each other in their influence on character, we need to be able to assess critically the images of the good life that these various communities communicate. The challenge of forming character for ministry is to create and sustain communities that support virtues fitting for ministry and then trust the power of the group to teach individuals what it means to be a certain sort of person.

To say character is formed in community through observation and imitation implies an enduring relationship with those who share a common quest for being good. This is what friends do for one another. We cannot become good persons apart from relationships with people who also want to be good, who share our aspirations, and who love us enough to help us achieve them. Whatever strength of character we achieve is not the result of our own efforts alone, but it is also the handiwork of friends who draw the best out of us. In this sense, we can say that who we become is as much gift as achievement. Consider Amy from our opening case. Her story shows how, to form character for ministry, we need people in our lives who share our dreams, ideals, values, cares, and concerns. We need people who agree with us about what matters most, and we need those who are willing to challenge us when we let our priorities slip. This helps explain in part why formation personnel are so concerned with the quality of the community that surrounds the candidates for ministry.

Within this community of friends are certain individuals we notice who embody more clearly than others the character we want to imitate. Amy had Mike, her best friend, to be her moral model and mentor. Our moral models are the ones who make true the saying, "It's not what you say; it's who you are." Their characters so fascinate us that they capture our imaginations and move us to want to be like them. So we watch them like hawks to see how it is done. We are drawn to the goals of one, the style of another, the spirit of a third. We watch them "doing their thing" and learn from them the skills that make them worthy of imitation. Through a process of observation and imitation, we begin to develop a character like theirs. This poses a great challenge for vocation directors and formation personnel to be models of moral character fitting for ministry.

However, simply being surrounded by good models is no guarantee that we will become good the way they are. Modeling is effective as a means of forming character when we are ready to learn from our models and are motivated to imitate what we see because we find their behavior desirable for ourselves. We find ourselves saying, "Yes. That's the way I want to be, too." Every candidate seeking to form character for ministry needs to witness and then to imitate moral models of ministry. What we learn through these models about ourselves and about relating to others will have effects far beyond the boundaries of this special relationship.

We live in a big world in which there are many people competing for a privileged place in our imaginations. But there is only one who is the exemplary image of Christian moral character. The whole Christian tradition points to Jesus as the paradigm of virtue.[35] As paradigm, Jesus is our primary example of what a minister's character ought to look like. He is the master. We are the disciples who try to conform our lives to his, not by copying his life point for point, but by harmonizing our lives with his by way of analogous behavior. This is what we mean by imitating Christ.[36]

We can be fascinated by Jesus' style of life the way we are fascinated by role models arising out of our families and friends. A major difference, however, is that we physically interact with our family and friends. We see them and talk to them in the flesh. When it comes to Jesus, we have access to him through the Gospels that tell his story. So the spiritual practice of praying with scripture is an essential discipline in the formation of ministerial character. We believe that by prayerfully and imaginatively engaging these stories under the power of the Spirit and in the life of the church, we will be able to capture their meaning and so imitate Jesus in our day in ways that are consonant with his life in his day.

Whenever I have asked men and women in ministry what they find so fascinating about Jesus that they would want to make him their paradigm and be his disciple, they describe different characteristics and refer to different Gospel episodes to illustrate them. However, what seems to emerge as an outstanding characteristic of ministry that they seek to imitate is the way Jesus modeled inclusive love through a service that liberates and unites and not as a force that dominates. Some have pointed to his miracles as works of liberation. Others see his parables as judgments on the use of power that excludes.

But the most illustrative image that ministers almost always mention as the most fascinating for expressing the character and virtue of the pastoral minister is the foot washing scene at the Last Supper. This story from John 13:6–10 is used as the Gospel reading on Holy Thursday in conjunction with the Pauline text of the institution of the Eucharist (1 Cor 11:23–26). When taken in that context, coupled with our understanding that it takes the place of the institution narrative of the Eucharist in the Gospel of John, the action of Jesus in washing feet highlights even more the distinctive style of servant leadership that is to characterize the pastoral minister in a eucharistic community.

In this scene, when Peter sees Jesus, the master, acting like the servant, he knows that something new is afoot. It is not the picture he has in his imagination of the structure of power in the community. So Peter resists being washed. If he complies with this washing, he would be accepting a radical reversal of the very structure of domination upon which he depends for his power. His resistance suggests that such a conversion, both in his imagination and in his life, is more than he is willing to undergo. But faced with losing his share in Jesus' destiny, Peter caves in. When he is done, Jesus spells out the meaning of his behavior. If the disciples are to share in his destiny, then the dynamism of his radical love and humble service must pass into their lives and on to all people. When Jesus deliberately reverses social positions by becoming the servant, he witnesses to a new order of human relationships in the community in which the desire to dominate and establish superiority has no place. Power in the disciple is not for domination but for service. As a community formed by the love of Jesus, this way of leading the community must become the sign of God's liberation and salvation in the world.[37]

When our manner of imitation is shaped by analogy rather than by trying to copy Jesus point for point, we will always face the question of appropriate imitation. Are we being faithful to the example of Jesus, or is our moral exemplar no longer recognizable in our witness? One check against our version of imitation is the witness and endorsement of the community of the church. To be a faithful disciple requires a community. We learn the way of loving service by being initiated into it. To sharpen our capacity to discern appropriate analogies for imitating Jesus requires that we participate in the life of a community pledged to be faithful to him. The community's spiritual practices, doctrines, and moral principles set parameters on analogies that are the appropriate imitation of Jesus.

Jesus has shown the way of inclusive love and liberating power. The details are now left to us. We have to think analogically from his example how to love as we have been loved so that we witness to the vision of Jesus that all peoples will be brought under the inclusive reign of divine love. Each of us will live as a disciple in a way that corresponds to our openness to the Holy Spirit. However, unless we establish strong bonds of solidarity with others who share in the vision and mission of Jesus and participate in their life, we will not be able to remain committed to discipleship.

Given this description of moral character as our moral identity and the dynamics of forming character by imitating what we see expressed in the lives of moral models and mentors in the community, we now draw out some significant implications for the formation of ministers. Highlighting some of the more significant ones can serve as a fitting conclusion to this chapter.

IMPLICATIONS FOR MINISTERIAL FORMATION

SELECTION

Selection is the most important step in the formation process. Long before candidates enter the formation program, their habit formation, and so character formation, is well advanced. As we saw in the earlier treatment of virtues as habits, character does not go into reverse easily. The arc of conversion is long, not short. So we can expect that the kinds of habits we form prior to entering ministry influence, more than we might want to admit, the kind of minister we will become and the style our ministry will take. It is not unusual to see the character a candidate brings through the front door of a formation program to be, by and large, the very character that walks out the back door at the end of the process. Some fine-tuning may go on, but radical changes are rare. People generally stay "in character." We generally dismiss atypical behavior or give it little attention because, since it is so uncharacteristic of the candidate, we feel that it does not represent their true self. This experience is confirmed time and again by formation personnel. It should help us to be more realistic about the influence formation personnel and programs have on shaping or certainly changing the character of ministerial candidates.

Formation personnel are often held responsible for the quality of candidates and their ministry. While they do share some of the responsibility, formation personnel and programs are not as influential as many people think they are. As an old expression has it, "You cannot make a silk purse out of a sow's ear." If a person does not possess at least incipient habits that are necessary for pastoral ministry, then that person should never be recruited for ministry. Or, to switch metaphors, if we want to produce a twelve-carat gold ring, we had better begin with some gold ore. Theologically we would say, "Grace builds on nature." The responsibility of the formation personnel is to fine-tune those habits of the candidate that will enhance the ministry of the church and to challenge and try to reform those that handicap it. Such a responsibility suggests that carefully selecting candidates is the most important step in formation.

The insights of virtue ethics call for a selection and formation process that engages positive discernment. This means that we are not trying to identify impediments to ministry, but we are looking for behavioral signs of habitual patterns that indicate that our candidates already demonstrate an ability to live the style of life and to exercise the ministry for which they are being recruited and formed. It is naïve (and nonsacramental) to think that ordination or commissioning will suddenly render someone capable of ministry. The behaviorally oriented interview and assessment process promulgated by Fr. Raymond Carey of the Archdiocese of Portland, Oregon, in his workshops with vocation directors and seminary personnel are an example of what virtue ethics requires in the selection process.[38]

EMOTIONAL DEVELOPMENT

One of the key aspects of ministerial candidates' character is their emotional development. In chapter 1, on the nature of having a vocation, I indicated the importance of having relational skills under the "gift" dimension of a vocation. That same concern fits here, too. Since the ministry is essentially relational, we want our ministers to be sufficiently emotionally developed so that they will be able to respond with appropriate emotion and foster trustworthy relationships and not become dependent on those they serve, nor manipulate, demean, or abuse them. No one should be accepted for ministry who shows signs of being emotionally tone deaf, rigid, or distant. Nor should candidates display a relational style that is arrogant or quarrelsome, controlling or intimidating. Candidates should be sufficiently developed emotionally so as to be self-disciplined, able to motivate themselves and control their own impulses. They ought to be self-aware and self-possessed in order to be attuned to the emotional overtones in people's words and actions, and be open to others in a hospitable, nondefensive manner.

A key emotional capacity is empathy, the ability to know how another feels, to take their perspective, and to respect differences in how people feel about things. Empathy is the root of caring and compassion. In order for ministers to develop good relationships, we need to be able to form affective attachments and have the ability to take a reasonably detached view of our own wants when they conflict with other people's legitimate claims. We need to be able to listen well and to ask appropriate questions, to distinguish between what someone is saying or doing and our own reactions and judgments. We need to be able to recognize what our emotional reactions are telling us about what is going on in the situation and where we stand so that we can cooperate, collaborate, resolve conflicts, and negotiate compromises without losing our integrity.

SPIRITUAL PRACTICES

Spiritual practices have a great potential to shape our lives around Christian attitudes and values. Every ministerial formation program includes opportunities to engage in spiritual practices—private prayer, Mass, devotions, retreats, fasting, and so on. We engage in spiritual practices primarily to show our love for God and to deepen our relationship with God. They are truly acts of worship, first of all. Their morally formative aspect is an indirect effect. William Spohn is emphatic on this point: "If the intent of worship is not God but personal growth, then God is being reduced to a means, which is a form of idolatry."[39]

While maintaining the priority of spiritual practices to express our love for God, ministerial formation is also interested in their potential in forming character. Prayer, both personal and communal, is the most obvious practice to express our spirituality. Cultivating the habit of prayer provides a place for us consciously to connect with God and to begin to see our whole lives in relation to God. By attending to God in prayer, we discover that we are forming dispositions befitting the attentiveness of a prayerful person.[40]

For example, praying with scripture can become a way of schooling the emotions so that we are drawn to care about what disciples ought to care about, and it can sharpen our perspective and nudge us closer to seeing from God's point of view. Walking around inside biblical images and the emotions that accompany them can help us discover new ways of being faithful to what discipleship demands of us. Prayerful reflection on the parables, for example, can develop openness to the unexpected and a sense of humor that will catch the incongruous as an epiphany of grace. Prayers of intercession can strengthen our capacity for solidarity, empathy, and compassion.

The Eucharist can strengthen our religious identity and nurture our dispositions to gratitude, forgiveness, and solidarity. Paul Wadell answers the title question of his article, "What Do All Those Masses Do for Us?" by saying that they form us into persons with a new vision that opens us to the attitudes and virtues of Jesus.[41] Gathering to confess our sins, to hear the word of God, to profess a common faith, and to share a common food can help us identify with the vision and values reflected in these ritual actions. As we are welcomed and forgiven in the Eucharist, so we are to be hospitable and liberating in like manner.

When engaged with the right intention, spiritual practices like these have the power to form our imagination, emotions, and dispositions so that our experiences of loving God and being loved by God can give rise to moral sensibilities that will extend the range of love's influence on the world.

FRIENDSHIPS

As I said earlier, acquiring a Christian moral character is a cooperative adventure.[42] Who we are as individuals is highly influenced by the quality of our relationships. So we need to watch the company we keep. To whom we talk, what we talk about, and how we live together are the training ground for our character. Christian moral formation requires that we be in the company of stable, enduring relationships with those who share and try to live by a Christian perspective on life.

Friendships are the most enduring relationships of all.[43] I have already emphasized that friendship is the school of virtue. Friends influence our attitudes, values, and perceptions. Nevertheless, friendships formative of moral character must be more than superficial acquaintances or codependent relationships. Friendships are marked by mutual enjoyment and care of one another, a desire for what is best for one another, the commitment to seek one another's well-being, and the freedom that allows for growth at each one's own pace. The company of good friends enlarges our imaginations, and our friends teach us how to be with and care for others by being genuinely empathic, loyal, just, generous, and gracious. In other words, being friends with a few opens the imagination to ways of being friendly toward many. Candidates for ministry ought to be able to demonstrate their ability to build and sustain friendships.

MENTORS AND MODELS

Another kind of relationship that influences ministerial moral formation is the candidate's relationship with mentors and models. The mentoring relationship is the more formal of the two. It is an intentional, time-limited apprenticing to someone who embodies the kind of life to which we aspire. Under a mentor, we not only learn what to do through observation and instruction, but we also pick up the spirit of how to do it. To be a formative agent in ministerial life, the mentoring requires not only the mentor's explicit attempt to pass on a vision and style of life but also the candidate's openness to receive it. No mentor is going to have an influence on anyone who is not open to being influenced.[44] This vision of mentoring is the inspiration embodied in the Mantle of Elijah Program of St. Mary's Seminary and University in Baltimore, a formal program for mentoring newly ordained priests.

Modeling relationships, by contrast, are less formalized and are not as self-conscious. Modeling in ministerial formation illustrates the axiom, "Good people form good people." Arguments alone are not enough to instill virtue. Someone must also capture our imaginations and, by so doing, open us to a world of possibility. In a formation community, this means that the identity and integrity of the formation personnel figure more prominently than the content of the curriculum of study. We are formed more by the impact a particular person has on us than we are by the content of subject matter. Teachers or formation directors capture our imagination with their character and style. There is something about them that we want for ourselves. Formation personnel are models for ministerial candidates more than they may want to admit. The dynamics of observation and imitation in the formation of character are so strong that formation personnel need to attend to them in order to make the formation environment an effective community of learning.

COMMUNITY'S CULTURE

A proper social understanding of the person underscores our dependence on the community to shape our emotions, imaginations, and virtues. Social scientists are telling us that character is greatly influenced by the cultures in which we are socialized. By culture here, I mean the patterns of meaning that a community uses to interpret and evaluate what is going on.[45] These patterns of meaning are not so much taught as caught by participating in the community's rituals, symbols, organizational patterns, and way of life. Once they get into our bloodstream, they predispose us toward certain feelings, dispositions, and actions.

Moral cultures provide metaphorical frames that support the reasons, restraints, motives, and incentives for living in one way rather than another. In other words, moral cultures provide the "whys" of moral behavior. Why seek a peaceful resolution of conflict rather than a violent one? Why do the right thing when it is not in your self-interest? The answers are found largely in the moral cultures with which we identify. Sociologist James Davidson Hunter has studied the moral cultures characterizing America and the role of those cultures in influencing moral behavior. While social scientists typically name a range of factors, such as race, age, class, ethnicity, and gender to account for moral judgments, Hunter contends that the most important factor cutting across all of these is an underlying attachment to a moral culture.[46] We acquire such an attachment through sharing common practices, such as joining together in social service projects, having meals together, praying together, spending leisure time together, and sharing stories of our experiences that reveal their common meaning.

The challenge of his research to formation communities is to ask how well we are facilitating an attachment to a moral culture that uses Christian metaphors to shape the pastoral imagination so that a Christian moral culture serves as the primary interpretive framework for making sense of life. When images of faith form a great part of the framework within which we interpret our experiences, then they can become a great influence on our character and action. Our moral imaginations are shaped by these religious images as we participate in the life of the community and its spiritual practices that help us develop our friendship with God.

In this chapter, we have reflected on ministry by turning to virtue ethics. Ministerial formation programs can benefit from the insights of virtue ethics in order to select suitable candidates and to provide the communal context along with the moral and spiritual practices that will fine-tune good characters for ministry. Attention to ministerial character inevitably begs for a description of the virtues fitting a virtuous minister and the habits ministers ought to practice in order to become virtuous. Sketching a profile of the virtuous minister is the task of the next chapter.

4

THE VIRTUOUS MINISTER

Dear Sr. Mary Alice,

Emily has requested that I send you a letter of recommendation on her behalf to accompany her application for a teaching position at St. Louise School. I have known her for five years as one of our outstanding religious education teachers. I am happy to recommend her for this new position, though we will miss her greatly from our teaching staff.

On our faculty, Emily was an exemplary role model for her students. In fact, her most powerful form of teaching was through her example. The way she faced each day showed all of us how to handle a variety of life's challenges, from the discouragement that can pull us down when our plans get thwarted to the need to change when we meet the unexpected. She has a great ability to adapt and be flexible to the differing needs and circumstances of our students. In the classroom, for example, she showed this capacity in the way she customized assignments on a certain topic for different skill levels. She employed a significant degree of creativity when designing lesson plans, assignments, activities, and assessments.

Patience and humility are two of her other special characteristics. Emily demonstrated patience in the way she would take time to explain seemingly simple topics, repeatedly if necessary, without sounding frustrated or belittling the struggling student. She would even stay after school to give extra attention to aid the remedial student. In the classroom, as in our staff meetings, she demonstrated patience in the way she maintained a level head in the midst of confusion and sometimes conflict. When confronted with negative behavior, she would articulate her position clearly without becoming harsh.

I believe all of this was possible for her because she is such a humble person. While as a teacher she had control of many aspects of the classroom, there were still some things that she knew that she could not ultimately control. But she knew her limits, and she was open to learn. Her willingness to grow in her own self-understanding as well as to work at her ongoing edu-cation to remain competent became a model for us all.

These qualities of flexibility, patience, and humility stand out as stable characteristics that I am sure you can count on in the future. It is for reasons like these that I highly recommend her for your school.

Letters of recommendation like this are a common way of giving a profile of someone's moral character. They isolate the characteristics that give us a picture of another's moral identity. Emily is a teacher being recommended for another teaching position. What about ministry? What character traits (or good habits) would you want to find in someone aspiring to ministry so that you could recommend him or her to this professional role with confidence?

Chapter 3 showed that virtues are those qualities of character that we need in order to have a rich and authentically good human life. By applying the method of virtue ethics to ministry, we must ask, "What kind of person should a minister become?" Or, what are the characteristics of an "excellent" minister—the minister who is all he or she is meant to be? This chapter draws further on virtue ethics to name the virtues that we need to cultivate and practice to achieve excellence in ministry.

Since ministry is inherently relational, we need a virtue that informs each of our relational ways of being in ministry. James F. Keenan has proposed a relational model of the cardinal virtues that serves this objective well.[1] Adapting his proposal, I propose a portrait of ministry that embodies at least the virtues of charity, justice, fidelity, self-esteem, and prudence. Of course, there are other virtues we would expect to find in ministers as well. In workshops, sometimes I have invited participants to list their nonnegotiable virtues. I have accumulated quite a list! We all have our favorites. I briefly discuss some of mine: gratitude, generosity, compassion, humility, holiness, and courage. I sketch what each virtue entails and identify some practices we might engage to cultivate and to express the virtue.

CARDINAL VIRTUES

CHARITY

When we consider charity, our tendency may be to think first of some loving thing we do for others, like donate to the hurricane relief fund or hand over a quarter to the panhandler with a cup standing on the corner. However, with charity as a cardinal virtue, this would be putting the cart before the horse. So it is wise to follow the sage advice that says, "First things first." One of the towering insights of Johannine theology is that God has made the first move to love us: "In this is love, not that we loved God but that he loved us" (1 John 4:10); and again, "We love because he first loved us" (1 John 4:19); and, "You did not choose me but I chose you" (John 15:16). In short, charity reminds us of the bottom line in moral matters: God has the first word and the last word. That word is *love*. The primary meaning of charity as a cardinal virtue is that God's basic disposition toward us is the disposition of love. Our whole life of virtue is living in response to grace—the love we first receive as a gift of God's graciousness. Like the parents who give their child money to buy them a Christmas gift, so God's love is the unearned gift that enables us to love in return.

Therefore, from God's side, when we say that charity is about love, we mean primarily that it is the defining characteristic of God. As 1 John 4:7–8 reminds us, "God is love," and the love we have for one another comes from God. God's loving us enables us to love in the ways the other virtues incline us to do. In 1 Corinthians 13, Paul admonishes us to open ourselves to this gift of love and to show its true identity in a life of virtue by being patient, kind, and all the rest.

From our side, when we say that charity is about love, we mean that "to be loving" is our primary disposition by virtue of belonging to God through the gift of divine friendship.[2] We can understand having this proactive energy for love by understanding whose we are. Faith recognizes that we belong to God through creation and in the new creation of the incarnation where Jesus' life-death-resurrection manifests God's enduring love for us. As Paul reminds the Corinthians, "You belong to Christ, and Christ belongs to God" (1 Cor 3:23). Since we bear the imprint (character) of the one unwaveringly disposed to love us, we are so disposed as well. "Just as I have loved you, you also should love one another" (John 13:34) gives us the most succinct statement of the New Testament's vision of the moral life. God's loving us calls us to love. The first and greatest commandment, Jesus says, is, "You shall love the Lord your God with all your heart, and with all your soul, and with all your mind." The second follows, "You shall love your neighbor as yourself" (Matt 22:37–39).

Traditionally we have talked about charity, humanly speaking, as an "infused" virtue, in contrast to the other virtues that we "acquire" through practice. To say charity is an infused virtue means that God's friendship (love) is a free gift that keeps on giving. It is always working in the background as the animating principle of all the virtues and referring them back to God. Without charity none of the other virtues is possible. The virtues, while retaining their own identity, participate in charity so that all the virtues are, in a sense, "acts of charity." Just as a single ray of light gets refracted into multiple colors by passing through a prism, so charity gets refracted through the prism of acquired virtues. This is what we mean when we say that charity is the "form," or inner rationale, of all the virtues.

I like to think of charity as the form of the virtues as analogous to my dad's being my baseball coach. He taught me the fundamentals of enjoying the game by drawing out of me and giving order to my own capacity to play ball. But he never took my place on the field. When I played my position, all that he gave me freed me to be my best. When I played the game, his teaching me the skills, cheering me on, and motivating me to be my best passed through the prism of my performance. To be effective, his loving affirmation and encouragement needed my face, hands, and feet. In the same way, charity needs the other virtues to be effective in deed.

Charity, as the form of all the virtues, plays in a thousand places and wears a thousand faces, but we never meet charity face to face. We meet charity in and through all the other virtues. In other words, the virtues specify the form charity takes in different circumstances. That is why we can say that ministers are charitable when they are just, faithful, generous, compassionate, courageous, and all the rest. These other virtues express what charity demands in a particular situation. These virtues do not exist apart from charity, since living virtuously is living in, by, and through God's love. We express charity through virtuous actions when we show love for God, others, and ourselves.

Ministers, like any baptized persons, express love for God through acts of piety, or what we call spiritual practices: celebrating the sacraments, reading the Bible, saying our prayers, doing acts of kindness. I come back to piety again under the virtue of holiness.

Charity also loves what God loves, and so we love our neighbor and we love ourselves. In ministry, when we act charitably by loving another, such as by going out of our way to make time for someone in need, or by doing random acts of kindness like sending a "Thank you" note to a staff member for a job well done, or even when we express "tough love" by holding a colleague accountable, we are expressing a fitting response to God's friendship, since a friend tries to get along with the friends of a friend.[3]

Charity is also expressed in appropriate self-love, such as when we take care of ourselves by means of good nutrition, adequate sleep, days off, time with friends, prayer, and reflective reading and study that help us to remain competent and to refine our professional skills.

Nurturing our friendship with God is fundamental for ministers. It grounds all our virtues. God's love for us and our love for God is the animating relationship for all other relationships. It is where our moral life begins, how it is sustained, and it is also the goal toward which living morally is moving. Since we are united to God in love, we must learn to cooperate with God in loving what God loves in the multiple relationships that make up our lives.

Practices that cultivate and express charity are found in the other virtues. The following descriptions of the virtues are an attempt to show what charity looks like not only for the minister, but also for any Christian who shares in the universal call to holiness to bring forth charity for the life of the world.[4]

JUSTICE

Justice is the virtue of interdependence in that it governs the ties that bind us together. Since everything about being human is social, justice seeks to nurture and protect the deep interconnectedness that exists between one person and another. Justice does not understand society as a loose association of individuals who stand side by side, bound together merely by self-interest. Justice, by contrast, understands personal existence only in terms of the interconnections that bind us with others, the Earth, and with God. Justice stands in stark contrast to the liberal forces of our culture that take independence and separation as the norm.

Justice in the life of the minister is continually drawing our attention to others. It reminds us that we are not the center of the universe. There are other centers of life, and we are to give proper weight to their claims upon us. With justice we know that human life is a shared life, that cooperation is better than playing the "Lone Ranger," and that give-and-take is better than grab-and-go. A just ministry is ordered to the common good. It forces us to recognize that, while there are some things that we want for ourselves or our favorite sectors of the church community (such as our youth group or our benefactors), we might not pursue them right now so that the good of the whole might be better served.

The common good is the well-being that we strive to achieve by living in solidarity with and for one another. It is not the sum total of individual goods, nor is it simply the good of the majority. While the common good respects the interests of individual persons, it ultimately upholds the good of the whole to be more important than the good of any one individual. It includes not only the well-being of the human family, but also the well-being of the church as a community of faith and the well-being of the Earth in its biodiversity. It believes that the individual will flourish only insofar as society as a whole flourishes. Justice reminds us that the needs and interests of others are really inseparable from our own so that our own flourishing as individuals is tied to how well others fare. The common good keeps in tension the best interests of the individual and the well-being of the community as a whole. Its achievement depends on the generosity of individuals and the church as an institution to seek those actions and policies that will provide for the good of the individual as well as for the good of others.

A just ministry is at work when we provide to the community the service we say we can provide by virtue of our role. A just ministry does not take advantage of one's role by giving priority to satisfying one's own needs and interests, but it gives due deference to the needs of those we are called to serve. A just ministry also observes criteria for fairness in employment practices, such as in procedures for hiring and firing and for fair compensation. It is at work when we act inclusively in offering service so that whole groups of people do not get neglected or marginalized from our spiritual care, such as the youth, the singles, the elderly, the shut-ins, the gay and lesbian community, and so forth. Moreover, a just ministry cooperates with social and ecclesial policies that promote collaboration among the churches and social agencies to share resources, such as shelters for the homeless, food banks, and the treatment and prevention programs for those with HIV/AIDS. Justice also opposes any financial arrangements that mismanage funds or curry favors through financial privileges. Justice opposes any structures and practices in which people are victimized sexually through harassment or abuse. Justice requires that we take time to educate ourselves about the society in which we live, its institutions, policies, and practices. We also need to develop the skill of social analysis to understand the impact that social structures have on others, especially those whose voice cannot be heard because they lack access to power in society or the church.

Some practices that cultivate and express justice are

Keeping informed about major social issues of the day
Collaborating with community agencies on projects of mutual concern
Serving each person and sector of the parish without discrimination
Encouraging a preferential option for the poor
Promoting a sustainable creation

FIDELITY

If justice is the virtue of honoring relationships in general and applies universally and impartially, then fidelity is the virtue of honoring particular relationships and favors partiality. Fidelity, and its companion virtues of loyalty and trustworthiness, weaves into one fabric the warp of a pastoral relationship and the woof of a covenantal one. It is the virtue that imitates God's covenantal loyalty to us (Exod 34:6; Hos 2:16 and 11). In the New Testament, God's fidelity is fulfilled in

Jesus. The very title, *Christ*, witnesses to Jesus as fulfilling God's promise to be faithful by sending the promised one, the Messiah, who would be the new covenant.

As we saw in chapter 2, a key feature of forming a covenant is the action of entrusting and accepting trust. In a covenant, we place into another's hands something of value to ourselves. In ministry, we covenant by being entrusted with the secrets, sins, fears, hopes, and need for salvation of our parishioners. In making this act of trust, they give us power over them and trust that we will not betray them by misusing our power by controlling, dominating, or manipulating them to serve our own interests. Fidelity is the virtue that safeguards the vulnerability of the other by holding in trust what has been entrusted to us.

In some relationships, such as marriage and friendships, the act of entrusting and accepting trust goes equally in both directions, so that the relationship is equal and reciprocal. However, the pastoral relationship is different. It is more one directional, since the act of entrusting falls more on the one seeking the pastoral service than it does on the pastoral minister. For this reason, pastoral relationships are not equal. In such a relationship of inequality, fidelity in the minister is all the more important, since we can easily take advantage of the other by abusing what has been entrusted to us.

If we want to be virtuous in the way fidelity requires of the pastoral minister, then we need to engage in practices that strengthen fidelity: respect physical and emotional boundaries in a relationship; keep secret what has been confided to us; honor others even in their absence; don't become a source of gossip; protect another's best interest when in a position to do so. One of the signs of growing in the virtue of fidelity is the ability to distinguish the various kinds of relationships the pastoral minister has with people—for example, personal relationships such as friends, business partners, colleagues, employer-employee, neighbors, pastor-staff, and pastoral relationships—and then to manage each appropriately without confusing one with the other. We ought not to mix or confuse personal relationships that are free and reciprocal with pastoral relationships, such as when the pastor becomes the spiritual director of the secretary, or the youth minister dates someone from the youth group. These "dual relationships" threaten fidelity by harboring potential conflicts of interest that can lead to playing favorites or exploiting the other's dependency.

Developing in fidelity requires self-esteem and involves a sufficient degree of self-possession to commit to another and to sustain that commitment over time through honest communication, a willingness to put aside one's desires for self-gain in order to seek the good of the other, and an ability to sustain the relationship through difficult times. We grow in fidelity by nurturing friendships. Being a friend with a few nurtures the ability to be faithful toward others.

Some practices that cultivate and express fidelity are

> Avoiding unnecessary dual relationships and monitoring the inevitable ones
> Respecting the physical and emotional boundaries in a relationship
> Refraining from fostering dependency in those we serve
> Keeping secrets and not becoming a gossiper
> Acknowledging the limits of our abilities and availability
> Remaining competent in our skills for pastoral ministry
> Following through on promises and commitments to be with and for others

SELF-ESTEEM

Self-esteem is the virtue by which we accept ourselves as being worthwhile apart from our achievements. It takes root in being blessed by others, from hearing others say "I love you," believing it to be true, and then living in ways that show we like what we have heard and have come to know.

"Do you love me?" is the persistent cry of the heart. We feel valuable when we know someone loves us. Charity reminds us that grace is the first move in love. God has taken the initiative to love us. Charity says that we are not so much the ones searching for love as the ones searched for. We matter to God in a most serious way: "I have called you by name, you are mine" (Isa 43:1). In the New Testament, one of the favorite images of Jesus for those whose lives are grounded in God's love is the child. The child is such an apt image for living under the reign of God because the child's worth is grounded in the generous love of the parents and not in something the child has achieved. That is what we are like before God. God's love bestows our worth. The act of faith on our part is to believe that to be true, to accept that we have been accepted and to claim our worth. That may be our most difficult act of faith, but it is foundational to self-esteem and to becoming a virtuous minister.

Our beliefs about God and images of God can also enhance or impede our quest for self-esteem. We need to examine our images of God for the subtle influence they can have on our sense of self-worth and our style of ministry. These images imbed themselves in the elusive corners of our subconscious and continue to influence what we think of ourselves and how we conduct our ministry. Before we can experience the love of the God of Abraham and Sarah, Moses and Miriam, Mary, Jesus, and Paul, some of us still need to destroy a whole pantheon of distorted images of a distant god who keeps book on us and waits for us to trip up so that we can be marked down as a loser. All of us need to find ways to assimilate and reinforce the fundamental biblical insight that God is love and that "God loves me." God loves us when we are in sin just as much as when we are out of sin. All we need to do is to live out of this love. The scriptures never tire of repeating the word of God's love. The prophets extol God's love; Jesus lived by the truth of God's love; and Saint Paul spoke about it out of his own experience.

We can build self-esteem through the spiritual practice of listening to God say "I love you" by meditating on the biblical stories that help us to understand divine love as the true source of our worth. Knowing that we are accepted by God and will never be abandoned by God can give us unending courage to live by self-respect in friendship with God and to care for ourselves appropriately without compromising our commitment to serve the best interests of others.

While self-esteem is ultimately grounded in accepting God's love for us, it is nurtured through other relationships. We will not feel our life as grace or gift of God unless someone values us. Another's esteem for us nurtures self-esteem. We sense ourselves as cherished by God when we feel valued and cherished by others. When we feel forgiven, accepted, or served by another, then we begin to feel our own self as graced and are inspired to be gracious to others. We come to know the love of God for us through the human love of others. The image we have of ourselves is largely the product of what others have told us that we are. So it makes a great deal of difference whom we let into our inner circle of influence and how they relate to us and name us. A kind word of affirmation and a smile of recognition are important.

Compare the following examples: Ysaye Maria Barnwell's song, "No Mirrors in My Nana's House," is a song about self-image, its source, and the effect of relationships on self-esteem. In this song, a black woman sings of seeing the beauty of everything, especially herself, through her Nana's eyes. Without mirrors in the house, she can only see herself the way her Nana tells her that she is. In her Nana's eyes, her black skin, her flat nose, and her frumpy, baggy clothes are beautiful. In her Nana's house, she knows only love. She does not know hate. However, if such love can build up, cruelty and inattention can bruise deeply, or even destroy. The experience of living in Nana's house stands in stark contrast with the experience of Vivian, the prostitute, in the film *Pretty Woman*. After telling of how her mother mistreated her as a child by locking her in the attic as a punishment, Vivian says, "When people put you down enough, you start to believe it. The bad stuff is easier to believe."

Self-esteem is the virtue of appropriate self-love. The second half of the Great Commandment tells us that self-love is important, for we are to love our neighbors as we love ourselves. One of the greatest things that we can do as ministers to serve others appropriately is to begin by liking ourselves, by enjoying who we are and what we do. The danger, however, always lies in the extremes of self-hatred that neglects self-love on the one hand and, on the other, loving ourselves excessively to the neglect of our commitment to act in the best interests of others. This is self-love not as virtue but as the vice of selfishness, which is giving undue preference to one's own interests while neglecting to attend to the legitimate interests of others.[5]

The virtue of self-esteem is the responsible care for ourselves in a holistic way. Ministerial training programs in recent years have given more emphasis to the importance of self-care and the self-reflection that accompanies it. This is as it should be. After all, it is what makes loving others appropriately possible. Caring for ourselves appropriately requires critical self-knowledge. So we need to take time to watch ourselves go by. This is the discipline of making a periodic review of life. This includes not only recognizing how we have used our gifts but also admitting to the limits of our knowledge and skill so that we work within the limits of our competence. Critical self-knowledge also includes an ability to recognize the warning signs of when we are beginning to cross the boundaries appropriate to the pastoral relationship, are beginning to use the other for our own needs, and are no longer acting in their best interest. We care for ourselves, too, when we set boundaries for healthy living by not working long hours with little time for exercise, proper nutrition, sufficient sleep, friends, prayer, and reflective reading. Virtuous self-love also involves establishing significant, supportive relationships with those who can be cheerleaders to encourage us and prophets to challenge us. It also includes developing our relationship with God by nurturing the regular practice of spiritual disciplines.

The virtue of self-esteem avoids a false perfectionism when it acknowledges our human capacity for evil. It enables us to affirm our good tendencies while feeling secure enough to correct our bad ones. Common experience reminds us that our lives are a tangled web of good and evil. The uncanny insight of my five-year-old niece revealed this basic truth. I asked her once what color she would be if all good people in the world were painted blue and all the bad people were painted yellow. She thought for a moment and then matter of factly said, "I'd be streaky." She had it exactly right. She said what is true about all of us. We are all streaky. We need to recognize that there is some good in the worst of us and some bad in the best of us, and we need to help others recognize this in themselves too, lest we mislead others by a false image of holiness. Because sin is real, no one will ever achieve total personal integration in this life. But we also believe that these dark forces are always encompassed by a greater power for good.

To live with appropriate self-love is vitally important for exercising the other virtues. For example, without self-esteem, what looks like humility is really a cry for recognition; what looks like generosity is really manipulation, a cry for love. We can speak truth to power with courage when we accept our own worth. We can give freely what we have freely received only when we know ourselves to be fully accepted by a love that makes no conditions. We have a special term for that. We call it *unconditional love*. When we accept the original blessing of our being loved by God—completely and unconditionally—then we can love others freely, without manipulating them in order to win their love in return.

Some practices that cultivate and express self-esteem are

Listening to God say, "I love you," by praying with the scriptures, such as Isaiah 43:1–5 and 49:15–16, Hosea 11:8–9, John 15:9, Romans 8:38–39

Keeping "sabbath" in one's life by making time for leisure, days off, hobbies, vacations, beauty, prayer, and retreats

Getting proper nutrition, adequate sleep, and regular exercise

Working within the limits of our competence

Continuing to refine professional skills and knowledge through ongoing study and supervision

Developing friendships compatible with our commitment to ministry

PRUDENCE

Prudence brings goodness to life by putting the virtues into practice in the right way, at the right time, and for the right reason. Unfortunately, the virtue of prudence is often mistaken for its look-alike—a cautious timidity ("no guts"), opportunism, expedience, or a calculated self-protectiveness that generally gets translated into the moral imperative "Be careful." However, prudence as a virtue is much more robust than these caricatures. As a virtue, prudence denotes exercising good judgment about what is appropriate. It is the virtue of discernment, for the work of conscience is completed by the prudential judgment about what to do. Prudence enables us to act in the best way possible in the circumstances based on an accurate perception of what is really the case and the reasonable deliberation about what response is most fitting.

All acquired virtues are expressed through prudence because acting virtuously is neither blind nor ignorant but involves intelligence and freedom. So prudence is not simply one virtue among others. It is the executive virtue; the others are executed through it. Prudence cuts through illusion and self-deception brought on by self-interest and our selective attention to what is going on. It sorts out competing claims among the virtues so that we can determine how to work for justice, keep faith, and exercise appropriate self-love.

Prudence also presumes a vision of the good life toward which we are always striving. From a Christian perspective, the good life is to love God and to love our neighbor as we love ourselves. Prudence helps us know what shape love will take in our general, particular, and unique relationships. Since what love will look like in those relationships is not fixed in stone, prudence must perceive the morally relevant features at stake in one's experience and discover the form love must take that best fits both the person who must act and the context calling for action.

Given the vast array of unpredictable and complex situations in which we must act, it is inconceivable that we will act ethically without the moral perception that allows us to see the situation as one requiring careful deliberation. But there is no formula for making a decision that will produce the right answer or guarantee that our actions will be the best expression of virtue. Moral principles can guide us, and the moral authorities in our communities can inform us. Nevertheless, neither principles nor authorities can ever tell us precisely what is the best way to act in a situation. In a morally complex world, where determining the best course of action cannot be reduced to an algorithm, our decision ultimately emerges from the quality of our prudence.

Thomas Aquinas gave perhaps the best description of the parts of prudence;[6] I summarize his vision here.

Prudence remembers past experiences, our own and others', to see if there is anything similar in the past to this new experience that can serve as a guide in determining what to do now. For this reason, we do not expect to find much prudence in young people or even in those who are "young" at a new role, like being a minister. The young do not yet have enough experience relative to their role in ministry to learn by comparison or to draw analogies. Without much experience, we need to follow the guidance of rules and the supervision of those in authority who have more experience.

Prudence cannot deliberate accurately about what to do until we can distinguish the morally relevant features of the situation from what is peripheral, know which principles apply, and look into the future to anticipate what values will be protected and what will be lost in the consequences of our actions. Prudence also partners with humility to seek counsel from others, especially those whose experience gives them a greater vantage point to see what we might miss. Prudence taps the wisdom of those with broader experience of living through similar situations. Thus the important role of supervision and mentoring programs in ministry.

Prudence thinks through the relevant factors and imagines possibilities, difficulties, and outcomes that will come about from trading off the values at stake. This reasoning is done in a prayerful manner so as to be open to the Holy Spirit that guides in the process of sifting through factors and options in order to catch subtleties in the circumstances and to notice how one is drawn to act. Prudence is willing to give this process time. So it moves cautiously to guard against a hasty decision that would cause harm that could have been avoided or lessened if we had paid attention to more factors and considered more fully the consequences. In order to honor this requirement of time and prudence as a process, we need to avoid the habit of filling up every moment of the day with activity. We ought to create a rhythm of making quiet space for reflection.

However, when there is little time to think thoroughly about what to do, we must rely on the lead that comes from having practiced prudence when we had the chance. Acquiring the skill of prudence gives us an uncanny ability to do what is right even when we cannot slow ourselves down to think about it as much as we would like. All of this leads toward making a decision that will be true to one's self and to an action that fits the particular circumstances.

Some practices that cultivate and express prudence are

Taking time to be silent and still
Fostering the discipline of self-reflection
Paying attention to details and discriminating among their
   degrees of importance
Consulting with an openness to learn from the experience of
   others
Working with a mentor, spiritual director, counselor, or friend
   who can keep us honest with ourselves
Coming to a decision in a timely manner

Besides these cardinal virtues, others fill out the richness and complexity of ministry. The everyday virtues I especially value are described next.

EVERYDAY VIRTUES

GRATITUDE

Everyone lives with a fundamental stance, or governing perspective, that shapes how we interpret what is going on and respond to it. For some, unfortunately, this stance is egocentric, defensive, or resentful. They are often the ones who try to turn everything into possessions that never become gifts. Such a stance has no place among Christian ministers. Ours is the fundamental stance of grace. We begin with thanks for being surrounded by gifts that can never become possessions. Gratitude, more than any other virtue, helps us understand why we should want to be moral in the first place: because we live in a world of grace where God's action is the ultimate basis of morality. When grace has the first word, then the moral life becomes an exchange of gifts, a living dynamic of receiving and giving with grateful hearts.

The commission Jesus gave his apostles when he sent them on their first missionary journey can be loosely translated as "Give freely to others what you have received freely as grace" (Matt 10:8). It houses the biblical imperative grounding gratitude as the foundational virtue of the moral life that seeks to imitate God's gracious action toward us. Two Johannine statements of New Testament ethics summarize well the shape our moral life ought to take in response to how God acts toward us: "Just as I have loved you, you also should love one another" (John 13:34), and "Since God loved us so much, we also ought to love one another" (1 John 4:11). These succinct statements outline the pattern for the moral life: we who have experienced God's acting beneficently for our well-being are moved to and ought to act lovingly toward others. We want to be good and do what is right principally because we are grateful for grace—for the ways we have been loved by God.[7] The writings of Paul also convey a strong imperative of gratitude as he models grateful living in the way he begins nearly all his letters with a word of thanks and then frequently exhorts his hearers to be grateful always and for everything (1 Thess 5:18; Phil 4:6–7).

Robert Emmons, in his popular book of positive psychology *Thanks!*, studies gratitude as a crucial component of happiness. For him, gratitude is the "knowing awareness that we are the recipients of goodness."[8] Gratitude acknowledges goodness in our life and recognizes from whence it comes. We nurture gratitude through memory. Remembering is what gratitude likes to do best. For example, in the United States we have designated a day for the nation to remember the year's harvest. We call it Thanksgiving. We interrupt our normal pace of life to "go over the hills and through the woods" to gather and to give thanks with and for family, friends, and food.

As religious believers, we remember, above all, that God is the giver of gifts. John Shea tells the story of one young boy finding God this way. We pick up on the story when the family shares a group grace before a festive meal. It is the five-year-old boy's turn to pray:

> He began by thanking the turkey which, although he had not yet tasted it, he was sure it would be good. This was a novel piece of gratitude and he followed it with more predictable credits given to his mother for cooking the turkey and his father for buying it. Then he began a chain of thankyous, surfacing hidden benefactors and linking them together. "And the checker at the Jewel, and all the Jewel people, and the farmers who feed the turkeys to get them fat, and the people who make the feed, and the people who bring the turkeys to the store...." His little Colombo mind was playing detective, tracing the path of the turkey to his plate. This litany went on for some time and ended with, "Did I forget anyone?"
>
> "God," said his older brother.
>
> "I was just getting to him," the child solemnly said, unflustered.[9]

When we practice the presence of God as a spiritual discipline, for example, we perceive the work of God's grace in all the gifts that we have received apart from our achievements and in all the people who have extended themselves to us beyond our asking. "Now Thank We All Our God with Heart and Hands and Voices" is a hymn of praise that is always at the ready, and always appropriate, whatever the occasion.

To remember in thanksgiving is also to remember times when we thought we would not make it—someone died whom we loved and needed; we lost a job; we got divorced; we were terribly sick. We remember that we were ready to give up. But we didn't. We remember that we are here. We made it! We got through the worst day of our life. When we see where we are, making our way out of the dark, we remember that we could not have made it to today if we had only ourselves to depend on. We remember that a strength other than our own pulled us through, a wisdom greater than our own opened the way.

Gratitude affirms our fundamental religious conviction that we are not our own explanation for living. We owe all we have and are to something beyond ourselves. That is why we can chuckle at Bart Simpson when he gathers his family for dinner and prays, "Dear God, we paid for all this stuff ourselves, so thanks for nothing." We chuckle because we see the bigger picture that he misses. We know that we are more receivers than achievers. While the Simpsons may very well have earned their money, they are missing the goodness that comes independently of our efforts, including the opportunity that was given to earn the money in the first place. When we remember, we know whom to thank, and we see that we are here today because of grace.

The very nature of having a vocation to ministry means not only that God has made the first move toward us by acting through all that attracts us to ministry, but it also means that God is the source of all the gifts that make our ministry possible. The awareness of God attracting us and gifting us can and ought to engender gratitude. Like the five-year-old boy's prayer before his festive meal, remembering all the experiences that make us want to thank others for what they have done to make ministry possible for us is an occasion for gratitude to God.

The Eucharist is our chief spiritual practice of remembering grace. No wonder we put it at the heart of ministerial spirituality. At the Last Supper, Jesus instructed his followers to "do this in remembrance of me" (Luke 22:19); and, as the preface of the eucharistic prayer reminds us, we are "always and everywhere to give thanks." In the Eucharist, we gather to thank God for being the recipients of gifts freely bestowed. However, eucharistic spirituality does not leave us complacent with the satisfaction that we live by grace. Rather, eucharistic remembering nurtures these gifts and directs us to give freely what we have been freely given. We celebrate the Eucharist as a judgment against ourselves if we fail to develop our gifts and hoard what we have received as a possession to be protected and not as a gift to be shared.

Gratitude as a virtue is a disciplined way of living. Like all virtues, it comes by choice and through practice. Each time we choose to be grateful, the next choice is a little easier, a little less self-conscious. But still the choice to be grateful does not come without effort. As James Gustafson is quick to remind us, the affirmation on which gratitude depends—that God is good and wills our well-being—is only in part confirmed by experience.[10] We must be careful not to push by hard experiences to an easy gratitude when life is tough. It is difficult to be grateful to God, for example, when those whom we have trusted betray us, or when the church gets rocked with scandal and we are forever looked upon with suspicion. It is difficult to be grateful when innocent children are painfully and brutally taken from us through random acts of violence in a schoolyard, or when all that we worked for in building a home or small business is swept away by a hurricane, flood, or fire.

The survivors who can still find reason to be grateful in the face of atrocities that would seem to make grousing trump gratitude always move me. Yet they do not point to those who are better off, nor pity themselves for having gotten the worst of it, nor look for what is missing in their lives, or rehearse the "if onlys" that would have made everything turn out differently. They have every reason to do so, and no one would fault them. However, they seem to choose gratitude. They look over life and notice how much of who they are is not of their own doing. The goodness that they know, even in the worst of times, is there as a gift of God and of caring friends. About the presence of thankfulness in the face of unmerited evil, Robert Emmons concludes that "gratitude is not simply a form of 'positive thinking' or a technique of 'happy-ology,' but rather a deep and abiding recognition and acknowledgment that goodness exists under even the worst that life offers."[11]

Grateful people are, at the bottom, happy with themselves, with others, and with what they have. Even under adverse conditions, grateful people are not miserable. They can wrap themselves in resentment if they want, but they choose not to. For they still find a thousand reasons to thank God for the good experiences of the past, even though these may have come in small sizes and with less frequency than they desire. This means that gratitude is a choice we make to respond to whatever happens to us with an openness that receives it as a grace.

Some practices that cultivate and express gratitude are[12]

Taking an inventory of the ways we have been gifted by others
Naming the people in our life who have made a difference
    for us
Practicing the presence of God and celebrating the Eucharist
    with memories of being graced
Developing our own gifts and nurturing the gifts of others
Saying "Thanks" when we receive a gift
Giving a gift as a sign of appreciation

GENEROSITY

When we recognize that what we have comes to us more as gift than as achievement, then we can give freely what we have received freely. Generosity flows from gratitude. It is the virtue of giving freely. Not to be generous is to be petty, stingy, or egotistical. In the spirit of the Psalmist, generosity asks, "What shall I return to the Lord for all his bounty to me?" (Ps 116:12).

Whenever I have asked ministerial groups to identify their non-negotiable virtues for ministry, generosity (along with compassion, my next virtue) always appears on their list. This is a good sign. For, while it is true that everyone is expected to be generous as part of Christian charity, ministers are expected to be even more so. We should not be surprised to be criticized for lacking proper ministerial character when people experience us as showing undue concern for ourselves over being available and ready to serve their needs. Ministers who are more faithful to their regimen at the gym than they are in meeting pastoral needs are a case in point. As ministers, we are expected to make our gifts available to others and, in the biblical idiom, to be willing to "go the extra mile."

Generosity, like charity that informs it, reflects the very character of God as self-giving love. The central symbol of God in the Christian faith, God is love (1 John 4:8 and 16), has been spelled out in the doctrine of the Trinity. This doctrine is normative for understanding who God is and who we are to be as images of God. About God, the doctrine asserts a relationship of mutual self-giving: God is eternally a giver or lover (Father), the receiver or beloved (Son), and the gift of love that binds them together (Spirit). About us, the doctrine affirms that we are essentially social and made to share. We cannot properly express ourselves as images of God apart from being in relationship with others and sharing our gifts for the sake of each person and the whole community. To be made in the image of God is an imperative calling us to live out of the fullness of the gifts we have received by putting them in service for the good of the community.

In pastoral ministers, generosity is the virtue that expresses well the covenantal spirit with which we are to fulfill our professional duty to act in the other's best interest. As we saw in chapter 2, the pastoral relationship as covenantal rather than contractual requires a flexibility and generosity that do not reduce ministry to merely meeting minimum requirements that we owe another because of some prior agreement. The generosity of the covenantal spirit makes us open to the unexpected. Such a generous posture is countercultural to a world that knows success only when self-interest wins out. However, generosity is a habit that is ready to subordinate self-interest to the best interest of the other, to put ourselves at personal risk or make some personal sacrifices, to adjust by changing plans that might cause us to suffer some inconvenience if necessary, and to try to make things work out so that everyone wins.

In this sense, generosity is the virtue of a good neighbor—self-sacrificing and interested in the welfare of others. The ideal of generosity is to love another for himself or herself rather than for what he or she can do for me. Without generosity, everyone who seeks our pastoral service will be seen as an opportunity for self-gain rather than as someone in need. But with generosity, we are free enough to resist giving pride of place to our own interests in favor of self-disciplined service to the community. The challenge of the virtue of generosity is to use our knowledge, power, and position in a way that will give greater preference to the needs of the other over our own. Such generosity makes little sense in a world where self-interest trumps service. But it makes a world of sense when put in the context of faith where we are called to imitate God's generosity of covenantal freedom of self-giving love, and to imitate Christ in the way he had a special feeling for those in need.

Like any virtue, generosity can be lost to its extremes. Miserliness only causes misery for others because it hoards one's gifts that could be a source of liberation and healing if shared. It fails to give freely what we have received freely. At the other extreme is the profligate prodigal who wastes wealth by reckless extravagance. What might look like generosity in its unsparing bounty can actually be a form of subtle manipulation in disguise. Those who are generous to a fault may unknowingly or, what is worse, purposefully play upon another's freedom to win their admiration and acceptance in order to advance their own interests in gaining recognition. Finding the mean between these extremes is not always easy for ministers whose temptation is to be more rather than less generous.

Generosity as a virtue needs its boundaries. The appropriate expression of generosity will be found when it partners with justice, fidelity, and self-love. Giving out of our gifts is not generous when we undermine the common good by serving one segment of the community to the exclusion of being available to others, or when we overwhelm the pastoral relationship by drowning the other with codependent care, or when we harm ourselves by overreaching our limits of time, energy, or personal resources. If we can honor our own needs for healthy living, then we may be able to transfer that same regard to others. To know where to draw the line on what generosity demands requires the keen moral sensibilities of the virtue of prudence.

Some practices that cultivate and express generosity are

Taking care of ourselves by maintaining our physical, emotional, social, and spiritual health
Sharing our resources, ability, and time
Responding with reasonable preference for the interests of others even if it means sacrificing some of our own
Being approachable as well as available to help people
Being actively concerned to protect justice
Serving without discrimination
Anticipating another's needs and how others will be affected by our own actions

COMPASSION

In my informal surveys, compassion is the other virtue that appears universally on the list of nonnegotiable virtues for ministers. It seems to be the virtue that most people identify with ministry. This is not surprising since the Christian moral tradition has long associated compassion with the central quality of Jesus and of God. It is the virtue embodied in the good Samaritan that we all know from the famous parable in the Gospel of Luke (10:25–37) that Jesus uses to teach about loving our neighbor.

When I have pressed ministerial groups to explain the meaning of compassion for them, I have found that many use it as an expression for love in general. But compassion is really a special kind of love. It is the virtue of suffering love, up close and personal. *Compassion* comes from the word for "womb." As its root meaning suggests, compassion is the gut feeling of empathy and identification with someone in need. It calls us to do as Atticus Finch advises in *To Kill a Mockingbird*: "Climb into someone else's skin and walk around in it awhile." Compassion is the ability to share in someone else's feelings, ideas, or experiences, to understand their motivations, thoughts, and fears almost as if they were our own. Unless our feelings are totally numb, we cannot stand to see another suffer. Seeing tears fall from another's eyes prompts tears to well up in our own. Compassion is at work here; we are being moved deep within us below the level of what the mind can grasp. I include compassion as essential to ministry because without it ministry would self-destruct. Unable to empathize, ministers would be cold and cruel, hard-hearted and indifferent bystanders. Or, they would fall into codependency in which they might feel the feelings of others but have no center of their own from which to respond.

Compassion has its roots in the very character of God and God's saving action toward us in Jesus. The compassion of God is Jesus' willingness to empty himself, become human, and take on the role of the suffering servant all the way through death and resurrection in order to reconcile us to God and to one another. Jesus did not sit on the sidelines as a detached observer of human suffering, but disclosed the character of God's love to be in solidarity with those who suffer. In speaking about God in maternal metaphors, Elizabeth Johnson further illuminates divine compassion to be like a mother moved by concern for the children of her womb. God as mother is concerned not only with the good of a privileged few but with the well-being of the entire world, and so her attention is turned toward those most in need. For Johnson, the compassionate God, spoken about in analogy with women's experience of relationality and care, can awaken in us responsible action in the face of suffering.[13]

God's compassionate struggle against destructive forces and for those in need moves those who are allied with God to do likewise. Compassion is a way of imitating God when we "suffer with" another who is suffering. Compassion is sharing in our vulnerability to suffering and it is reaching out to relieve what we can and to be a support in bearing what we cannot relieve.

However, suffering with another is hard because we often do not know what to do about another's suffering, how to explain it, or how to make use of it. Suffering, according to Dr. Eric Cassell in his work *The Nature of Suffering*, is a psychological or spiritual state characteristically marked by severe distress or a range of emotions induced by threats to our well-being and with the loss of our sense of personal wholeness, meaning, or control.[14] None of us is spared this reality. We know it whether it comes from pain and sickness, the deaths of friends and family, the loss of a job, loneliness, or the collapse of a dream such as living a long life or having a happy family. When we suffer, we lose our connection to God, to others, to our own identity, and to our sense of purpose in life. This sense of loss is heightened by the feeling of isolation from all those activities and people that once supported us.[15]

Ministering to suffering takes us out of the physical realm of medical attempts to alleviate pain or preserve health and into the metaphysical realm of human happiness or a meaningful life. This is the realm of philosophy, religion, and spirituality—the worlds of pastoral ministry. Clearly, we ought not to glorify suffering or portray it as a value in itself. Suffering is not one of those problems in life that provokes the question, "How are we going to solve this?" Suffering, rather, poses a subtler question: "How do we behave toward it?"

One way to behave toward it compassionately involves the willingness to interrupt one's routine and comfort so as to be with those who suffer in order to help them live with and through the suffering. It can take the concrete expression of providing religious symbols and rituals as a source of meaning and comfort. It can also take the form of meeting material needs such as finding a new doctor, or giving financial assistance, or modifying the sufferer's living environment. But whatever form it takes, compassionate behavior is not a one-time intervention limited to the moment of the precipitating event of suffering.

Compassion is the virtue of the long haul, not a quick fix. It is willing to go the distance with the sufferer as the process of suffering unfolds through various phases and as the needs of the sufferer change in the passing days, weeks, and months.

Another way of behaving toward suffering is to deepen our connectedness to others. Stanley Hauerwas captures it well when he says that for Christians, suffering cannot be separated from our commitment to community. Although, historically, Christians have not had a "solution" to the problem of suffering, Hauerwas says, "They have had a community of care that has made it possible for them to absorb the destructive terror of evil that constantly threatens to destroy all human relations."[16] The challenge to ministerial compassion is to bind the suffering and nonsuffering into the same community. Through the cooperation of health care facilities, schools, churches, mosques, and synagogues, we can provide an antidote to the isolation that threatens to cut off those who are suffering from a network of social support.

A third form of compassionate ministerial care includes attention to the spiritual dimensions of suffering. The inability to integrate the experience of diminishment into a framework of meaning is a real threat. One's spiritual vision of life helps sustain a framework of meaning that supports our movement through the experience of suffering and to respond in a way that bears witness to love. A story I once heard from a hospice nurse makes this very vivid. She spoke of how she used small, plain wooden crosses, like the Franciscan Tau cross, that fit into the palm of the hand and can be gripped when someone is afraid. At such times, sensory identification with the suffering of Jesus enabled the patient to experience emotionally—not simply affirm intellectually—that another has known our fear of death. In this mode of caring, patients more easily may feel connected to one who understands, and they may not feel so alone. Compassionate care like this keeps a person connected to communities of shared meaning wherein they find the affirmation and consolation as they confront the fundamental ambiguity of their condition.

However, virtuous "suffering with" is not always a matter of doing something to relieve the suffering. As Daniel Callahan has pointed out in his book, *The Troubled Dream of Life*, there is a more subtle demand to compassion than the burden of relieving suffering. It is not to focus on trying to explain suffering, but to be present, often in silence and helplessness, to the one who suffers. It is like the friends of Job before they tried to explain things through their theology. As the text says, "They sat with him on the ground seven days and seven nights, and no one spoke a word to him, for they saw that his suffering was very great" (Job 2:13). When suffering cannot be overcome, compassion takes the form of accepting the suffering that another must endure. Such may be the case when the suffering comes from courageously standing up for one's convictions, or when a parent suffers by accepting a child's need to make mistakes for the sake of the child's social and moral development. In instances like these, compassion partners with patience, fidelity, and courage to suffer with the other.[17]

Some practices that cultivate and express compassion are

Being with another in whatever he or she is enduring
without blame, judgment, or projection of one's own
preoccupations

Listening attentively to the meaning of what another is
experiencing

Following through on promises and commitments to be with
and for others

Being present to the evening news and letting the circumstances
of others move our hearts and maybe even bring us to
tears

HUMILITY

We often miss the importance of humility because we confuse it with its fraudulent forms, such as refusing to affirm our talents and accomplishments, to discount our own gifts, to be overly submissive and become a doormat for someone else's arrogance, or to display uncritical docility that is unwilling to have an opinion.

To understand humility properly as a virtue for ministry, it helps to remember that *humility* and *human* have the same word root: *humus* ("earth"). God took the dust of the earth and breathed life into it (Gen 2:7). We have been destined for humility ever since, and we are reminded of it in our Ash Wednesday liturgy, "Remember, you are dust and unto dust you shall return."

Humility, simply put, is being down to earth about one's self. Humility is not having gifts and then doing our best to deny them. Rather, it is the realistic acceptance of our power and limitations, of what we can do and what we cannot do. Humility like this is possible when we have acquired the virtue of self-esteem.[18] A professor of mine gave the best functional definition of humility I have ever heard. "Humility," he said, "is the willingness to be who you are and to do what you can." This clearly situates humility between the extremes of pride (acting as though I had no limits) and self-effacement (ignoring my real abilities and accomplishments).

Humility is the willingness to be who we are. So the first movement in acquiring the virtue of humility is to cultivate our capacity for true self-knowledge about what we can do in the world.[19] That begins with recognizing and accepting that we are creatures, not the Creator. This means that we are gifted to do some things, but we do not have all the gifts to do everything. We are limited and dependent. But we bridle at limits, and we try to make it on our own. But we can't.

My favorite lesson on facing limits humbly comes from Ernest Hemingway's *The Old Man and the Sea*. In this story, Santiago, a Cuban fisherman, hooks a fish of heroic proportions. He lets out his line and follows the fish out to sea beyond the limits of its strength and his. Finally, on the way back to shore, sharks lock in on the fish lashed to the side of the boat. They attack and tear the great fish to pieces, despite the old man's valiant defense with knife, tiller, and oars. When only the eighteen-foot skeleton of the fish remained, the old man confesses that he should not have gone out so far. Going beyond his limits ruined them both.[20]

As with the old man, so it is with us. Humility does not come easily. Like the old man, we too seem to have a particularly difficult time knowing our limits, knowing how much is enough and sticking with it. More often than is good for us, we go out too far. Theologically speaking, we would say that we run ahead of our graces. In pastoral ministry, this can take the shape of counseling cases beyond our competence or proposing parish projects that are beyond our resources of time, money, and personnel.

Our culture does not make it easy to be humble in this way. Our culture holds up an ideal self whose dignity depends on the ability to control outcomes. In addition, if there is one criticism of people in ministry that I hear often, it is that they love to be in control. However, humility forces us to ask, To what extent is living with absolute control the only kind of life worth living? Certainly, no one wants to deny that we need some degree of freedom and control if we are to respect personal dignity. But the freedom of humility is less the freedom to control outcomes and more the freedom to choose an attitude. Recall what Viktor Frankl said in his reflection on surviving the concentration camps: "The last of the human freedoms [is] to choose one's attitude in any given set of circumstances, to choose one's own way."[21]

The fact that we are limited and dependent is clear. The question for humility as a virtue is, Is that okay with us? Do we resent having to ask for help? Are we open to what we don't know or can't do? Do we lose our dignity and worth if we don't have absolute control, or can't do everything, or can't do perfectly even what we can do? Humble pastoral ministers know how to accept help without being humiliated, they can say "No" to requests that are beyond their limits without feeling guilty, and they can say "Thanks" to a compliment without having to make excuses. The humble are able to consent to, affirm, and celebrate who they are.

Humility is also the willingness to do what we can. That is to say, the humble are able to be part of the action, but they don't have to be the whole show. They can let go of what is beyond their ability and beyond their control and invite others in to share the burden and the benefit. The growth of collegial collaboration among ministers is a sign of humility. The humble are able to contribute what they can, then stand back and trust in the gracious work of God acting through the gifts of others who can do what they cannot.

Signs of running ahead of our graces and assuming more control than is rightfully ours are behaviors such as growing cynical, anxious, depressed, highly critical of others, defensive, short tempered, and suspicious of the basic honesty and goodwill of others. When we start to show signs like these, we need to ask just how much of the situation bothers us for objective reasons and how much bothers us because it reminds us of our own limitations that we do not want to accept. Without humility we tend to exaggerate our importance and put down others so that we feel more valuable. People who cannot live with themselves as they are seem to try to do their best to make sure others cannot either. Humility keeps us honest with what is troubling us so that we can deal with it as it is and not look for a scapegoat in other issues or other people.

The deadly enemy of humility is pride, the vice of thinking and acting as if we had no limits. Whereas humility lives with limits creatively and graciously, pride is grossly competitive, unable to enjoy an achievement for its own worth but only to the extent that it is better than someone else's achievement. The proud cannot take delight in anything for its own sake but only because it is good by comparison. With a disposition like that, the proud make their gifts become walls that alienate rather than bridges that unite. Humility, on the other hand, enables us to affirm and to celebrate what we have, to recognize that even if we do not have it all we are still secure enough and good enough, and then to be open to what others can give.

Some practices that cultivate and express humility are

Facing our limitations and accepting God's mercy there
Working within the limits of our competence, and asking for
    help when more needs to be done
Accepting a compliment without making excuses
Acknowledging the accomplishments of another

HOLINESS

Humility is the fertile soil of holiness. In fact, humility is one of the doors through which holiness enters the world. Holiness touches into the spiritual depths of a minister, for it expresses our longing for God, our dependence on God, and our love for God. While our hunger, dependence, and love for God are expressed through all the virtues, they get focused in holiness.

We try to satisfy our hunger for God through spiritual practices. The old-fashioned word for this is *piety*. However, piety, a perfectly good religious term for a virtue, has become so bruised and battered by mishandling that few, if any, want to own it as a virtue. Just the mention of this term turns people's minds off like a switch. Others wonder why any one who wants to promote spiritual practices would continue using it. Today we would rather say that we want to deepen our spiritual life, or we are striving to be holy. But pious? No way. We seem to recognize it more as the vice of superficial religion, a characteristic of plaster saints, simpletons with naïve notions of God and of how God acts in the world. A pious person connotes someone of such stifling moral perfection, with their judgmental, holier-than-thou attitude in matters moral and religious, that we would run the other way if our paths crossed. No wonder, then, that no one in my surveys of ministerial groups has ever used "piety" as a nonnegotiable virtue for ministers. The closest they have come is to speak of "prayerfulness."

There was a time when piety had great depth of meaning as a virtue of profound reverence, awe, and perduring faithfulness to God upon whom we are absolutely dependent.[22] Piety is the virtue that involves both deep human affections from being moved by one's experience of God and a deep, responsive love that expresses our faithfulness to God. Piety brings together not only our love for God but also our humility in living dependent on God. It expresses our gratitude for the gift dimension of our lives and our generosity and compassion in the ways that we cherish the gifts that make up our lives.

Holiness, or piety, in the pastoral minister does not set us on a pedestal above everyone else. As a virtue, holiness as piety is the way we give witness to God as the center of life, love, and value. Holiness or piety finds strength, focus, and direction from our relationship with God nurtured not only in personal prayer and public worship, but also in working for justice in the community. We can see and feel the faithful commitment of holiness in personal authenticity, in a nondefensive leadership style, and in the commitment to justice and reconciliation.

Some practices that cultivate and express holiness are

> Participating in the communal prayer of the church as well as in taking time for quiet to fill our senses with the presence of God
> Learning about our faith so that our piety may be grounded in sound understanding
> Living out of an inner freedom that enables us to be flexible and nondefensive
> Being open to the religious experience of others
> Being able to make our own experience of God available to others through preaching and celebrating religious rituals

COURAGE

Last, but certainly not the least, is courage, the virtue of a brave heart. It is the virtue universally admired for protecting and promoting the dignity of conscience and personal integrity. Who among us does not yearn to possess courage and dread to be accused of cowardice? Courage is the apex of character; cowardice its nadir. If there is one aspect of ministerial character that has come under scrutiny as a result of the sexual abuse scandal more for its absence than its prominence, it is the integrity of ministers, both personally and corporately. Integrity takes courage.

In the midst of all of our diverse ministries, we share a common experience: we all face adversity. It comes in a variety of forms. We have to deal with difficult people or malicious rumors that threaten to ruin our reputation; we face temptations to give in to fear or to concede to the intimidations of someone more powerful than we are; sometimes we have to speak candidly to the pastor or the bishop or confront a colleague about misconduct; we have to move on after a successful tenure as a pastor or teacher and resist the temptation to interfere with those who replace us when they change everything we worked so hard to establish; we sometimes struggle with the tension between being an officer of the church and being one's own person; we meet unexpected events that bring us face to face with our limits, such as our personal inadequacies of knowledge, skill, or energy; we get sick; we grow older and weaker; and we all face death. If we are not going to let such threats do us in, then we need courage, both physical and moral.

Rooted in the Latin word for heart, *cor*, courage is the virtue of a brave heart. It gives us the energy, creativity, and strength to face appropriately whatever threatens us, especially those things we would rather not have to face but know that we must if we are to be true to our self.

For classical authors, the paradigm of courage was facing the fear of death. For Aristotle the model of courage was the soldier on the battlefield.[23] For Thomas Aquinas, martyrdom holds primacy of place as an exemplary act of Christian courage.[24] Stories of courageous people are one of the most powerful ways to recognize what courage looks like. In literature, Stephen Crane's short novel, *The Red Badge of Courage*, is one of the great fictional depictions of Aristotle's vision of courage in battle. Robert Bolt's famous play, *A Man for All Seasons*, depicts the courage of Thomas More as an embodiment of the martyr's courage extolled by Thomas Aquinas.

But we do not have to limit courage to the ability to stand against the fear of death. Courage helps us face the fear of anything that threatens us, not only physical death. When we are threatened with bodily harm, then we need physical courage, or "intestinal fortitude," as our high school football coach liked to call it. This is the courage that enables the linebacker to charge the running back, the cancer patient to face surgery, or the holiday shopper to stand up to the would-be mugger. However, when the threat is social disapproval, the loss of our job or reputation, or compromising our convictions so that we lose our self-worth, then we need moral courage, or the heartfelt commitment to values that trumps our fears.

I think the defining characteristic of courage in ministry is the ability to act on the strength of our heart's commitment to what we value. This is moral courage—the ability to be our own person and to stand up for what we believe. Moral courage is what we find in the prophet, the social reformer, or the corporate whistleblower. This is the courage that promotes integrity. That is why I think so many of us admired the courage of Rosa Parks and Martin Luther King Jr. to fight nonviolently for civil rights, and why we can say that Sojourner Truth was courageous in her campaign against slavery and for women's rights, and that Dorothy Day was courageous for standing against violence and for the poor. We admire these people because they had the courage to be their own persons and to act on the strength of their commitment to what they believed was important about life. When we measure our lives against people like these, we hope that we will never have to admit that, when a question of injustice came to us, we did not have the courage to raise it.

Three elements define moral courage: fear in the face of a threat; a willingness to endure danger; and standing up for the values that we say we live by.[25] We know when a situation requires courage because we can feel the fear in our bodies—we start to perspire; our hands, filmed with sweat, clench tightly; butterflies flutter in our stomach; our bowels rumble; we shiver; our knees tremble; we have the mental wish to run the other way. Nevertheless, in the idiom of John Wayne, the courageous are those who may be shaking in their boots and scared to death, but they saddle up anyway.[26]

If fear of some danger is the first characteristic of courage, then the second is the willingness to hang in there when doing so is hard. Courage perseveres. Enduring danger is difficult because we know the cost is great. We may lose our job, our reputation, or even our life. Turning away from danger when the going gets rough only erodes whatever courage we may be bringing to face the danger. When courage collapses, we put ourselves at risk of selling out to those who shout the loudest or simply hold positions of power. If we sell out, then we are on the road to resigning ourselves to live with injustice and allow immoral people, policies, and structures to prevail. Courage, though, restrains our fears and endures danger so as to serve the common good by working to change the situation.

We are able to persevere because of the third element of courage: a heartfelt commitment to value. In the sexual abuse crisis, we witnessed a lack of courage and a loss of integrity not because the priest abusers and some bishops who kept quiet about it did not have values, but because they did not act on what they laid claim to be values about personal dignity, sexuality, and justice. One of the dangers of not standing for what we believe to be true is that we may fall for anything, and so risk losing our soul. But neither would we be acting courageously to seek a change in policies and practices if we rushed recklessly into speaking truth to power. Courage finds its way between the extremes of cowering cowardice (the timidity that does not stand up for one's convictions for fear of making a mistake or of offending someone) and foolhardy bravado (the irrationality that does not calculate how best to proceed on the basis of insight, imagination, and consultation). Courage is the virtue of appropriate fear and confidence seeking to do what is right by enlisting the virtues of self-esteem, prudence, and humility.

Courage protects our integrity because it enables us to act on what we believe really matters. In this way, courage is the virtue that upholds the dignity of personal conscience. Our conscience is the ultimate court of appeal once we have done the hard work of forming it. We let our integrity suffer when we allow any person, institution, or authority to replace conscience in the name of being loyal or obedient. More than one pastoral minister has shared with me the tension they feel when caught between an official position of the church and the reality of their own pastoral experience and insight gained from prayer, study, and serious reflection. Taking a stand in the name of conscience is not stubbornly clinging to the familiar and the comfortable; it is witnessing to integrity. Acting with the courage of our convictions is the well-earned prerogative of those who follow through with their responsibility to discover what is right and good, identify with it, and be willing to pay the price for being so committed.

To uphold courage as a virtue for ministry that protects personal integrity is to encourage everyone to have the courage to be their own person. Instead of submitting unquestioningly to authority, we commit ourselves to coming to greater clarity on where we stand and why we stand there. Living with the courage of our convictions does not mean that we have to have a fully articulate position on every controversial moral or political issue that arises—the war in Iraq, stem cell research, gay marriages, health care reform, capital punishment, abortion, euthanasia, and so on—but we ought to be committed to discovering what really matters to us rather than to seek only what is safest or most acceptable to others. We cannot claim to have integrity if we act simply on the basis of what someone else says we ought to hold.

If there is one lesson that the stories of courageous people have taught us it is that we cannot run from our fears without suffering a great cost to our self. Just as we do not become courageous by making one bold move, so we do not lose courage in one instance. It withers away, bit by bit. Small betrayals driven by the fear of losing acceptance or approval, especially of those in authority, erode courage. Courage deteriorates when we fail to think critically, remain silent before an issue we deeply care about, or when we allow something that we know to be wrong to continue. These kinds of avoidances corrode courage because they make us comfortable hiding behind our fears when, in the image of John Wayne, "saddling up" and taking fear along for the ride would be more costly. Before we know it, we become compromised. We have lost our soul. However, having the courage to face everyday tests of our integrity helps us to determine how we will respond when we come face to face with a significant moment of truth.

Since courage only shows itself in the face of a threat, these practices are ways to prepare ourselves to be courageous when the threat arises:

Reading biographies or memoirs of courageous people
Clarifying our convictions by talking about what really matters
    to us with someone with whom we feel safe
Volunteering an opinion or skill

So there you have my vision of the "virtuous minister." Right now you may be feeling the way one of the participants in my workshop felt after hearing this description of a virtuous minister: "Where can I meet this person?" No one may embody all of these virtues fully, or excellently, I admit. But one of the characteristics of virtue ethics is that it orients us to growth and development. It gives us a vision of the kind of person we can aim to become, and it inspires us to set ourselves in the direction of that goal, even if we never fully become that kind of person.

Moreover, I am making no claims that this is the one and only ideal expression of the virtuous minister. The communion of saints testifies to an enormous variety of ways to be virtuous in ministry. Saint John Vianney (the Cure d'Ars) was not Oscar Romero, and the Little Flower was not Dorothy Day. Yet each models virtuous ministry for us in different ways. This chapter has only tried to set out from my limited perspective the qualities of character that I think are nonnegotiable for ministers if we are to be sacraments of Christ and agents of God's reign of peace and unity among all peoples and with the earth.

I am very much aware that commending any list of virtues invites others to ask why this list rather than others. Any list underwrites a certain conception of what counts for an "excellent" minister. You may want to add a few of your own or drop a few of mine. You may also have different interpretations of the virtues in my list. The specific meaning of a virtue can change over time and in different cultures. Virtues, remember, are not action specific. How we express a virtue depends a great deal on our culture, personality, maturity, and the context in which we live. Analogies are always possible, but there will also be differences in how we exemplify the virtue. For example, the courage of the soldier facing enemy fire is different from the courage of the pastoral associate who must speak truth to the power of the pastor or bishop, or of the bishop who must confront one of his priests about professional misconduct, or of the pastor who must rein in a difficult staff person.

Furthermore, you may have noticed some overlap in my description of the virtues. This is not unusual, since it is difficult to draw precise boundaries around the behaviors that belong to each virtue. They naturally blend into each other and do not exist in isolation from one another. At any rate, I hope this profile of the virtuous minister has stimulated your own thinking of the kind of minister you want to become in serving the mission of the church. Achieving excellence in ministry requires a host of virtues working together to give coherence, direction, and wholeness to our lives as disciples modeled after Jesus, our paradigm of the virtuous minister.

5

THE DYNAMICS OF POWER

Fr. Frank is in his third year as associate pastor. In learning how to negotiate relationships with the pastor, the parish staff, parishioners, the clerical world of the diocese, and the diverse cultures of the parish, he has come face to face with the ambiguity of power in the pastoral ministry. On the one hand, he feels that he doesn't have any power, since he is not the one in charge. Furthermore, his duties in the parish had already been defined for him before he got there. He felt powerless by not having any room to negotiate these duties. On the other hand, he sees how influential he can be over parishioners, especially through his preaching and in the respect they show him as their priest, even though many do not really know him apart from seeing him preside and hearing him preach on Sunday.

While Fr. Frank tries to find his way around in the parish, he mixes with a great variety of people in many different capacities. This gets confusing as he moves back and forth between firm boundaries and weak ones as he tries to get close to everyone and yet remain their priest. Sometimes he steps out of his role as the parish priest and tries to make himself a peer and friend, especially with the youth group. At the same time, he is very firm in making sure that the youth activities are properly supervised by adult parishioners. He has a few favorite families that he spends time with on his day off.

Fr. Frank is starting to wonder whether he is confusing his role and relationships in the parish and compromising his pastoral effectiveness. Where does he draw the line between being their priest and being their friend?

What can Fr. Frank teach us about power in the pastoral relationship? Chapters 3 and 4 focused on the personal identity of the minister. They showed that acquiring a virtuous character requires that we have certain sorts of relationships with others. The centerpiece of chapter 4 was the portrait of a virtuous minister painted with the various hues of the virtues. This chapter continues to examine the relational character of ministry by focusing on the dynamics of power in the pastoral relationship.

The first section of this chapter describes the ecclesial warrants for examining the dynamics of power in pastoral ministry. The second section analyzes personal power in the pastoral relationship and the wisdom of boundaries for safeguarding our capacity to influence another and the environment. The third section considers the influence of social power on ministerial behavior. Social power is the interaction that goes on among us to form the organizational culture that helps or hinders the exercise of personal power in the pastoral relationship. It creates a paradox of power for the pastoral minister. The final section of this chapter proposes the criteria of justice and liberation to assess power in the pastoral relationship.

ECCLESIAL WARRANTS

Of the various models of the church that shape our self-understanding, three especially provide warrants for analyzing power in pastoral ministry. These are the church as hierarchy, as communion, and as sacrament.

CHURCH AS HIERARCHY

Catholics have long been accustomed to describing the church primarily in terms of its hierarchical structures. The familiar hierarchical model stratifies the community in pyramidal fashion with the laity making up the base and having minimal power. Then in ascending order of power and status come the vowed religious, priests, and finally the bishops at the top. In this model, we all know where we belong and what our role is to be. This long-standing model of the church has given Catholics a strong sense of corporate identity, institutional loyalty, and a stable organization under a clear chain of command to support the aims and teachings of the church.

The stratification of power in this model creates a clear distinction between the laity and the clergy. It has encouraged the laity to view clergy as set apart with special virtues and power. Power spells privilege, especially when a role entails a divine calling. Clerical power is further supported by the loyalty of the faithful who trust that clergy are of strong moral character and will always act with their best interests in mind. However, since pastoral relationships are fundamentally marked by the inequality of power, this hierarchical stratification creates enormous potential to take advantage of the vulnerability of those seeking pastoral service.

From a sociological point of view, then, instances of the misuse of power, such as sexual abuse or financial malfeasance, should not come as a surprise, since we organize ourselves in power-over relationships with little or no oversight or mutual accountability between the stratified layers of power. A hierarchical model warrants examining the inequality of power and how it must be managed well if we are to promote the mission of the church and not undermine it. Attending to the professional aspects of ministry creates the possibility of nurturing both justice and fidelity that disposes us to be accountable for our use of power and to maintain boundaries that create a safe haven for those whom we serve.

CHURCH AS COMMUNION

When everything is going well, the hierarchical model stands in creative tension with the communal model. However, when these models collide, scandals like those of sexual abuse, financial malfeasance, and the misuse of ecclesiastical power can result. The communal model of the people of God upholds a spirit-filled community in which we hold different roles, responsibilities, and offices in the church. While some persons in the church have by ordination a new relationship to Christ and to the body of the faithful, at the same time the communal model recognizes that we are fundamentally equal through baptism.[1]

This model has nurtured the growth of lay ministries that have brought the laity into relationship with clergy in ways the hierarchical model could not envision.[2] Collegiality and collaboration are two of its

119

mechanisms that promote solidarity in governing the church and shared participation in carrying out its mission. This model has given rise to the notion of the parish as "community" or "family" under the direction of a ministerial "team." But these communal metaphors can too easily presume an equality of power that is really not there. In fact, clergy are still in a position of greater power than the laity. Ministering out of a presumption of equality and not from the reality of unequal power too easily leads to violating the boundaries of one's role and mismanaging power.

For all the good the communal model of the church has done to affirm and call forth the baptismal dignity of each person and to nurture diverse gifts in the church, this model without proper nuance can easily obscure the boundaries and lines of accountability that must exist to respect the differences of power in a pastoral relationship. In this model, accountability can be lax and boundaries blurred in the name of baptismal equality, shared ministry, the pastoral "team," and the parish "family." So this model of the church has more to gain than to lose by attending to the wisdom of boundaries and structures of accountability that may guide the right use of power. The church would be more authentically communal if everyone acknowledged their power, if boundaries were protected, and if we had some commonly recognized standards against which to hold one another accountable for our ministerial conduct.

CHURCH AS SACRAMENT

The church as sacrament is a third model that warrants examining the dynamics of power. According to *Lumen Gentium*, the church is to function as a "sign and instrument of communion with God and the whole human race" (*LG* no.1). The sacramentality of the church lies in everything that makes it visible to the public—the witness of its members, its religious and social practices, and its organizational structures. If the church is sacrament, then there should be some coherence between what the church signifies and the way it structures itself and practices ministry. These visible realities of the church are to sign forth the unity of all under the rule of divine love.

The church enhances its sacramentality of divine love when its own structures and practices embody the same values it wishes to offer to the world. The 1971 synodal document *Justice in the World* asks for nothing less. In that document, the bishops claimed that the church must not only offer to the world its social teaching, but it must embody that teaching in its structures and practices:

> While the Church is bound to give witness to justice, she recognizes that anyone who ventures to speak to people about justice must first be just in their eyes. Hence, we must undertake an examination of the modes of acting and of the possessions and life style found within the Church itself. (#3)

Being just and doing the work of justice are constitutive dimensions of the church's sacramentality. To the extent that the church's own structures and practices are unjust, its mission is compromised. If the church is going to speak to people about justice, then, as the bishops said, "it must first be just in their eyes." A just ministry embodies the virtue of justice not only disposing us to the ties that bind us to one another but also to the rules of action that reach beyond the dynamics of the pastoral relationship to shape the ecclesial structures influencing the way we provide ministerial service.

These, then, are three models of the church that emphasize the moral challenge for a just ministry to manage the dynamics of power in pastoral relationships and ecclesial structures so that the church can be a more effective sign and agent of God's reign of love.

PERSONAL POWER

THE PROFESSIONAL PASTORAL RELATIONSHIP

The professional pastoral relationship is the primary interest of the first part of this chapter. We are at risk of unethical behavior when we treat a pastoral relationship as if it were a personal one. Such confusion is understandable when we realize that what constitutes a professional pastoral relationship is not always clear. We are in a much more ambiguous relationship with our people than other professionals are with their clients. Doctors, lawyers, and therapists, for instance, generally meet with their clients in well-defined settings and for a clear purpose. It is uncommon for them to socialize or work side by side with their clients in other institutional or social settings. As a result, what constitutes a professional relationship for them, and when one is in a professional relationship with them, remains fairly clear.

However, we do not always enjoy the same clarity of distinction in our relationships. Spiritual directors, for example, may be able to define their relationships with directees much more clearly than pastors can with their parishioners. However, parish-based ministers, like Fr. Frank in the opening scenario, meet with their people in a great variety of settings, not just the office, and they socialize with their people or work along with them on diverse projects, not just religious ones. As a result, pastoral relationships can easily overlap with other kinds, such as personal, social, or business ones. Consequently, sometimes it is difficult to distinguish when we are in a professional pastoral relationship and when we are not. This was certainly the case with Fr. Frank. All the more, then, we need to understand the dynamics of power in these mixed relationships. Where do we draw the line between a personal and private relationship on the one hand, and a professional pastoral relationship on the other? What kind of behavior is appropriate in each?

I do not consider all relationships that we have as automatically being professional pastoral relationships. By a professional pastoral relationship, I mean one in which we are

> Acting as a representative of the church so that people can draw from our special authority and competence to meet a religious need (for example, pastor serving parishioner; spiritual director serving directee; catechist serving students)
>
> *or*
>
> Serving in a supervisory role over others (for example, pastor to staff; director of religious education to catechists)

122

THE NATURE OF PERSONAL POWER

Like Fr. Frank, many of us are ambivalent about power. Some are in awe of the power people give us over their lives by entrusting us with personal secrets even without knowing whether we are trustworthy. Others, especially women, feel powerless because of ecclesial and social structures that exclude them from some positions of leadership. Many of us do not like to be told that we are powerful. Having power seems to be contrary to the kind and style of service that ministry stands for. We are suspicious of power because it connotes domination or being "one-up" on another, or it suggests the capacity to coerce or intimidate people into doing what they might not otherwise do. Nevertheless, power need not reduce people with whom and for whom we work to people over whom we have control. Power can also be liberating or enabling. Power can be a loving influence that releases the goodness in another. Love and power need not be in opposition.

Perhaps the easiest way to get a handle on the power we have is to see it as a capacity to influence. It is what enables us to make things happen or not. In this sense, everyone has power, but we do not all have it to the same degree. Power as influence is always relative to our resources. One of the most important self-examinations we can do is to name our sources of power, for we are most at risk of ethical misconduct when we minimize or ignore our power.[3]

Where do we get our power to influence? James and Evelyn Whitehead have organized sources of legitimating power under three major categories: institutional, personal, and extra-rational.[4]

INSTITUTIONAL SOURCES OF POWER

The most obvious institutional source, and the easiest to recognize, is that of official appointment. When some form of public validation legitimates our personal power, we speak of having "authority." When we get ordained, commissioned, installed, credentialed, or even hired for a position in pastoral ministry, the community recognizes us as someone with religious authority and with power to act on their behalf. From this institutional endorsement comes power in our role, title, distinctive garb, or symbol of office. Our institutional power is enhanced further by the expectations people have of anyone with institutional legitimation.

The Catholic tradition has enshrined the institutional power of ordination in its sacramental theology of *ex opere operato*. This means that the validity of the sacramental celebration depends on the fact that the minister is duly ordained, and not on his moral worthiness. Graham Greene's "whiskey priest" in *The Power and the Glory* is an extreme example. Although he had lost his faith, the people of his village pressed him to say Mass for them because there was no other priest to turn to. Because of his office, he did. The Mass was valid independently of his faith and morals. The example of the whiskey priest exercising sacramental power and authority is straightforward. His cultic role was clear, and so were the expectations of the villagers. However, such is not always the case. *De jure* authority does not guarantee equivalent *de facto* power. Personal sources of power will often condition and qualify the influence of an officially appointed pastoral minister.

PERSONAL SOURCES OF POWER

Simply because of who we are, each of us brings personal sources of power to the ministry. They are many: our virtues, gender, age, size, physical attractiveness, experience, reputation, emotional stability, language skills, personality, charisma, knowledge, or competence, to name a few outstanding ones. Whether we want them to do so or not, these personal sources of power are at work in pastoral relationships to enhance or weaken our influence on others. Because we all bring a host of these personal sources of power, we really cannot say that we are "powerless" in the relationship. We have power simply by showing up as the persons we are. We are more or less powerful in relation to those we serve, depending on our resources of influence relative to theirs.

I want to single out "competence" as the one source of personal power that has tremendous significance for pastoral ministers. In chapter 2, I took the position that competence in theological reflection is the professional aspect of the gift dimension of our vocation to ministry. One of the primary goals of theological reflection is to help people name their graces by seeing more than meets the eye. Ministry is about helping people see. We are the ones to whom people go so that they might be able to see their lives through the lens of faith. Take the ministries of preaching and spiritual direction, for example. These ministries stand out as prime opportunities to do some lens grinding, to influence the way people see themselves and their experiences in relation to God. The ethics of preaching and direction underscores the importance of calling to these ministries those gifted with this skill of reflection.

Because we are recognized as religious authorities, our interpretations of experience strike many as the most truthful. Our way of seeing things is taken as the way the church sees them, or even more, as the way God sees them. One woman who was a victim of her pastor's sexual abuse specifically saw this way of using power operative in her experience. She was a teenager when the abuse began. When she looked back on how she experienced her pastor's power, she said, "He had a lot of power over me personally, too, in terms of naming me. I was very young. I was still trying to figure out who I was. I'm still trying to figure out who I am. But at that time, whatever he said was Gospel."[5]

People rely on our theological competence to assist them in finding meaning by celebrating life's experiences sacramentally or by relating their experiences in life to the stories of faith or to our religious convictions, such as our beliefs about God's love in Jesus, about sin and grace, and about crucifixion and resurrection. The question, however, will always be whether we are using the rituals, symbols, and stories of our religious tradition accurately and wisely. The strong reaction against those religious leaders who wanted to declare that AIDS is God's punishment for sin reflects, on one level, a sensitivity to the great power that a minister's evaluation of a crisis can have on the way people understand and accept themselves. It also reflects the ability of many people to recognize theological incompetence that interprets God's relationship to us in a way that is incompatible with most of our tradition's understanding of God.

The significance of competence as a personal source of power can be clearly seen in the lack of it. Official appointment as a pastoral minister invests us with enough authority to get people to approach us for help. However, after an initial grace period of unquestioned acceptance, the power of official appointment alone may not give people enough confidence to engage us in ministerial service. For example, the authority of a pastoral care minister can quickly wane when people discover that he or she does not have the knowledge or skills to communicate a perspective of faith to someone who is sick, dying, or bereaved. The trust necessary to sustain the pastoral relationship is based on the confidence that we are competent to address people's religious needs. People simply give more power to those who are good at what they do. While official appointment (and *ex opere operato* theology) may compensate for the lack of competence up to a point, in time incompetence will undermine whatever credibility we may have had by virtue of institutional sources of power and authority. It follows, then, not only as a moral requirement, but also out of a personal desire to be of service, that we should become and maintain our competence in what we profess to be for the community.

EXTRA-RATIONAL SOURCES OF POWER

Symbolic Representation

I introduced symbolic representation as a source of power in chapter 2 as a professional aspect of the call to ministry. Here I draw out its significance as a source of power.

The power that derives from our being symbolic representatives of the holy is frequently misunderstood and often strongly resisted or denied. Many who are inexperienced in ministry are frightened and confused by its power. I have heard some express it this way: "Can't you see it's only me? Don't lay that 'God' trip on me." I hear in this expression the refusal to accept what is happening when one becomes a representative of the holy, and the attempt to deny or at least dilute one's power by making oneself just like everyone else. We are like everyone else in so many ways (thus, "It's only me"); but there is also something different about us. We bring "something more" to ministry than just ourselves (thus, the "God" trip). We experience this difference when we are both praised or blamed beyond what we deserve. This is not surprising because we represent the sacred for people.

Symbolic representation gives added significance to our presumed competence. Since we are representing the One who gives meaning and purpose to life, there is a "sacred weight" that adds more seriousness to what we say and do. Perhaps this explains somewhat why there is so little questioning of our preaching, teaching, or counseling. After all, we are perceived to be speaking not just for ourselves, but also for the church or even for God. People trust these sources to be truthful, and so we are readily given the benefit of the doubt when speaking for the church or God.

The representative role also helps explain, in part, why others believe that we are worthy of trust without having done anything to earn it or show it. Their trust is based not only on past experiences of pastoral ministers, but also on expectations they have of what we represent—a trustworthy God. Because of our representative role, we must be all the more careful to interpret the world accurately, to represent the church fairly, and not to exploit the vulnerability of those who trust that we will act in their best interest.

As a corollary of symbolic representation, we often find ourselves to be lightning rods for people's religious projections. We become, in a sense, the conduit into which people channel their deepest hopes and feelings about God, about their salvation, or about their moral life. Their projections only magnify our power over them. This was the case with two victims of professional misconduct by pastors who were asked by the Evangelical Lutheran Church of America to share their stories. When asked how they experienced their pastor's power, one said:

> I saw him, maybe not that he was God or that he was Jesus, but that he took on that role, and he made his vow to God to pastor the flock, you know, to be shepherd. And so, when I look back on it, I saw him in that role and he could have told me to do anything, and I would have believed him, and I would have done it.

The other said:

> I found myself, when I was praying to God, sometimes praying to God the Father and thinking of this pastor. I would pray passionately to be like him one day, to be compassionate as he was one day.[6]

One does not have to be in ministry long to experience how the power of representing "something more" attracts people's religious hopes, fears, guilt, joys, and angers. We must face the fact that people's projections are inevitable. Projection is part of any relationship, and it is especially acute in relationships with persons in authority. Since we cannot get rid of projections, we need to learn how to work with them. Projection is not unhealthy. As a matter of fact, it is a common process of letting people's unconscious hopes, fears, and defenses become conscious. The anger, fear, guilt, and need that people project onto someone else appear to be what he or she is really all about. Nevertheless, in fact, the real meaning of what people think is out there actually lies within them. If we do not become defensive about people's projections, we may be able to use them to help people clarify their thoughts and feelings about God and their relationship to God. So we need not run from projections. We need to hold them in trust and gradually return to the people what really belongs to them. Being a symbolic representative of the holy is a gift that we need to nurture responsibly. If we can befriend the power of symbolic representation, then we can direct it to liberation.

Religious Authenticity

The power of religious authenticity is what we feel when we meet someone whose life flows out of personal faith. The Whiteheads describe religious authenticity according to three themes derived from a study by the Alban Institute, an interdenominational center focusing on parish life:

1. Personal genuineness
2. Nondefensive leadership style
3. Spiritual leadership[7]

Personal genuineness is the matter of being present and responsive to people without hiding behind a professional role. When we are genuine, people see us in a human way and get a glimpse of our personal life of faith. A nondefensive leadership style arises from a realistic acceptance of ourselves. If we can befriend our limitations and feel at ease with who we are, then we do not have to expend any energy defending an idealized image of ourselves. We can redirect that defensive energy into creative ways to adapt to the needs and goals of different groups. We exercise spiritual leadership by using religious convictions, symbols, and rituals to help people find a connection between their personal story and the stories of faith.

These, then, are some of the sources of power that we bring to the pastoral relationship. There can be no question that we have power over those we serve because we have the resources that will satisfy their religious needs. However, having power over another does not mean that we have to be exploitive. The core ethical challenge of the pastoral relationship is the prudential handling of its inequality of power. We turn next, then, to the demands of the virtue of fidelity that governs the interpersonal relations in ministry characterized by an inequality of power.

BOUNDARIES

The first demand of fidelity is to set and maintain boundaries. Boundaries set limits. They separate me from you, my space from your space, what is mine from what is yours. We recognize them as necessary and helpful on the highway as guardrails that keep us from falling off the cliff, or as the white lines that separate the flow of traffic. We know them in baseball as the foul line and in football as the sideline. Chalk on our shoes is a clear sign that we have stepped out of bounds. In life and in pastoral ministry, we can get "chalk on our shoes"[8] when we cross the line by the way we speak to and about others, by the way we touch them, and even by the way we look at them. We can also get chalk on our shoes by throwing things at them, by sending messages (e-mails), by giving gifts, or by postings on billboards or bathroom stalls. In sports, in life, and in ministry, boundaries are for safety and fair play in reaching one's goal.

In workshops on boundaries in ministry, I have sometimes met resistance to the notion of boundaries, though not as often since the sexual abuse scandal. The resistance is often rooted in the negative connotations associated with boundaries, such as barriers or walls that divide and exclude. Boundaries in this sense only undermine the spirit of ministry that aims to liberate and nurture our life in the Spirit. Even though boundaries do separate, they need not alienate, especially when they are established and maintained as an expression of fidelity. Positively speaking, boundaries are the way we set limits that create a hospitable space wherein others can come in and feel safe with someone who makes room for them and accepts them. In the safe space created by clear boundaries, those seeking pastoral service can trust that we will not take advantage of their vulnerability. Then they can be free to focus on their own needs and experiences without having to deal with ours.

All relationships have boundaries, but they differ according to the nature of the relationship. In personal relationships of friendship, in which two people seek to meet the needs of each other, boundaries are flexible. Each party shares mutually in the responsibility to maintain them. However, in a pastoral relationship, such as spiritual direction or a pastor's supervising the secretary, boundaries must be more clearly defined, and we have the greater burden of responsibility to define and maintain them. Establishing and maintaining clear boundaries is what fidelity in a just ministry requires.

COMMON BOUNDARIES

Some of the common boundaries that any minister must establish and maintain are those of time, space, and person.

Boundaries of time give security, safety, and respect to the other; they show commitment to the other's interest by starting and stopping meetings on time, by setting enough time to complete a project, and by taking on a limited number of projects in order to honor our promises and to safeguard our emotional, mental, spiritual, and physical health. In multicultural settings, we need to learn how to accommodate different interpretations of time. For example, Hispanic and Asian cultures are more flexible about starting and stopping meetings at a set time than Euro-American cultures are. Negotiating appropriate boundaries of time in a multicultural setting requires understanding and flexibility on all sides.

Boundaries of space respect limits on where ministry occurs. Changing the setting or the environment can confuse, threaten, or distract the one seeking the pastoral service. For example, moving a pastoral meeting from the office to the coffee shop can change, or at least confuse, the meaning and purpose of the relationship. Place helps keep each one's role clear and to support the purpose of the meeting. Space can also ensure the confidentiality of the pastoral relationship. Spaces that are too open to the public (for example, offices separated only by shoulder-high barriers, or too easily invaded by distracting external noises or activities) can violate boundaries that ought to protect the private nature of the pastoral meeting.

Boundaries that respect the person honor physical and emotional limits. We get chalk on our shoes when we invade another's physical space by sitting or standing too close, by making physical contact (hugging, "bear hugs," or kissing) as a gesture of "pastoral" concern without asking permission, by meeting one on one when no one else is around, especially when one or the other is a minor or an emotionally fragile adult. We can cross emotional limits by giving and receiving gifts of a personal nature, by getting too involved in another's life through frequent phone calls or e-mails of personal interest, or by spending too much time together alone, by ridiculing another's experiences or beliefs, by commenting on another's body and appearance, by eliciting unnecessary details of another's experience (especially sexual ones), by showing excessive interest in another's personal activities within family life or among friends, by gossiping with confidential information, and by fostering dual relationships that confuse roles and create conflicts of interest.

CHALLENGES TO FORMING BOUNDARIES

The importance of establishing and maintaining boundaries can easily be undermined by some prominent forces at work in society and in the church: for example, the ethos of postmodernism, the feminist movement, the reactionary defensiveness to a litigious environment, and an ecclesiology of community.

Because of an ethos of radical autonomy, postmodernism resists any suggestion that we must put limits on our behavior or that we ought to abide by standards in professional relationships. Boundaries only interfere with exercising free choice. We see this manifest frequently in clothing and automobile advertisements that entice us to break with convention, to be daring, and to live without limits. These ads implicitly deny that relationships that respect limits can ennoble and build up personal and social life.

For some feminists, boundaries are a vestige of patriarchal practices that shut out the possibility of realizing some of the prized feminist values of mutuality, vulnerability, and friendship. According to one such feminist view, no relationship should be prevented from becoming mutual;[9] "friendship" should be the primary analog of the ministerial relationship.[10] Other feminists, however, recognize that nonmutual relationships are not necessarily oppressive and abusive. The dynamics of power in relationships need not be mutual to be ethical. Denying the inequality of power in the pastoral relationship leads only to avoiding the difficult challenge of using power appropriately.[11]

At the opposite extreme of these two views is a reactionary defensiveness that some feel we must assume in our highly litigious environment. The great cost, financial and emotional, of the sexual abuse crisis makes some feel that one can never touch anyone again in a pastoral relationship, especially a child, or that one can never be alone with anyone behind closed doors. Some ministers feel that such caution is extreme, even paranoid. Others are not so sure. However, ministry cannot survive with such aloofness. We are just as wrong to withhold authentic emotional connection as we are to touch another in ways that are confusing or abusive. Genuine connection with people is essential to ministry. It requires the prudential sense of what fits in often very confusing settings.

The ecclesiology of the spirit-filled community in which everyone is "one in Christ" and so enjoys the evangelical equality of the baptized can contribute to fuzzy or weak boundaries. For all the good that such an ecclesiology has done to affirm and to call forth the baptismal dignity of each person, to nurture diverse gifts in the church, and to foster collaboration and collegial styles of ministry, we cannot forget that there are real differences among ministries and between ministers (even on the same ministerial team) and the faithful. Vatican II teaches, for instance, that priests differ essentially and not only in degree from other ministers (*LG* no. 10). While there are times when pastoral ministers of all kinds enjoy equality with all the baptized (*LG* no. 32), we cannot level the necessary distinction of role and status in a church that is hierarchically structured.

To insist on clear boundaries is not to be patriarchal and want to keep the laity in their place. While boundaries can get lost in the name of evangelical equality and when promoting shared ministry, we should recognize that the inequality of power exists in pastoral relationships. Our responsibility is to maintain boundaries that are neither too fuzzy nor too rigid in order to shape the kind of relationship that will provide appropriate pastoral service while protecting the vulnerable from exploitation. Fidelity and prudence can meet this challenge, especially when informed by the keystone principle of professional ethics—the fiduciary responsibility.

The Fiduciary Responsibility

Our professional fiduciary responsibility is to exercise our power and authority in ways that will serve the religious needs of those seeking our service, and not to exploit their vulnerability but to give greater preference to their best interests over our own. Being faithful in the pastoral relationship requires that we first acknowledge the various sources of power we have in pastoral ministry. When we lose sight of the power gap between us and those seeking our pastoral service, we pave the way for betraying our commitment of fidelity by exploiting the vulnerability of those seeking our service.

Marilyn Peterson's provocative book, *At Personal Risk*, makes this point very clear. Her thesis is that professionals are most at risk of unethical behavior when they minimize or ignore their power. She documents quite convincingly that professionals who refuse to accept the authority that comes with their role, or who are not clear about the extent of their power over others, can easily misuse their role and abuse their power in ways that violate the boundaries they are morally bound to protect. Her work shows that the person in the best position to help others is also the person in the best position to hurt them. Once hurt, only with reluctance will people trust again. When one victim of sexual abuse by her pastor was asked, "What do you struggle with today?" she said, "Well, it's very hard to regain the sense of trust, not only trust in pastors, but also trust in people and trust in the goodness of the universe."[12]

A moral principle that can guide our fiduciary responsibility is this: The greater burden of moral responsibility falls on the one with the greater power. Even though the other person in the relationship may try to manipulate the situation and is responsible for his or her manipulative behavior, we are nonetheless obligated to maintain the boundaries of the relationship because we have the greater power to do so.

The Lure of the Friendship Model

It is tempting to reduce or ignore the inequality of power in the pastoral relationship and treat it as if it were a friendship. When we make the pastoral relationship a peer relationship between friends, as Fr. Frank of the opening scenario did with some members of the youth group and with some families, we risk falsifying its real nature and putting ourselves at greater risk of unethical behavior.

In her analysis of different styles of pastoral leadership, Martha Ellen Stortz has identified various facets of friendship to show that several of them conflict with what ministry demands. Her seven facets of friendship are these:

1. *Choice*: Friends choose each other.
2. *Similarity*: Friends have certain things in common (same school, taste in food, interest in sports).
3. *Mutuality*: Friends hold certain things in common (beliefs, commitment, vision, goals).
4. *Equality*: Friends are equal in power and status.
5. *Reciprocity*: Friends give and receive equally.
6. *Benevolence*: Friends love the other for themselves and not for utilitarian benefit.
7. *Knowledge*: Friends invite truthful self-disclosure.[13]

By examining each of these facets of friendship, we can see that ministry correlates easily only with benevolence, in the sense of acting in service to our neighbor. Friendship and ministry correlate with mutuality in the sense of sharing evangelical equality signed in baptism and nurtured in word and sacrament. But there is no mutuality in the roles we play, or the power and authority we have in the community.

The demands of ministry clearly come into direct conflict with the other facets of friendship. Stortz points out that friendship as a matter of choice implies the possibility of exclusion. If we choose some within the community as friends, we risk dividing the community along the lines of those who are in and those who are out. One does not have to be in parish ministry long to know that a sure formula for creating factions in the parish is to become friends with a family or a person in ways that show we are enjoying the benefits of friendship *only* with them to the exclusion of all the rest in the community. A tes-

timony from Marilyn Peterson's study of boundary violations in professional relationships illustrates one cleric's experience of the divisive-
ness of making parishioners friends:

> My own ideology was very much the ideology that is rein-
> forced in the church. I believed in a shared ministry. I
> believed that people in the church should be friends. I didn't
> want to set myself apart as superior. I felt that the minister
> needed to be part of the group. Having your primary friends
> be outside of the congregation didn't fit with this ideal picture
> of friendship and community. Therefore, my best friends
> were members of the congregation. Now I know that each
> person's participation in the church is influenced by the one-
> to-one relationship with the minister. If the minister is best
> friends with one or two or three people, that's going to have
> an influence on the life of the whole congregation. It makes
> an in-group and an out-group, and things like that are really
> deadly for a church.[14]

People are much more conscious of signs of favoritism than we
imagine. The more exclusive and possessive a friendship is the less
authentic it is. Authentic friendships, by contrast, promote inclusive,
universal love. They are more in line with the commitment of ministry
to be of service to the whole community for they help to make one
more loving and caring toward others.

To continue with Stortz's categories, *similarity* of common experiences in the church is getting harder to find as people become more
mobile and continuity of traditions diminishes. *Equality* is enjoyed
through a common baptism but diminishes when we assume different
roles and functions within the community. Today's golf partner can be
tomorrow's annulment case. *Reciprocity* demands mutual giving and
receiving. However, pastoral relationships are not a two-way street in
any "equal" sense. It is expected that ministers will make more sacrifices for others than they would make for themselves. *Knowledge*
demands that friends allow themselves to know and to be known by
each other. However, in a pastoral relationship, intimate sharing goes
primarily in one direction. Those seeking pastoral service must disclose intimate knowledge about themselves in order to satisfy their

needs. But ministers can be effective in meeting those needs without disclosing any personal, intimate knowledge about themselves.[15]

I find Stortz's analysis to be very helpful for clarifying the difficulties of using the paradigm of friendship for pastoral relationships. Nevertheless, we ought not to conclude from this analysis that friendships must be absolutely *avoided* in ministry, or that we are *never* to minister to a friend. Ministry cannot be so clearly departmentalized. Since different ways of relating to the same person can make life messy at times, we need to be careful where we draw the line. For example, a pastoral administrator shared with me her experience of a personal relationship that opened the way to a pastoral one. Her friend was having marital difficulties and so turned to her first for help. By being pastorally present to him, she was able to help him sort out his issues and then make an appropriate referral for further counseling. This was a pastorally and ethically correct exercise of ministry. The key to it is that she made a referral and did not try to engage her friend in long-term counseling. She drew the line where it was necessary to respect their friendship *and* her pastoral role.

Not all pastoral relationships are equally vulnerable and so do not demand the same degree of trust, or of soul searching and self-disclosure. For this reason it is quite common, and ethically appropriate, for priests and deacons to witness the marriage of friends, or to baptize the children of friends (or one's own in the case of a married deacon), or even to bury their parents. However, it is another matter to try to be a spiritual director to one's friend or to give long-term pastoral counseling to a friend. The vulnerability demanded in these ministries tends to conflict with the intimacy and mutuality of friendship.

Perhaps a way to grasp the personal and professional dynamics involved in developing friendships through pastoral ministry is to consider relationships on a continuum. On the far left is the professional relationship of the pastoral minister. On the far right are the intimate personal relationships of family and lovers. In the middle are friendships. The further we move from left to right, the more we concede the power and authority of our pastoral role and compromise our professional commitment to the other. When we become a friend, we have crossed the line from a professional to a personal relationship. We are no longer relating to the other out of our professional role as a pastoral minister, but as his or her friend. Our friend would now need to turn to someone else to serve his or her religious needs, since we have compromised our professional commitment in this regard. Fidelity would even require that we help the person find another pastoral minister who can meet his or her religious needs.

Mixing a personal and professional relationship puts us at greater risk of violating trust. To safeguard against such a violation and to keep the relationship clear, we might ask ourselves these questions:

Which role is dominant for me in this relationship?
Who am I for you in this relationship?
Who are you for me?
Whose needs are being met here?

The answers to these questions will help us to define more clearly those situations in which it is appropriate to relate as peers and friends and so meet each other's needs, and those in which the difference of role and status must be acknowledged. Thus, the purpose of the relationship remains focused on meeting the needs of the one seeking pastoral service.

DUAL RELATIONSHIPS

When we interact with another person in more than one capacity, we form a dual relationship. This happens, for example, when as teachers we make a student our golf partner or baby-sitter, or, as pastors, we become long-term counselors to someone on our staff, or, as youth ministers, we date someone from the youth group, or, as spiritual directors, we seek the financial services of one of our directees who is also our broker. Dual relationships are like trying to wear two hats at the same time.

The strict prohibition of dual relationships is a well-established principle in the helping professions. Doctors, for example, are not to serve as the primary physician for members of their own families. Therapists are not to socialize with their clients. The wisdom enshrined in their restrictions warns about the great potential for harm that comes with mixing roles with the same person. Multiple relationships can be inappropriate and even wrong because they are fertile ground for impairing judgment, harboring conflicts of interest, and exploiting the trust of dependency. If applied as strictly to the pastoral ministry as to other professions, this prohibition of dual relationships would mean in practice that we are not to serve as a pastoral minister for someone who is also our employee, friend, financial advisor, spouse, doctor, therapist, sibling, student, teacher, client, lover, or any other relationship that creates a conflict of interest for us and for them.

However, must pastoral ministers be as strict about dual relationships as other helping professionals? I do not think so. Pastoral ministry is not exactly parallel to the helping professions, even though we share with them many of the same skills and objectives. As full members of the community, we provide servant leadership in a holistic way, not just in specialized religious functions. We stand for and mediate the presence of God in the whole of human life, not just in the specifically religious sector. While those of us with very specialized ministries, such as spiritual directors and chancery officials, may be able to avoid mixing roles with those they serve, many others cannot.

Moreover, while avoiding multiple relationships as much as possible is a good rule for governing professional life, many of us are not in a position to follow it absolutely. Realistically and sometimes out of necessity, we inevitably blend several roles and functions. For example, in seminaries it is common for a faculty member to be in multiple relationships with the same student in the roles of teacher, spiritual director, confessor, advisor, evaluator, prayer partner in small prayer groups, team member of a committee, community member of the school, and social partner in community events. In a parish, a pastor will have to supervise and show pastoral concern for an employee of the parish who may be experiencing marital difficulties, burnout, or some other personal difficulty that deserves pastoral attention. In small towns, ministers have few alternatives for therapists, doctors, contractors, or even friends.

Managing the inevitable dual relationship is one of the greatest professional ethical challenges we have to face. What guidance can professional ethics offer to navigate dual relationships in pastoral ministry?

1. *Avoid dual relationships as much as possible.*

The wisdom of prohibiting multiple relationships as a general rule should tell us that while many dual relationships are already built into much of pastoral ministry, we ought not to create more than what

already comes as a given in our ministry. Dual relationships can be wrong because they are fertile ground for

Impairing judgment
Harboring potential conflicts of interest
Exploiting the trust and dependency of the vulnerable

Our judgment can be impaired when we are emotionally involved with the other. Conflicts of interest can easily arise when a relationship creates competing demands. For instance, one campus minister shared with me the bind she found herself in when she let one of the staff members use her as a marriage counselor over an extended period of time. She was caught, on the one hand, with being his boss and holding him accountable for his performance and, on the other, with being his minister who was trying to be supportive. She came to realize that she could not be both for him at the same time.

2. Dual relationships are not necessarily wrong in all circumstances.

Some ministries, like those in religious formation houses and pastorates in small towns, inevitably and unavoidably entail dual relationships. In seminaries, the very professionalism that seminaries try to instill in the seminarians can be undermined by the experience of these inevitable dual relationships. Thus in the seminary as in the pastorate, we need to heed the wisdom of boundaries while in such relationships.

3. Dual relationships become problems when roles get confused and boundaries are not respected.

Dual relationships do not have to become problematic if we are

Being honest about the kind of relationship we have
Paying attention to our own needs
Satisfying personal needs beyond the limits of the dual relationship
Keeping the pastoral role as the primary one in the relationship
Monitoring the development of the relationship, for example, through therapy, supervision, and/or spiritual direction

By following such guidelines, some pastoral ministers have been able to establish friendships with members of the parish whom they have gotten to know over the years. These dual relationships have not necessarily become a hindrance to effective ministry, but in fact have been healthy for both parties. So, to insist only on rigid boundaries that absolutely prohibit dual relationships for all pastoral ministers in every setting would be as crippling to ministry as allowing flexible boundaries to prevail.

4. Dual relationships can become a problem when we are not satisfying our needs appropriately.

Often the people we meet in our ministry are the most accessible and attractive ones to whom we turn in seeking to satisfy personal and social needs. We can easily end up using them more than ministering to them. This is what happened to Fr. John Madigan, according to this excerpt from an interview he gave regarding his experience of burnout and his process of recovery:

> I had always believed that my needs for intimacy would be met by the parishioners in terms of their responding to what I was doing, by going to their homes and meeting the families. But I've found that it's not a dual relationship, and that I can't expect parishioners to meet my needs. In terms of friendships, my needs have to be met outside of my parish work. When I develop friendships within the parish, there's the struggle of being close to parishioners when conflicts arise. Then I'm put in compromising situations. It may seem like a wonderful idea that the parishioners are your family, but in effect they really aren't. They have their own concerns and needs and I am there in the capacity of pastor.[16]

Fr. Madigan's experience reminds us that pastoral ministry is primarily for the benefit of the people. Our aim is to act in the best interests of those we serve. They have every right to expect that their interests will take priority in our hierarchy of interests.

To accept the responsibility to monitor our own needs and to discipline ourselves to satisfy them outside the professional relationship belongs to the virtues of fidelity and self-esteem. Marilyn Peterson's observation about professionals violating boundaries is instructive here:

> Most of the time, professionals find that their misuse of the client did not grow out of some malicious intent or unresolved psychological issue. Rather, the violation happened because they were unaware of their needs and the client was convenient. Using him or her made their life easier. Within this reality, professionals begin to grasp how they used their greater power in the relationship to cross the boundary and take what they needed from the client.[17]

The self-discipline involved in submerging our own needs in order to meet the needs of those seeking pastoral service is part of the freedom we ought to have to live out our vocation and manifests the virtue of fidelity that guides our service. Peterson adds that to understand why we cross boundaries, we have to examine the rationalizations we use to disregard limits. Perhaps we think the pastoral relationship is over, or that our behavior is not really interfering with the goals of the relationship, or that we are doing what any minister would do. Rationalizations like these or any others only allow us to avoid facing the responsibility we have to find acceptable alternatives. Peterson argues that what really leads to crossing boundaries is that we have "either minimized the relationship or equalized the power differential."[18]

I believe that dual relationships, while not always wrong in the pastoral ministry, generally ought to be avoided. At least we ought not to create more than those that already come with our particular form of ministry. Those dual relationships that we cannot avoid need to be carefully monitored. When we are in dual relationships, we must monitor these relationships and make an honest appraisal, often with the help of a friend, a spiritual director, or a therapist, of the effect the dual relationship is having on us and on others. After all, the purpose of avoiding dual relationships is to guarantee an unambiguous space for people who seek pastoral service to get their needs met without our own needs and projections getting in the way. Dual relationships in ministry are instances of ambiguous situations that call in the end not for a legalistic set of rules to be set up in minute detail, but for a keen moral sensitivity, prudential discernment, and a virtuous character that can strike the balance between self-interest and the interest of the other.

One pastoral minister shared with me why she believes that dual relationships are not necessarily harmful in ministry and how she evaluates them. She was arguing, in effect, according to the axiom that general principles (such as, pastoral ministers ought to avoid dual relationships as much as possible) apply generally. She cautioned that if dual relationships are the only kind we have, then we are surely in a danger zone and a disaster is waiting to happen. Her way of keeping a watchful eye on her relationships was to pay special attention to her own vulnerability. She said, in effect, that if we know that we are in a more vulnerable place than usual because of the stresses in our life, then we need to keep firm boundaries. However, when our personal life and our ministry are satisfying our needs for creativity, nurturance, and acceptance, then having dual relationships may not put us at such a great risk for blurring boundaries and exploiting the dependency of others. Whenever in a dual relationship, the guiding question is, "Whose needs are primary here, mine or theirs?"

This is good pastoral wisdom—to be cautious about dual relationships without unequivocally condemning them. Careful scrutiny of dual relationships in ministry is certainly necessary, for probably nothing will provoke the judgment of being "unprofessional" or "unethical" more quickly than our taking advantage of the vulnerability of the one seeking our pastoral service.

Accepting and working with the differences of power in the pastoral relationship is a true test of character and one of the major breakthroughs of maturing professionally as a minister. In a culture like ours that promotes aggressive power, we are conditioned to exploit to our own advantage whatever power we have. People with power tend to be oblivious to how others perceive them and are likely to take risks with their power because they do not believe anyone will ever call them to account. This attitude seems to be implicit in the clerical culture of the church, as the sexual abuse scandal showed. But one of the sure ways of using power rightly is to understand what having power does to us for better or worse. At one extreme, it can enable us to relate to others in ways that draw out the best in everyone. At the other extreme, having power can so lower our inhibitions that we act in cavalier ways unmindful of the influence we really have on others. When we accept our power and authority as ministers, we have to curb our desire to be equal in all ways with everyone else, we have to change our assumption that pastoral relationships are peer relationships, and we have to realize that we influence others by who we are, by what we do, and by how we do it.

However, power is paradoxical. Although we might acknowledge that we have personal power because we have resources of virtue, experience, role, theological competence, pastoral skills, and the like that give us the capacity to influence others, we do not have to be in ministry long to feel powerless, even with all these resources. The feeling of powerlessness comes from finding ourselves at the mercy of many structural features of our social and ecclesial worlds over which we have little or no control. Our personal power is limited or enhanced by the forces of social power that influence greatly how we interpret what is going on and how we respond to it. Professional ethics also needs to consider the realty of social power.

SOCIAL POWER

Up to this point, the analysis of the dynamics of power has focused on the individual pastoral relationship and on personal power as a capacity to influence it. This relationship is marked by an inequality of power in which the one seeking the pastoral service gives up equality and is forced to trust and to become dependent on the skill, competence, compassion, and general professionalism of the pastoral minister. Appreciation of the dangers for abuse from the inequality of power has produced a great deal of professional attention to the wisdom of boundaries in such a relationship. However, the dynamics of power are not restricted to our own personal power or to the individual pastoral relationship. There are also dynamics of social power within an organization's culture.

Social power is primarily a matter of relationship, not possession.[19] It is not a capacity we have to influence others, but the relational dynamic within an institution or community that shapes the way we think, feel, and interact with one another. The reality of personal power in the pastoral relationship is complemented by social power, or what goes on among people, and often behind the scenes, in the institutional setting.

The flow of social power gives rise to patterns of relating, to defining roles, to establishing expectations, to assigning status, and to establishing ways of behaving that become a normal part of the minister's life. All these structures together (role differences, expectations, status, patterns of behavior), along with the underlying and often unspoken assumptions that support them, create what social psychologists call the organization's culture. This is what Fr. Frank of the opening scenario is still trying to figure out.

ORGANIZATIONAL CULTURE

The most visible aspects of a culture are the lines of authority among the various constituencies in the organization, the way a group arranges its physical space, the way people dress and address one another, the language or jargon people use in reference to one another and their common tasks, the use of symbols of status and titles of office, the mission statement of priorities, and the pattern of relating among the members of the group, such as who can talk to whom directly. However, according to social psychologist Edgar H. Schein, deeper down a culture is really all about "*basic assumptions* and *beliefs* that are shared by members of an organization, that operate unconsciously, and that define in a basic 'taken-for-granted' fashion an organization's view of itself and its environment."[20]

Perhaps some examples of secular organizations can illustrate what is at stake in the dynamics of social power. Take the *Columbia* shuttle disaster. The public explanation for it was that a piece of foam broke loose during launch, hit the wing, and damaged the protective tiles forming the heat shield for reentry. While all this was true, there was a cause deeper than damaged tiles. It was NASA's organizational culture. The report of the Accident Investigation Board spoke of a "broken safety culture" that suppressed the mutual interdependence that encourages the free interchange of experience and perceptions among the employees who were knowledgeable about potential problems. While particular individuals must be held accountable, an analysis of social power focuses our attention on the stifled dynamics of the give-

and-take of mutual interdependence that prevented sound decision making from happening.

The story of NASA's broken safety culture that took exceptional courage to address from within is also the story of Enron, where managers could not offer suggestions to correct unethical practices without exceptional risk to their futures. Moreover, it is the story of the church, in which a culture of silence and loyalty, called clericalism, undermines establishing and implementing procedures of accountability between bishops and priests, bishops and the people, and the priests and the people. Behaviors that those outside the ecclesial and clerical culture would recognize as unacceptable have become normalized on the inside, so no one pays any attention to them.

Schein's analysis shows that the organization's culture is often quite different from what the organization explicitly says it stands for in its statement of mission and values. His analysis of organizational culture helps explain, in part, much of the mysterious and seemingly irrational things that go on in the church, such as the kinds of behaviors that get rewarded, the importance of protecting the public image of the church, how much risk one can take in raising questions or challenging each other across peer groups or up and down the hierarchical ladder without being marginalized or fired, who can talk to whom directly while others must communicate indirectly, who can have which roles and who can't, and the secrecy and silence that conceals many internal transactions. Schien's analysis also underscores the importance of those coming into ministry to learn "how we do things around here" if they are to get along in this ecclesial world.

What makes the interplay, and sometimes conflicting forces, of personal and social power difficult to grasp is that we live in several intersecting cultures at the same time, and the influence of these cultures is often unconscious and subtle.[21] In the church, for example, we live within an American culture, the Vatican culture, the clerical culture, a culture among bishops, a culture among priests of a local region, and the emerging cultures of lay ecclesial ministers. We not only have these cultures, but a culture can also have us. For example, the process of being socialized into the clerical culture blinds us to the subtle influence this culture has on the way we think, feel, and behave. "Insiders" do not see the influence of these human constructs, whereas an "outsider" or newcomer, such as a lay ecclesial minister, identifies them easily. The worst thing that can happen to newcomers is to adapt to a dysfunctional situation, for then they become part of the sickness. According to Schein, if there is ever going to be any change of behavior in the group, then it will begin by surfacing and confronting its underlying assumptions.[22]

These assumptions take on a life of their own and work largely unconsciously to shape the way members of the group relate to one another and share common interpretations of everyday events. James and Evelyn Whitehead offer a telling example. When "the way we do things around here" is that the men always do the organizing, the women bring the food, the youth group cleans up, and the priest leads the prayer, then the pattern of relating has become so predictable that no one notices whether the person assigned a role really has any special ability for it. It is just assumed. Since the assumption is that leaders and followers can never trade places, then the leaders begin to exercise their authority independently of the dynamics of the mutual interdependence that constitutes the group. As a result, the leaders become immune from the accountability that comes with living interdependently and sharing responsibility for the mission of the institution.[23]

THE CLERICAL CULTURE

For some decades now, priest associations have developed as ways for priests to support one another as intimate companions trying to hold fast to gospel values and to meeting pastoral demands in a healthy way. Such positive developments in the clerical world should not be confused with clericalism, a vice characterized by using clerical status to claim privilege or special treatment. Its sense of elitism can be manifest in many ways: the unearned respect given to clerics, an unquestioning deference to their word ("Father knows best"), social privileges ("Father deserves the best"), exclusivity (being ordained into "the club"), entitlements (receiving exemptions from normal constraints on behavior coupled with low expectations regarding professional performance), and the lack of any significant accountability structures (the "wink and nod" of tolerance).[24] The clerical culture is morally dangerous. A clerical attitude can easily lead to exploitation.

The Dynamics of Power

From the sexual abuse crisis, we have learned what can happen when there is an uncritical acceptance of the implicit rules and communication patterns of clericalism, like the fraternal silence or "wink and nod" that facilitate an abuse of power by freeing clerics from the normal constraints that would keep them in line. The crisis has made us aware of the hidden assumptions and overt behavior patterns of this culture so that we are now in a better position to evaluate and reform it.

While the clerical culture affects both the ordained and nonordained, it is not the whole story about priests or pastoral ministers generally. Developments in theology and in ministry can support this effort to reform the clerical culture. For example, one of the benefits of the ecclesiology of communion, mentioned at the beginning of this chapter, is to look upon different gifts and functions in the church not as adversarial or competitive, but as complementary. This perspective underscores collegiality and collaboration, and not control, as the way forward to enrich the life of the whole community. Moreover, this ecclesiology supports a relational interpretation of ministry that enables us to appreciate each other's serving the church and its evangelical mission as "co-workers in the vineyard," as the title of the 2005 United States Conference of Catholic Bishops' document on lay ecclesial ministry suggests. A too lofty theology of the priesthood could reinforce clericalism if it divorced the priest's sacramental representation of Christ from his other relationships in the church and from the spirituality of ministry that emphasizes service and pastoral charity.

In ministerial training, clerical and lay students are studying together in some seminaries or at least working together side by side in common pastoral services. This mode of training provides the condition for the possibility of eroding clerical culture. In addition, we also find efforts to reorganize the leadership of parishes so that running the parish no longer belongs just to the pastor. Many others are working in partnership with the pastor to share responsibility for the many facets of parish life. Inviting parishioners to use their skills in running the parish is a way of transforming the clerical culture of exclusivity and control and replacing it with inclusiveness and collaboration.

Another hopeful sign is the growth of ministerial support groups that foster intimate companionships among ministers. These groups provide an opportunity to have "accountability partners" to whom we become answerable in a trusted circle of support. They can affirm us when we are doing well and challenge us when we grow careless. Already well established are the highly organized programs such as the *Jesus Caritas* and Emmaus programs. Other groups require less formal gatherings for reviewing life, socializing, prayer, and discussion.

Another sign of hope is the U.S. Bishops' *Basic Plan for the Ongoing Formation of Priests* (2001) that calls for developing mentoring programs for priests at certain transitional points in their life and ministry. One such well-structured program is the Mantle of Elijah Program of St. Mary's Seminary in Baltimore that serves newly ordained priests in many dioceses. Both the growth of support groups and the emergence of mentoring programs provide opportunities for peer review and accountability, even if informal, that are missing in the clerical culture.

THE CALL FOR ACCOUNTABILITY

A just ministry calls for reforming the clerical culture by introducing structures of accountability that will keep alive the mutual give-and-take of social power. Accountability begins with establishing some clear qualifications for admission to pastoral ministry. This is a giant leap beyond merely inviting volunteers to step forward. The lesson from virtue ethics applies here: selection is the most important step in the formation process.

Along with criteria for admission, we also need a rigorous course of preparation that gives the community confidence that graduates are competent in knowledge and skill. The U.S. Bishops' *Program of Priestly Formation*, their *Permanent Deacons in the United States: Guidelines on Their Formation and Ministry*, and the *National Certification Standards for Lay Ecclesial Ministers* all set forth some requirements for admission and performance.

In addition to careful selection and rigorous preparation, we need to create a morally safe environment in which to exercise a just ministry. The current outcry from the sexual abuse scandal can be read in part as a desire to live within a church in which all members feel safe enough to speak up, to admit error, and to challenge each other across peer groups or up and down the hierarchical ladder in ways that produce a collegial ministry. For example, consider a case like this: a lay pastoral associate, who has been working in the parish for a few years, notices how the pastor has begun to relate to a female staff person in ways that are flirtatious and professionally inappropriate. When the lay pastoral associate brings this behavior to the pastor's attention, the pastor is incensed and threatens to fire the lay minister. This case is a good example of a morally dangerous environment. The pastor pulls rank on the lay pastoral associate and pollutes the moral climate of the parish staff by resorting to hierarchical power. To speak up again and challenge the pastor in any way would take extraordinary moral courage.

One way to try to shape a better moral climate might be to introduce a code of ethics. Codes of ethics are emerging with such frequency that it is hard to keep up with the trend. Elaborating the core values of ministry and the moral implications of the professional role of the minister in the way codes do clarifies how ministers go about responding to their call to be signs and agents of God's love. However, for codes to be credible and effective, they need a moral environment and ecclesial structures that enforce accountability as a commitment to a just ministry. Without structures to support ministerial colleagues and laypersons in rewarding good performance on the one hand and reporting professional misconduct on the other, the code as an instrument of accountability is an empty promise. For any code to be effective, it needs to be at least accompanied by, if not preceded by, a change in the organizational culture and moral environment of the church.

Creating a morally safe environment for ministry in the church is not an easy task. To change the moral climate requires a critical mass of morally sensitive persons to emerge throughout all levels of the church—starting at the highest levels of leadership and moving throughout the ecclesial structures to include those in the trenches. These persons must encourage, model, and reward thoughtful discussion, creative problem solving, a willingness to call unprofessional behavior into question, and a readiness to admit to error. Such individuals will draw in others who are also committed to shaping the moral climate of the church but who may not yet have the moral courage to speak up. This is how moral courage will be strengthened within the church and how enough persons will emerge to change its moral environment.

To create a safe moral environment, a culture must introduce structures for reviewing ministerial performance. As the sexual abuse crisis has taught us, vertical accountability, or simply being accountable to someone higher up in the organization, is not enough. If we take seriously the communal and sacramental models of the church, along with the dynamics of social power, then we need the give-and-take of peer review groups (pastors, principals, chaplains, directors of religious education, and so on) and the input of those who are being served in the community. Only in this way will we affect the flow of power in the group. To do this we need to develop policies, procedures, and some instruments of evaluation and to create advisory councils that will guarantee mutual accountability and will follow through with supervision, disciplinary procedures, and sanctions for controlling deviant behavior. There must also be a greater openness of church leadership at all levels to public scrutiny and transparency of its procedures. We also need to make better use of structures already in place that make it possible for more people to be involved in issues that affect them and to have a voice about the flow of power in the community, such as pastoral councils and priests' senates at the diocesan level, and parish councils and school boards at the parish level. Those whose lives are affected need to have a say in shaping policies, goals, and budgets, and not just in creating the strategies that fulfill someone else's goals.

In conclusion, then, while virtue ethics focuses on the agent and helps us appreciate that persons of good moral character have the moral impetus to practice right behavior, we know from experience that acting virtuously in ministry is hard. It is hard not for lack of motivation to be good and to do what is right, but because influences on us from the culture, context, and structures of our social worlds strongly affect our behavior. While virtues dispose us to guard against contextual forces that might undermine virtuous behavior, virtues do not always prevail. Critics of virtue ethics tell us that virtue alone cannot guarantee right behavior. We must also attend to the dynamics of interaction in the work setting and to how they influence our interpretation of what is going on and the way we respond.[25] Although a just ministry must take social forces into account as seriously as it does character traits, social forces are not commonly a concern of codes of ethics. However, if we ignore social influences on behavior, we can too easily reduce ministerial misconduct to a lack of faith or virtue and focus conversion on personal change to the neglect of the cultural and structural reform that still needs to happen. Part of professional responsibility is to notice the social dynamics that help or hinder our pastoral ministry. Justice requires that we work to change what needs to be changed so as to transform an oppressive environment into a liberating one.

ASSESSING THE USE OF POWER

Efforts at structural reform for better holding the use of power to account need to be guided by ethical criteria that protect and promote the dignity of the person made in the image of God and that reflect the gospel witness of Jesus.

ETHICAL CRITERIA

Karen Lebacqz holds up the criterion of justice through liberation as the proper measuring rod for relationships that have power as their central dynamic force.[26] To assess our use of power, she asks, "Is liberation happening here?" Power is used rightly when it enables the other to become increasingly free. The normative perspective to which we turn in order to determine whether liberation is happening belongs not to us who hold the greater power, but to those we serve in the ministry. They are the more vulnerable, and so they are the ones in a better position to determine whether they are being oppressed or set free.

Our power in ministry, then, is used rightly only when we enhance another's freedom. We fulfill our professional commitment to serve the interests of others not by doing for them or giving to them in ways that keep them passive and dependent on us, but rather by enabling and empowering them to release their potential so that they might more fully participate in the common mission of the church. In his discussion of professional ethics from a Christian perspective, Darrell Reeck argues that the primary duty of the professional is to "empower" the one seeking professional service to come into his or her own freedom.[27] Service as empowering helps others to recognize their potential, and it encourages and guides them to develop it.

PSYCHOLOGICAL MODEL

Rollo May has developed a schema that can be useful for evaluating our use of power in the professional relationship along a continuum that shows how power can be used to oppress or to expand another's freedom.[28] At one extreme are *exploitative* and *manipulative* acts of power. These are expressions of domination. They presume a relationship of inequality and a determination to keep it that way. Exploitative power depends on force and coercion to remain in control. Manipulative power is more subtle in that it uses psychological means to retain control. Both undermine the covenantal commitment to seek the best interest of the other; they are disrespectful of the dignity of the person, and they represent the most abusive forms of power in a pastoral relationship.

Competitive power lies in the middle of the continuum. It presumes relative equality. If equality is absent, this form of power dominates and so can be destructive. However, when there is a relative equality of persons, competition can act constructively to bring vitality to a relationship. Since pastoral relationships do not enjoy relative equality, this form of power has too much potential for misuse.

Nutrient power presupposes the inequality of the parties in a relationship. But unlike the other forms of power over others, it does not act in self-interest but for the benefit of one who still lacks responsible freedom. It enables or empowers others to come into their own freedom. Nutrient "power for" correlates well with the covenantal bonds of the pastoral relationship.

Integrative power respects the freedom of others. It presumes an equality such as we find among colleagues. This is the kind of power that makes collegial and collaborative ministry possible, for it cooperates with another's gifts and interests.

Rollo May's schema helps us see that "power over others," which is inherent in the pastoral relationship, is not necessarily demonic. While the potential for abuse is there, the just and faithful use of power can also open the way to liberation. The moral challenge is to draw upon the virtues of justice and fidelity to direct our use of power away from dominating others through exploitation and manipulation and toward liberating them through nutrient and integrative acts of power.

THE MODEL OF JESUS

We have a model of this use of power in the ministry of Jesus. He rejected the use of power that dominates or promotes oneself over others in favor of power that serves others by empowering them. Several scenes in the Gospels give us examples of Jesus insisting that those who share his values must reimagine power and its use in human relationships. The devil, Jesus' own disciples, as well as the political and religious leaders of his day, often serve as foils of Jesus' loving use of power.

Matthew and Luke portray Jesus at the start of his public ministry being tempted by the devil to build his ministry on the demonic power of domination. The temptation scene (Matt 4:1–11; Luke 4:1–13) can be read as a conflict over power: demonic power would use domination in the name of doing good. Jesus insists that such power corrupts and will only defeat the good in the long run. In each temptation, Jesus witnesses to his trust that God reigns through the power of nurturing love. When Jesus is tempted to obtain power over the world at the price of acknowledging a world governed by demonic power, he rejects this possibility and instead worships a God who rules by love. The rest of his ministry shows him preaching and working for a new order of human relationships in the community whereby the desire to dominate has no place.

The disciples, too, act as foils to Jesus' image and use of power (Mark 9:38–40; Luke 9:49–50). They want to stop a man from casting out demons in Jesus' name because he is not one of them. Jesus, however, protests: "Whoever is not against us is for us." The disciples want to control the good and to make themselves superior to another who is not one of their company. After all, they, not this stranger, are the official exorcisers. The fact that a man now lives free of demons is insignificant to them. What matters is that they did not work the wonder. The one directed by divine love does not want to usurp the good; the arrogant, who seek privilege and domination, do.[29]

A fresh understanding of power is seen in the conflict between Peter and Jesus over forgiveness (Matt 18:21–35). "How often should I forgive?" Peter asks Jesus. Peter knows that Jesus is prone to forgiveness, so he makes a liberal estimate, "Seven times?" "Not seven times," says Jesus, "but, I tell you, seventy times seven times." The contrast here shatters Peter's image of the power of ministerial authority and the nature of human relationships. Jesus responds to Peter with an image of inclusion. Peter, who has just been given the keys, is looking on human relationships through an image of power that can exclude by locking some out and others in. Jesus challenges that understanding with an image of ministry that creates hospitable space, that has room for others even in their sinfulness.[30]

We can also see this liberating power at work in the scene of Jesus' healing the bent-over woman in Luke 13:10–17. This time the religious leaders are foils to Jesus' liberating power. Jesus calls to a woman who has been bent over by an evil spirit for eighteen years. First, Jesus addresses her as a "daughter of Abraham" to show that she is included and equal in dignity to the "sons of Abraham." Then he places his hand on her and she stands up straight. She who was once weak is now strong. Friends of Jesus rejoice over her liberation, but the officials of the synagogue who observe this are angry over his doing the work of healing on the Sabbath. The power that liberates by making the weak strong is too challenging to them. Arrogant power of control wants to keep some weak while others remain strong. Jesus exercises the power that challenges behavior that seeks domination.[31]

The passion story ultimately brings the issue of power to a climax.[32] In Gethsemane, Jesus' opponents come with familiar instruments of power that guarantee control: betrayal, arrest, swords, and clubs. Jesus has no such weapons. Those who hold positions of control according to the social structure of that day, the Sanhedrin and Roman procurator, abuse him. Roman soldiers torture him with the very symbols of domination—a purple robe, a crown (of thorns), and homage (of spittle and blows). The ultimate weapon of the power of domination is public execution on the cross. In the crucifixion, the power of domination is raging out of control.

Yet the very success of this power is its own subversion. By dying on the cross, Jesus does not resort to legions of angels to destroy the evil of those who appear to be in power. If he did, then his kind of power and theirs would be the same. The only difference would be in the size of the muscle. Jesus resorts to the only kind of power he knows—divine love—and offers forgiveness. The cross reveals the emptiness of all oppressive power. As in his ministry, so in his death, Jesus exercises a power that gives life: "And just as Moses lifted up the serpent in the wilderness, so must the Son of Man be lifted up, that whoever believes in him may have eternal life" (John 3:14–15). The passion and death of Jesus reveal the steadfast love of God unmasking the arrogance of power that nailed him to the cross. The same steadfast love invites us to become followers of Jesus and to use our power as a source of life and freedom for others.

In the pastoral relationship, the use of power is the key moral issue. We inevitably have power over those seeking pastoral service because we have something they need. Our fiduciary responsibility protects their vulnerability, for it obliges us to maintain clear boundaries and to subordinate self-interests to serving their best interest. The ministry of Jesus models for us a power that need not be oppressive but liberating. He demonstrated the criterion of justice through liberation in the way he set people free. As disciples, we are called to do likewise.

This concludes my sketch of the pastoral relationship as the context for exercising a just ministry. Its centerpiece is the dynamic of power, both personal and social. The wisdom of boundaries safeguards the right use of personal power by protecting the vulnerability of those seeking the pastoral service and by creating a safe haven that enables their liberation. The dynamics of social power require attending to the mutual interdependence of responsibility for the community through structures of accountability that ensure an open and transparent process of directing the flow of power within the community. Jesus models for us the right use of power as liberation to nurture the gifts of those we serve so that together we can witness to the reign of God in our midst.

6

SEXUALITY

Fr. Joe is in the third month of his new assignment as associate pastor of an inner-city parish, St. Boniface. He completed five years at his first assignment as associate pastor in the suburban parish at St. Jerome's. He was well liked by the parishioners there. They found him to be what a minister should be—dedicated, caring, and sensitive. He worked hard and for long hours—often late into the night. While at St. Jerome's, he earned a good reputation as a spiritual director.

Before he left St. Jerome's for his new assignment, Jill, a new parishioner who is married and has two small children, began to see him for spiritual direction. It means a lot to her that Fr. Joe gives her time because she knows that many people, mostly women, are making demands on his time. Fr. Joe's busy schedule buffers him from any feelings he might have toward the women who come to see him. He is largely unaware of being sexually attracted to any of his parishioners, especially his directees.

Jill continues to see him for direction, even though he is now associate pastor of a new parish many miles away from his first assignment. Fr. Joe has been so busy with his transition to a new ministerial setting that he has not yet established any bonds with his new staff or his parishioners. Jill is the only person who represents stability for him at this time. Fr. Joe enjoys his sessions with Jill and has a relaxed rapport with her. Before and after their meetings, the two share a hug and kiss on the lips. He has even been to her home in the suburbs to enjoy a backyard barbecue and the pool with her husband and children.

However, as Fr. Joe becomes settled in his new assignment, meeting for spiritual direction and going to her home on Sunday afternoons for dinner begin to taper off. Jill becomes confused when Fr. Joe is less available for social meetings. He tells her that meeting socially as they have been is really interfering with their spiritual direction relationship. He gives her the name *of another director she might want to see and apologizes for making their professional relationship so confusing.*

Sexuality is utterly fascinating and profoundly ambiguous. The lure of sex both excites us and confuses us. On the one hand, we revere sex as a gift from God that can expand the human spirit by opening us to communion with God and all human reality, and, on the other, we praise sexual abstinence as a way to holiness. Sex can satisfy our longing to connect with another, and it can deepen our loneliness. Sex can be tenderly healing and violently abusive. It can be the sacrament of our deepest desire to be in communion with God and delight us with a taste of divine ecstasy, and it can be a commercial transaction without any emotional investment.

We know that sexuality is a pervasive, powerful force in our lives, yet we are uncertain about what it means, where it fits in our lives, and what to do about its provoking of strong feelings, attractions, and desires. Since everyone seems to be trying to figure it out, I would not be surprised to hear that many people begin reading this book at this chapter. For some it will be the test case for the worth of the whole book: What does he say about sex? Let me put it up front, succinctly. The special vulnerability of people seeking our pastoral services requires that we have only one concern: to be a religious resource in serving their needs for ministerial assistance. To mix a personal sexual agenda with this professional one is to cross the boundary into unethical behavior. Therefore, sexual conduct in the form of sexual abuse, exploitation, and harassment violates professional ethics and is always wrong. Other forms of visual, verbal, and physical contact are ambiguous and sometimes wrong. We bear the greater burden of responsibility to maintain the boundaries despite any suggestive behaviors or explicit requests from those seeking our pastoral service. In the opening scenario, the burden of responsibility for maintaining boundaries falls on Fr. Joe. When he realizes that he has created fuzzy boundaries by mixing professional and social relationships with Jill, he reclaims the boundaries by drawing clearer lines in their relationship.

As pastoral ministers, we are not sexless people. Whether married, celibate, or neither, we are fully sexual persons. We have all the sexual attributes of being male or female; we can appreciate others as sexual beings; and we have the capacity to exert sexual attraction and to be sexually attracted. As an old story goes, when a seminarian asked

an elderly priest when he would cease to be bothered by sexual temptation, the priest said, "I don't think we can count on that until we are
dead for at least three days!" This is hyperbole, of course. However, its
kernel of truth is that sexual dynamics are always at work in every
human interaction. We do not grow out of it, and we cannot escape it.
The pansexual theory of Freud went so far as to maintain that human
motivation is rooted sexually. We may regard this position to be an
exaggeration, but we cannot deny that it contains some truth.

We are especially vulnerable to sexualizing behavior and crossing
boundaries because so much of our ministry is done behind closed
doors and deals with some of the most intimate and fragile areas of
people's lives—loss of love, grief, guilt, loneliness, low self-esteem. In
the context of privacy and under the influence of an emotionally
charged conversation, the sexual tension of the pastoral relationship
can become quite pronounced. It can be very tempting to use this situation to satisfy our own need for intimacy, affection, affirmation, and
pleasure. Moreover, we are even more vulnerable to sexualizing behavior if we are in significant denial of our own sexual issues, tend to use
sex to take care of our emotional needs, or are survivors of sexual,
emotional, or physical abuse.

The moral demand of the professional relationship is to keep the
purpose of the pastoral meeting at the center of our attention and not
the sexual energy and attractiveness of the interaction. However, if we
do not acknowledge the power of sexual longing that is linked to the
genuine care and concern we show for another person, then we risk
unethical sexual behavior. If we go wrong on sex, the harm caused can
be devastating. Because we are symbolic representatives of the holy, to
victimize anyone sexually can be taken as being exploited by the
church or even by God. Moreover, as the sexual abuse crisis in the
church has clearly shown, nothing quite makes for sensational news in
the public's eye as a sex scandal in ministry does.

This chapter examines what it means to be a sexual person in the
public, professional role of ministry. It unfolds in four main sections.
The first section lays out the nature of the sexual conduct being called
into question. The second defines several forms of sexualized behavior.
The third makes an ethical assessment of sexual conduct. The fourth
offers some suggestions for the prevention of professional misconduct
in the area of sexuality.

SEXUAL CONDUCT

"Sexuality" and "sex" are related but distinct realities. Sexuality is the more comprehensive one. It includes sex but much more as well. "Sexuality," according to the *Catechism of the Catholic Church*, "affects all aspects of the human person in the unity of his body and soul. It especially concerns affectivity, the capacity to love and to procreate, and in a more general way the aptitude for forming bonds of communion with others" (no. 2332). This description encompasses both our affective capacity for intimacy (emotional and spiritual dimensions that enable us to form bonds of communion) and our physical, genital capacity to procreate. *Sex* is more narrowly construed to refer to our biological makeup (male or female), or *sex* refers to expressions of our sexuality in its physical, emotional, and spiritual dimensions, particularly in reference to genital actions resulting in orgasm and/or sexual intercourse.

Keeping these distinct but related understandings in mind, we may better appreciate what makes sexuality in the pastoral relationship both a promise and a peril.[1] The promise, or "joy of sex," is that it can be a resource for ministry because our sexuality already inclines us toward an interpersonal connection. Our sexuality can support our motivation for ministry because it reinforces our longing for union. Rooted in our basic need to love and to be loved, our sexuality supplies energy for creativity in the ways we express ourselves. It heightens our sensitivity and responsiveness to human needs, our passion for what we believe in, our commitment to those with whom and for whom we live and work, and our pleasure in being with others. Our sexuality can soften our interpersonal conflicts and increase our capacity for teamwork. It also makes us want to look our best, dress our best, and behave in ways that attract people to be around us rather than to make them want to avoid us. It is also a means for being tenderly present to those who are hurting as well as being passionately devoted to setting relationships right when practices, beliefs, institutional structures, or people offend human dignity.

God gives us our sexuality to expand our human spirit, to draw us out of ourselves and into relationship with others. In this sense, sexuality is intertwined with our spirituality. As James B. Nelson has shown, both drives yearn for a communion and a wholeness that will satisfy our restlessness and incompleteness. Such a longing is satisfied ultimately only in God.[2] For these reasons, our sexuality ought not to be seen as a barrier to grace, but as a means of grace, the power of God's love working through our sexuality to touch another with tenderness and healing and to create new life with another. By means of our sexuality, we enter into communion with God in and through our relationships with others and with all of life. Such is the mystery of the incarnation and the ultimate goal of living by the Great Commandment.

Along with this promise of our sexuality, there is peril. While our sexuality is a gift for ministry with its creative energy and drive to connect with others, it can easily overwhelm us and become a tragic instrument of abuse, exploitation, manipulation, and harassment. We need to be able to distinguish when we are responding to others out of sexual attraction from when we are serving them because of the call of ministry. Peter Rutter represents the perils of sexuality as "sex in the forbidden zone" in his book of the same title.[3] He describes sex in the forbidden zone as any sexual contact that occurs within professional relationships of trust. He estimates that 96 percent of forbidden-zone sex occurs between a man in power and a woman under his care. He emphasizes the vulnerability of any professional person to sexual conduct.

Rutter goes on to explain how common it is for two people, especially a man and a woman, working closely together in a relationship marked by trust and differences of power to feel sexual desire, to be flooded by sexual fantasies, and to long for sexual union. This is exactly what was going on between Fr. Joe and Jill in this chapter's opening scenario, even though neither had explicitly acknowledged it. While this can happen within any combination of sexual genders, Rutter finds that women in power exploiting men (as in Michael Crichton's novel, *Disclosure*[4]) or men and women engaging in homosexual exploitation is a very small percentage of forbidden-zone sex. Given the sexism in our society, sexual boundary violations are predominantly a matter of men in power over women.[5]

Rutter's analysis underscores that whenever we touch deeply the emotions of another person, we develop an intimacy with them that includes a tendency toward sexual contact. The intimacy that develops can make us oblivious to any sexual boundaries. However, when we recognize that passion is stirring, we have a choice, as evident in Fr. Joe's decision to draw clear boundaries in his relationship with Jill. The presumption in a professional relationship is that we will not allow sexual energy and attraction to obstruct the purpose of the relationship.

SEXUALIZED BEHAVIOR

What do we mean by sexualizing behavior that obstructs the purpose of the pastoral relationship and crosses the line of appropriate sexual boundaries? As the earlier description of the promise and peril of our sexuality shows, all of our behavior has a sexual dimension to it. Nevertheless, not all of our behavior needs to express an interest in the other person as a sexual partner. Sexualized behavior is verbal or nonverbal behavior that expresses a sexual interest in the other person, whether or not that person gives consent. Verbal sexualized behavior includes such speech as inquiring about the other person's sexual experiences or giving an account of one's own, commenting on another's body or appearance, and using risqué humor or innuendo in our conversation. Nonverbal sexualized behavior would be acts such as sexual intercourse, touching erogenous zones of the body, kissing on the lips, prolonged hugs, seductive dress or posture, creating a romantic atmosphere in which to meet, secretly photographing another, staring, giving intimate gifts, massaging, lap sitting, and leaning against the other. Sexualized behavior that leads to accusation of professional misconduct is generally some form of sexual abuse, exploitation, or harassment. Sexual fantasy, cybersex, and touching are more ambiguous. We take a closer look here at what each entails.

SEXUAL ABUSE

Sexual abuse is often interchangeable with *sexual exploitation* as the generic term that covers any form of improper sexual conduct. A more restrictive meaning of sexual abuse is using others who lack the ability or will to protect themselves (a child, an elderly person, or a physically or emotionally vulnerable adult) for sexual stimulation by the one responsible for their care. Examples of sexual abuse include such acts as incest, pedophilia (a primary sexual desire toward children between one and thirteen), ephebophilia (a primary sexual desire toward children between fourteen and seventeen), child prostitution, child pornography, exhibitionism, molestation, and rape. Notice that sexual abuse is not limited to the abuse of minors. It also extends to vulnerable adults.

In response to the sexual abuse crisis in the Catholic Church, the Bishops of the United States adopted on June 14, 2002, the *Charter for the Protection of Children and Young People* (the *Charter* was revised in 2005), and *Essential Norms for Diocesan/Eparchial Policies Dealing with Allegations of Sexual Abuse of Minors by Priests, Deacons, or Other Church Personnel* (the *Essential Norms* were revised in 2006).[6] The *Charter* is intended to protect victims and to promote healing. Among its provisions are the calls to provide outreach to victims, to establish review boards in every diocese, to make all church personnel mandated reporters of abuse and to cooperate with public authorities, to remove permanently from ministry a priest or deacon for even one offense of abuse of a minor, to publish diocesan policies, to establish national Offices for Child and Youth Protection, and to screen carefully seminary candidates. The *Essential Norms* present the process to be followed if a credible allegation of sexual abuse of a minor is made against a priest or deacon.

As a result of the sexual abuse scandals, we have become painfully aware of the kinds of behaviors that lead to accusations of sexual abuse. Praesidium, Inc., an abuse risk-management firm that works extensively with religious congregations, social service programs, schools, and youth development organizations, provides a list of the types of behaviors that have led to accusations of abuse. While some of these explicitly mention minors, many of them also pertain to the abuse of adults.

Meeting alone in isolated places
Showing favoritism
Engaging in physical contact that was misinterpreted
Wearing provocative or revealing attire
Giving money to a "special" minor
Meeting in homes and in bedrooms without others present
Being nude in front of minors
Sleeping with minors in the same bed

Giving special or secret gifts
Graphically discussing sexual activities or allowing others to
   do so
Keeping "secrets" about relationships
Failing to adhere to uniform or accepted standards of affection
Showing affection when no one else was around
Staring while others were dressing
Commenting on minors' bodies
Taking pictures while minors are dressing or showering
Shaming or belittling an individual

SEXUAL EXPLOITATION

Sexual exploitation is fundamentally a betrayal of trust in the professional relationship by using our personal, professional, or physical power to develop a sexual relationship with someone under our care or to take advantage of the other's emotional or physical vulnerability for our own sexual stimulation and satisfaction. Sexual exploitation includes, but is not limited to, such acts as intercourse, touching the erogenous zones, fondling of the breast or genital areas, kissing on the lips in a lingering and intimate way, deep embracing, disrobing, verbal comments expressing a sexual interest in the other or inviting sexual involvement, and dating the one with whom we are in a professional relationship.

Praesidium, Inc., identifies four types of exploitation. *Predatory* exploitation is purposeful, planned, and incremental behavior that often exploits a large number of victims. Predators know what they are doing and why; they use their influence and charm to break down barriers to a sexual relationship; and they groom their victims to become their sexual partners by making sure they have ample opportunity for access to their victims through shared work or social activities. *Situational* exploitation is the result of a combination of needs converging in the exploiter's life, such as the use of drugs or alcohol, stress, depression, rejection, burnout, or loneliness. Situational exploitation in ministry often follows upon our becoming increasingly dependent on a parishioner for intimacy. The convergence of two vulnerable persons—the minister and the parishioner—creates a sexual "perfect storm." *Seduced* exploitation is when we do not initiate but, because of our own vulnerability at the time, allow or encourage the other to intensify the intimate relationship. *Indiscriminate* or *sadistic* exploitation is when the exploiter gets sexual gratification from the pain and suffering inflicted on the other rather than from the sexual activity itself.

SEXUAL HARASSMENT

Sexual harassment, like abuse and exploitation, is not only about sex. It is also about power. Sexual harassment is any form of unwelcome touching or language expressing sexual interest. Its most egregious form is when we use our power to coerce another into unwanted sexual relations or to exchange sex for some other favor, such as a job, a promotion, a higher salary, or some other privilege. Such *quid pro quo* ("this for that") harassment is so clearly wrong that it is not even reputably challenged. A more ambiguous form is hostile environment harassment. This involves creating an intimidating, offensive working environment through unwelcome verbal, visual, or physical conduct of a sexual nature.

In his extensive study of sexual harassment, *Sex, Power and Boundaries*, Peter Rutter claims that the prime ingredient of hostile environment harassment is "unwelcome" sexual behavior.[7] What makes the behavior unwelcome is that it crosses the boundaries that define someone's emotional or physical space. To prevent sexual harassment, we need to anticipate another person's reactions to our behavior, because charges of harassment often arise over disagreements about boundaries. Behaviors that a reasonable person could regard as crossing boundaries and contributing to a hostile working environment include, but are not limited to, such actions as suggestive talk (such as risqué jokes, innuendo, teasing with sexual overtones, pressure for dates, phone calls, letters, or e-mails of a sexual nature); unwelcome visual contact (such as staring or giving a prolonged gaze, as in "checking someone out"); undesired physical contact (such as lap sitting, kissing, hugging, pinching, leaning against, cornering, patronizing pats on the head or shoulders, as well as the intentional touching of breasts, genitals, buttocks, or clothing covering any of these body parts); creating a sexually offensive working environment (such as by displaying derogatory posters, drawings, or cartoons); and ingratiating and overly solicitous behavior (such as pressure for sexual favors, comments or questions about sexual behavior or orientation, comments about clothing or physical appearance, compliments that are uncomfortable for the receiver, seductions, requests for social engagements, and sexual assault).

While harassment is most commonly spoken of as a dynamic of the workplace, professional ethics for ministers considers harassment wrong no matter where it takes place. Harassment shares with abuse and exploitation the misuse of the unequal power in a relationship for the purpose of manipulating and controlling a situation. Yet, hostile environment harassment may be harder to recognize because it can too easily be disguised as playful teasing. We who serve in the church can miss how harassing we can be, since we like to think of ourselves as always intending care and concern. "It's all in good fun, lighten up," we say. What we don't realize, however, is that we just crossed a boundary. The other person finds our teasing, jokes, and gestures to be offensive and demeaning. That we did not "intend" anything by them is not ultimately determinative; we can still be harassing. How others reasonably experience our ways of relating to them is always a morally relevant feature.

The exchange between Carol and John in David Mamet's play, *Oleanna*, illustrates the conflict between what is intended and what is received. The play is built on the breakdown of communication between the sexes on different levels of power and the slippery "he said/she said" of sexual harassment. Carol, an anxious college student, seeks guidance from John, her well-meaning but self-absorbed professor. They become entangled in a web of confusion, and she accuses him of sexual harassment:

> CAROL: My charges are not trivial. You see that in the haste, I think, with which they were accepted. A joke you have told, with a sexist tinge. The language you use, a verbal or physical caress, yes, yes, I know, you say that it is meaningless. I understand. I differ from you. To lay a hand on someone's shoulder.
> JOHN: It was devoid of sexual content.

CAROL: I say it was not. I SAY IT WAS NOT. Don't you begin to see...? Don't you begin to understand? IT'S NOT FOR YOU TO SAY.[8]

John discovers here that what constitutes sexual harassment is not his intention about sexualizing behavior but how welcome or not that behavior is to Carol. The question for someone like a human resources officer to resolve, for instance, is whether Carol was being reasonable about her charges. But the hard lesson for John to realize is that to prevent the charge of sexual harassment, he has to be able to read better in advance whether his behavior will or will not be welcome by the recipient. Upon seeing Carol's reaction, John should respond accordingly—acknowledge her discomfort and apologize. Peter Rutter advises that we can judge whether our behavior will be welcome or not on the basis of the kind of feedback we get from the recipient about the impact we are having on their sexual boundary. Being able to read the information we receive allows us to adjust our behavior in the future to prevent sexual harassment.

Sexual abuse, exploitation, and harassment are clear expressions of professional misconduct. No one questions that. While they are clearly identified as wrong, the range of other kinds of behavior is less clear.

SEXUAL FANTASY

Sexual fantasy is a scenario of a sexual nature played out in the imagination. More questions about sexual fantasy have arisen in my workshops on sexual boundaries than about the other forms of sexual behavior just described. Is it unethical to have a sexual fantasy of a coworker? Perhaps a question like this reflects deeply entrenched Catholic teaching on interior acts against chastity, particularly the infamous *delectatio morosa*—taking pleasure knowingly and willingly in sexual fantasies (a.k.a. "bad thoughts"). For a long time moral manuals taught that sexual pleasure must be confined to marriage so that all directly intended sexually arousing thoughts oriented toward intercourse outside of marriage are morally evil. Sexual fantasies that are purely spontaneous, however, do not fall under this judgment.[9] The valid insight of the traditional position is that fantasies in a nonmarital context, while not a completely indifferent matter, challenge personal sexual integration, which requires discipline and control in managing sexual fantasies in order to respect firm boundaries in personal relationships.

While a normally constituted person can limit overt sexual behavior, no one can avoid all sexual fantasies. The capacity to fantasize is human. Peter Rutter's study, *Sex in the Forbidden Zone*, clearly attests to how sexual fantasies happen with a good deal of frequency when people work together and experience closeness, comfort, familiarity, and trust. Having a sexual fantasy is completely natural and need not come under any negative moral judgment as evil in itself or as crossing another person's boundaries. The moral issue is not in having a fantasy but in using the fantasy to shape our social behavior. The moral challenge regarding sexual fantasy is to manage it so that we do not confuse it with reality and let it become the script of our social behavior. Rutter's analysis of sexual fantasy in *Sex, Power, and Boundaries* shows that the inability to contain a fantasy and to deal with the difference between fantasy and reality lies at the roots of sexual misconduct in professional life.[10] We cross sexual boundaries when we use the fantasy as the basis of our social judgments and bring our fantasy life into our public behavior. For that reason, we need to draw a bright line between what is within us and what is outside us, between our thoughts and our actions. When we confuse the inner world of our fantasy with the outer world of our sexual behavior, we have crossed the line.

Peter Rutter offers the following guidelines for managing fantasies and minimizing the chances of sexual boundary violations:[11]

1. *Identify your sexual fantasies.*

Fantasies bring together different parts of ourselves that usually function separately, such as our physical selves, our feelings, our memories of past experiences, our hopes and wishes. If we know when our fantasies are operating, we can more easily distinguish them from reality. We must respect the power that fantasies have to shape our social judgments and behavior.

2. *Acknowledge that fantasies are an unreliable guide to sexual behavior.*

The more powerful the fantasy, the more unrealistic will be its information about what is truly the case in our interpersonal relationships. Fantasies tell us more about what is going on within us than about what is going on in the external world.

3. Keep your sexual fantasies private.

To manage boundaries effectively, we must make sure the other person does not know what we are thinking. Therefore, we must refuse to engage in boundary-testing behavior, like flirting or talking about the fantasy with the person who is its object. Such sharing can raise the volume of the erotic dimension of the relationship to an intolerable pitch. We would benefit more by channeling the energy of fantasies by seeking their internal meaning by journaling or by sharing them with a trusted friend.

4. Take care of yourself physically and psychologically.

Physical fitness is a fundamental prerequisite to managing fantasies. At certain times in life, psychotherapy may also be necessary for good health. Being run down physically and psychologically puts us at risk of making poor judgments about how to handle fantasies and boundaries. Spiritual practices that cultivate an inner life can also help, since, as virtue ethics shows us, who we are inwardly affects how we behave outwardly.

5. Hone the feedback loop to recognize what is unknown.

Rather than using information from our fantasies to suggest how we might want to behave, we need to be able to determine what kind of behavior is out of bounds from the information being fed back to us from others. The information we receive as a result of our behavior allows us to shape our future behavior.

CYBERSEX

Sexual fantasy has spawned a whole new form of sexualized behavior called cybersex. In their extended analysis of cybersex, Jennifer Schneider and Robert Weiss define it as "any form of sexual expression that is accessed through the computer on the Internet."[12]

Psychologists Carnes, Delmonico, and Griffin organize the sex-related behaviors of cybersex under three categories.[13] First, we can access online pornography, audio, video, and text stories. Through the Internet, we can enter the largest porn shop in the world without ever leaving our desks! Not only can we log onto pornographic images and erotic stories through Internet browsers, but we can also exchange them via e-mail and through discussion or newsgroups. Second, we can have real time with a fantasy partner by carrying on virtual affairs through videoconferencing and voice chatting. Third, we can acquire multimedia software in the form of video games that are sexually charged or CD-ROMs of erotica magazines. Although interactive and available on the computer, this software is not a form of online cybersex since it is limited in its capacity to explore related sites or to relate to virtual partners. What makes the Internet so appealing for someone seeking sexual arousal and fulfillment is that many of these high-tech sexual activities come to us at no extra cost beyond that of our monthly Internet access fee and the electricity to run the computer. In addition to being virtually free for the taking, cybersex is alluring because it is so convenient, it is available 24/7, 365 days a year, it is safe from the risk of disease, and it allows us to remain anonymous (unless, of course, we are being monitored in a police sting operation). As Carnes and associates conclude, cybersex gives you "what you want, when you want it, at low cost, minus the 'messiness and hassles' of a person-to-person relationship, and with complete anonymity."[14]

Since cybersex is not "real" sex with anyone, what could be so wrong with it? For the merely curious who do not sustain an interest in the unreality of cybersex and for those who use the Internet to acquire sexual information, cybersex is not a morally serious problem. Delmonico and Griffin recognize that "for some, the Internet may be a healthy way to explore sexuality in a safe environment."[15] However, curious Web surfers who do not become problematic users of cybersex still face the challenge of satisfying their sexual curiosity and of ordering their sexual desire in ways that promote personal sexual integration without the negative effects that can come with regular use of cybersex.

However, for at-risk and compulsive users, cybersex is less morally ambiguous, especially when sexual behavior on the Internet begins to interfere with other aspects of life. While admitting that it is not possible to predict who will become a problematic user of cybersex, Carnes, Delmonico, and Griffin identify three categories of potentially high-risk users. The *discovery group* includes those who have no problems with sexual fantasy or behavior until they discover cybersex. Discovering sex on the Internet fosters compulsive behaviors they may never have experienced otherwise. The *predisposed group* includes those who have a history of problematic sexual thoughts or fantasies but have coping mechanisms in place to keep their sexual urges under control. The Internet fosters sexual thoughts and fantasies that may not have gotten out of control without the stimulation available over the Internet. The *lifelong sexually compulsive group* includes those who make the Internet one more way of sexually acting out. This group sees cybersex as a "safer" way of acting out since it does not require physical contact with anyone.[16]

The findings of these researchers disclose some important moral dimensions that we ought to heed if we are tempted to use or are already using cybersex as a form of sexual behavior. One is that many users escape to cybersex as a distraction from life's stresses or to bolster low self-esteem. Since acting out over the Internet requires less effort than risking a real relationship, it can keep the user from developing the communication skills necessary for relating on an intimate level. Moreover, the virtual relationships on the Net give a false sense of one's self-image and capacity for sustaining freeing and intimate interpersonal relationships, while objectifying the participants, often reducing them to body parts.

Cybersex is also a very isolating sexual activity. The compulsive users of cybersex, such as those who get hooked on it as a form of sexual addiction, withdraw from friends in the real world in order to make time for virtual friends, and they isolate themselves more by lying in order to conceal their involvement on the Net. Frequent and prolonged use of cybersex also erodes moral character because it can interfere with cultivating the virtues of chastity and fidelity. Interpersonal connections made in cyberspace do not require the same level of social skills and intimacy that real-life behavior does. The moral tragedy of cybersex is that it provides an escape from real-life relationships and contributes to weakening our ability to contain powerful sexual energies and fantasies. The consequence is that we begin to use our virtual sexual experiences as the basis for social judgments and involvement. The movement from behaving in the virtual world of cybersex to creating real-world sexual liaisons, to trading in prostitution, and to child pornography is not a long journey. These are serious moral wrongs. They are the tip of the iceberg floating in the sea of cyberspace addiction.

Sexuality

Carnes, Delmonico, and Griffin have provided an Internet Sex Screening Test that helps us evaluate our use of the Internet for sex and where we might be on a continuum of problematic behavior, from relatively harmless to addictive.

True or false:

1. I have some sexual sites bookmarked.
2. I spend more than five hours per week using my computer for sexual pursuits.
3. I have joined sexual sites to gain access to online sexual material.
4. I have purchased sexual products online.
5. I have searched for sexual material through an Internet search tool.
6. I have spent more money for online sexual material than I planned.
7. Internet sex has sometimes interfered with certain aspects of my life.
8. I have participated in sexually related chats.
9. I have a sexualized user name or nickname that I use on the Internet.
10. I have masturbated while on the Internet.
11. I have accessed sexual sites from other computers besides my own.
12. No one knows I use my computer for sexual purposes.
13. I have tried to hide what is on my computer or monitor so others cannot see it.
14. I have stayed up after midnight to access sexual material online.
15. I use the Internet to experiment with aspects of sexuality such as bondage, homosexuality, and anal sex.
16. I have my own Web site that contains sexually explicit material.
17. I have made promises to myself to stop using the Internet for sexual purposes.
18. I sometimes use cybersex as a reward for accomplishing something like finishing a project or enduring a stressful day.

19. When I am unable to access sexual information online, I feel anxious, angry, or disappointed.
20. I have increased the risks I take online (for example, giving out my real name and phone number or meeting people offline).
21. I have punished myself when I use the Internet for sexual purposes. For example, I've arranged a time-out from the computer or canceled Internet subscriptions.
22. I have met face-to-face with someone I met online for romantic purposes.
23. I use sexual humor and innuendo with others while online.
24. I have run across illegal sexual material while on the Internet.
25. I believe I am an Internet sex addict.[17]

While Carnes, Delmonico, and Griffin have designed this screening test for therapeutic purposes, we can use it to flag morally problematic behaviors—both as warning signs that we are being lured by cybersex and as indicators that we are already caught in the Net and are at risk for moving from online acting out to offline sexualizing behavior. The findings of these researchers shows that it is a wise practice to screen candidates for pastoral ministry about their use of sexual sites on the Internet or about their use of chat rooms as a way to relieve feelings of loneliness.

GOOD TOUCH/CONFUSING TOUCH/ BAD TOUCH

If cybersex is alluring because of its "safety" in avoiding physical contact, then the real world of touch poses a special challenge to containing the sexual energy of interpersonal relationships. "To touch or not to touch?" is a question more pressing today due largely to the defensive climate created by accusations of professional misconduct in the area of sexual behavior. How do we distinguish good touch from confusing and/or bad touch?

In the pre–Vatican II church, most clergy were, for the most part (as there are always exceptions), a group of "untouchables." As one priest who spent a good part of his ministry in the pre–Vatican II church said to me, "We kept our distance and our hands to ourselves." Then the theological and cultural developments in the 1960s and 1970s released us from bondage. We found a new freedom and appreciation of the power of touch to heal, affirm, and show care. Psychologists talked about the need to be touched in order to develop intellectually and emotionally in normal ways. In society, bumper stickers abounded with the message, "Have you hugged your ____ today?" (Fill in the blank with the class of people or pets whom you think most need affirmation and affection.) In the church, touching became an integral part of worship. Revised sacramental rites implemented the imposition of hands, the liturgy included the greeting of peace, the washing of feet, and, in some communities, the joining of hands while praying the Lord's Prayer.

We can find warrant for touching in the ministry of Jesus. Touching was the signature of his healing ministry. Nevertheless, just because Jesus touched does not mean that we have to do it, too. Jesus lived in a different era and culture. Each culture forms its own rules about ways to express ourselves. For example, Jesus did not live in the highly litigious society that we know today. While we want to be faithful to the mission of Jesus, we need to explore creative ways to continue it that fit our own times.

While I do not think that anyone wants to turn the clock back to the pre–Vatican II church and become "untouchable," we cannot proceed without realizing how easy it is to have our physical expressions of care and comfort misunderstood, especially a man's. Allegations of impropriety are discouraging many from putting a friendly arm around a shoulder or giving a reassuring hug. However, many tell me that they are more careful today than they used to be about whom, when, where, and what they touch. Here are some samples of the ways pastoral ministers have responded to my inquiry about the use of touch in their ministry.

> I don't touch children anymore. It's just too dangerous. I don't
>   even use the imposition of hands in reconciliation anymore.
> I only hug a person in clear public view where the context
>   leaves no doubt as to its meaning, and then only after the

other person takes the initiative. But I don't initiate hugs anymore, especially in the privacy of my office. I even keep the door of my office ajar when I am with a woman.

Now that I am in the parish by myself, I have become very careful whom I let into the rectory and when. I never pull the shades down whenever anyone is in the house with me, and I certainly will not be alone with a child.

I have become more conscious of the structure of the space where I meet students from the campus. It contributes to suspicion. I have put a clear glass door in my office, and I have stopped meeting with students in private after everyone has left the ministry center for the day.

I only touch the head, shoulders, arms, or hands. Nothing else. I don't let children sit on my lap anymore, and I have put a clear glass window in the door of the reconciliation room.

Through my experience with the pastoral care department, I have come to a greater appreciation of touching as a form of communication. I always ask myself, "What am I trying to say here? How will this be interpreted?"

My criterion is a public one. "Will this act pass public scrutiny? Could someone use this behavior to make me look bad?"

Everyone seems to be aware that touching can show care, or heal and affirm in unique and important ways. They know that when people are hurting and going through trials of loss, for example, touch is a pastoral asset that can be the bond of comfort and an expression of understanding. Aware of our power as symbolic representatives of God and the church, we want to be able to communicate a loving concern. To do this we have to make our way between the extremes of being cold and unresponsive and touching in ways that feed our own ego needs and erotic interests.

At the same time, we must be realistic that what is intended as a gesture of pastoral intimacy can, because of the link between touch and sex, be received as a personal intimacy with sexual interests. Consider this real-life incident:

The pastor was greeting people after Mass when a distraught woman, nearly in tears, approached him. She told him of her strained relationship with her husband and the painful divorce procedures they had begun. The priest put his arm around her shoulders in a gesture of comfort and moved her away from the heavy traffic of the exiting Mass-goers. The woman continued to talk about her pain and began to cry. The pastor held her more firmly in a comforting embrace. He did this in full view of the others who continued to pass by. There was nothing secretive about what he did or the distress the woman was in. After the woman calmed down, and just before she left, the pastor said to her, "I am happy that I was able to be here for you today and to hold you this way." The woman left, her eyes full of tears. Only later did the pastor learn how conflicted the woman felt when she left him. He learned that she was confused about what his embracing her meant and how to interpret his words, "that I was able to hold you this way."

While this embrace cannot be classified as abuse, exploitation, or harassment, it is, at least, a confusing touch. This priest did not seem to realize that his embrace, accompanied by what he said, could make the woman feel uncomfortable and confused not only about the touch but also about him, perhaps because of the trauma of her divorce. Physical gestures of human caring can too easily be confused with romantic, sexual interests, especially when they come with ambiguous words.

The pastoral ministry gives us access to people's lives on a great variety of levels. As this incident shows, some are quite intimate. We have more freedom to hug, to kiss, and to extend other friendly gestures of touch than any other profession. But the very ready access to intimate parts of people's lives and the freedom to touch create problems. People who seek pastoral services, especially at times of crisis, are very vulnerable. They can easily be led on. As one priest said to me,

"I am amazed at how trusting people are in their vulnerability. They give me incredible power over them. I feel that I could do almost anything to them and I wouldn't get any resistance. I have to be very careful with myself and sensitive to them."

Are hugging and touching inappropriate because they can be so easily misunderstood? Are they inappropriate because in the present social climate we make the ready association of touching with sexual advances of abuse, exploitation, or harassment? If not all touching is inappropriate or unethical, what guidelines can we use to tell the difference? What does the virtue of fidelity in the pastoral relationship demand of us?

I have talked with many pastoral ministers who are quite clear about how easy it is to cross from the good touch of pastoral caring, which is received as affirming and supportive, to a confusing touch, which makes the receiver feel conflicted and uncomfortable, to a bad touch, which is experienced as manipulative, coercive, intrusive, and frightening. But when I press for some guideline that helps them to determine when to hug or not to hug, they are less clear. They rely on "common sense" or "pastoral instinct." However, I must remind them that common sense is not so common and that not everyone's "pastoral instinct" is as sharp as theirs. We need a principle that expresses the wisdom reflected in their instinct and practice. As they explain how their pastoral instinct leads them, I hear a very sound moral principle at work drawing the line between good touch and confusing or bad touch. The principle is this: In relationships of unequal power, preference must be given to the perspective and judgment of the less powerful.

Whether a touch is good, confusing, or bad depends not on our intention or even on how it appears in public. It depends, rather, on how it is received! We cannot control that. Just think of how many filters our touch must pass through before it gets received. Among them are the person's past experience of being touched, emotional state, physical condition, feeling of freedom not to be touched, relationship to us, projections on us, and others. Not being able to control these filters that will influence how another receives our words and touches makes us especially vulnerable to accusations of "misconduct" even if our behavior is not abuse, exploitation, or harassment.

Prudence is the much-needed virtue when deciding whether to touch or not to touch. Prudence must take into account the many factors influencing how our ways of relating will be received. One pastor told me that, since he regards his parish as his family, he hugs everyone. If that is the case, then, I wonder how he respects anyone's freedom not to be hugged. Whose needs are really being met here? Touch that is not freely chosen will be confusing at best and bad at worst.

Another factor is the person's cultural heritage. Ethnic groups have their own unspoken rules and expectations about how they are to express themselves as sexual persons among genders and between genders. Just watch the way the greeting of peace is given in a multi-cultural parish these days and you will see what I mean. Some give a rib-crushing *abrazo*, others shake hands, and still others only nod politely. Culture and other filters of reception are the context and clues for how physical touch might be received. We must attend to these if we are to be prudent in the ways we touch in our pastoral ministry.

Lest you feel that you can never touch because we cannot rely on any gesture as carrying a general sense of being an appropriate display of affection, Praesidium, Inc., provides some examples of appropriate and inappropriate displays of affection.

Under appropriate expressions, they include:

Asking permission before touching
Hugs
Pats on the shoulder or back
Hand-shakes
"High-fives" and hand slapping
Verbal praise
Touching hands, faces, shoulders, and arms
Arms around shoulders
Holding hands during prayer or when a person is upset
Holding hands while walking with small children
Sitting close to small children
Kneeling or bending down for hugs with small children
Holding or picking up children three years old or younger

Among the inappropriate displays of affection are these:

Any form of unwanted affection
Full frontal hugs or "bear hugs"
Touching bottoms, chests, or genital areas
Lying down or sleeping beside minors
Massages
Patting children on the thigh, knee, or leg
Tickling or wrestling
Touching or hugging from behind

Games involving inappropriate touching
Kisses on the mouth
Showing affection in isolated areas such as bedrooms, closets,
    restricted areas, or other private rooms
Compliments that relate to physique or body development

To conclude where I began, "To touch or not to touch?" remains a perplexing question for us in this highly litigious and supersensitive climate created by the sex abuse scandal. Even Praesidium, Inc.'s examples of "appropriate" touch apply for the most part or as a general rule. We still need to draw on the moral sensibilities nurtured by the practice of prudence. Our prudential judgments can be aided by a clear moral framework of how to assess sexual conduct in ministry. To that we turn next.

ETHICAL ASSESSMENT

At first glance, two frames of reference come to mind within which to assess the sexual conduct of pastoral ministers. One is celibacy for some; the other is chastity for all. Celibacy is a professional obligation for those who have committed themselves to it. By definition, everyone is off limits sexually for a celibate. However, since celibacy is not the chosen life of all pastoral ministers, it is of limited value in assessing sexual conduct in pastoral ministry. Moreover, no research supports any causal connection between celibacy and professional misconduct in the area of sexuality. Furthermore, taking celibacy as the perspective for assessing sexual conduct might too easily make professional misconduct a psychosocial or spiritual problem and miss placing it squarely within the moral province of responsibilities that belong to our professional pastoral relationship.

Chastity is the virtue we generally invoke in matters of sexuality. According to the *Catechism* (no. 2337), in our journey toward becoming fully integrated persons, chastity seeks the integration of sexuality within ourselves so that we will express ourselves appropriately as sexual beings in all of our personal relationships. We have traditionally spoken of chastity as taking the forms of celibacy for those who profess it, conjugal chastity for married people, and chastity in continence for all others (no. 2349). The perspective of professional ethics enables us to see what is entailed by chastity in the professional pastoral relationship. Professional ethics sets limits on sexual conduct in pastoral ministry by underscoring the moral significance of what being professional demands of us by way of our character, duties, and responsible use of power in the pastoral relationship.

The virtues of justice and fidelity provide the orientation and overarching framework for evaluating sexual conduct in the pastoral relationship. In chapter 4, I sketched some characteristics of each of these virtues for directing pastoral behavior. Here I apply them to sexual conduct.[18]

JUSTICE

Justice governs the general relationships that a minister has with the community. It seeks to nurture and protect the complex interconnections that exist between us. As a virtue of the pastoral minister, justice defines our ministerial role as being disposed to subordinate self-interest in order to give a greater degree of preference to the good of the community and to provide the community with the resources and services that are proper to our ministerial role, even if doing so costs us some personal risk or sacrifice. Sexual conduct in a pastoral relationship, however, *violates our professional role* by taking advantage of the vulnerability of others by using them to satisfy our own needs for intimacy, affection, acceptance, or pleasure.

Justice is also the virtue that governs *restoring right relationships* when boundaries have been violated. Justice for the victim means providing help to regain self-esteem and trust in the church and in pastoral ministers. Justice toward us means getting us help to recognize the personal and professional issues that led to the boundary violation in the first place. Justice for the community from which we and the victim come means addressing its feeling of betrayal so that it can renew its trust in the church and in the pastoral ministry generally. Justice in the church means developing policies and structures of accountability to protect against future incidents of misconduct and to respond to victims, communities, and offending pastoral ministers. We have been experiencing good work on all these fronts at the national and diocesan levels in response to the sexual abuse crisis.

FIDELITY

If justice governs general relationships, the virtue of fidelity, with its companion virtue of trustworthiness, governs the relationship with a particular person. Fidelity is the virtue that holds in trust what has been entrusted to us in the pastoral relationship. It requires that we *respect physical and emotional boundaries* in our particular relationships and that we not confuse the one-directional pastoral relationship with the reciprocal personal relationships. Sexual contact in the pastoral relationship violates fidelity by privileging self-gratification over attending to the needs of the other.

In chapter 5, we saw that the pastoral relationship is not a peer relationship of the sort we enjoy with friends and colleagues wherein we can satisfy each other's needs mutually. Instead, the pastoral relationship is one directional, not mutual, so that it is characterized by the inequality of power. The simple fact of being in a professional role creates a power gap between us and those we serve, which, in ministry, is enhanced by the numinous quality of our being linked with God and all things holy. We are sought out for our expertise in matters religious, for being a representative of the church, and for our position of leadership in the ecclesial community. The parishioner, lacking these resources, needs us to provide religious services and leadership. In relationships where one party is stronger than the other, or more in control of the encounter, fidelity is guided by the principle "*Do no harm.*" In unequal relationships, the person in the best position to help another is the very same person in the best position to hurt another. The greater burden of responsibility lies with the one who has greater power to avoid, to prevent, or to minimize harm.

The harm we can cause by misusing our power is immense. In addition to physical harm that may be caused by forcing sexual acts on another, there can also be significant psychological and spiritual harm. Psychologically, victims can lose their ability to trust not only us but anyone else. Their self-esteem can be damaged by having been made a victim of someone else's gratification. They may become socially isolated if their ability to form healthy relationships has been affected. They might become sexually confused or withdraw into a defensive isolation. Spiritually, the psychological harm can take on cosmic proportions by shaking the foundations of their faith when they project onto God as betrayal by one who represents God.

The flip side of the negative obligation to do no harm is the positive *obligation to empower* others to become more in charge of their own lives and not to keep them dependent on us for how they live their lives. We can do this by maintaining boundaries that provide a safe place for people to be vulnerable without the fear of being exploited. This means not only that we not initiate sexualizing the pastoral relationship but that we must say "No" to any sexualized behavior toward us. To permit the other to seduce or manipulate us into sexualized behavior is also a misuse of our power. The burden of proof always remains with us, who have the greater power, to show that any visual, verbal, or physical touch of ours is not taking advantage of the other's vulnerability. Sexual contact that reaches beyond the pastoral intimacy that comforts, supports, and empowers is ethically wrong as an abuse of power.

For sexual conduct to reflect fidelity, each partner must be able to give *free and informed consent* to it. However, the inequality of power and the ignorance of the risks to harm can compromise valid consent. Valid consent for sexual contact requires a context of mutuality, equality, and a capacity for understanding risks of harm. However, the inequality of power in the pastoral relationship compromises these conditions of valid consent. Moreover, children and vulnerable adults are especially at risk, so that their inability to give valid consent makes sexual contact with them always wrong.

STRATEGIES FOR PREVENTION

In light of the nature of sexual conduct and the ethical assessment just considered, I close this chapter with some strategies for preventing professional misconduct of a sexual nature in the pastoral ministry. I have acquired this list of strategies not only from the resources of Praesidium, Inc., but also from the feedback and examples I have gotten in the many workshops I have held on the issue of boundaries in pastoral ministry. While this is not an exhaustive list, it does represent what many pastoral ministers have found helpful. It can be a good review for those who want to examine more closely their own practice, or it can be a good start for those who are looking for some helps in establishing a better discipline of maintaining boundaries.

1. *Recognize our risk factors.*

At the beginning of this chapter, I mentioned how we are especially vulnerable to crossing sexual boundaries because of some working conditions of the ministry, such as working in privacy, dealing with intimate areas of life, having conversations that are emotionally charged, and so on. In addition to these generic features of ministry, there are some personal ones that can put us at risk of crossing boundaries, too. No preventative measure quite takes the place of critical self-knowledge. So, a first step toward preventing sexual misconduct of any sort is to recognize several risk factors for misusing our relationships for sexual purposes. Among them are these:

> Lacking experience with romantic relationships, or failing to appreciate our own vulnerability to attraction and closeness, can easily lead to mistaking another's attraction to what we do for personal attraction and romantic interest
>
> Lacking the social skills or self-confidence necessary to maintain a nonpossessive and independent adult relationship, especially with those who push boundaries, can make us vulnerable to the manipulation of seduction
>
> Loneliness or isolation from friends and family, or working on our own without access to supervision, can leave us with no one to talk about what we are experiencing and so we overload our pastoral relationships with personal needs and interests
>
> Stress and the inability to manage moments of discouragement can leave us vulnerable to another's attraction to us or ours to them because of our need for affirmation and acceptance
>
> Working with vulnerable people (the lonely, the abused, the emotionally disabled) but without the skills for this kind of ministry can lead to inappropriate behavior in the name of trying to be caring
>
> Being too available by meeting for too long and too often can create confusion about the nature and purpose of our relationship

Becoming dependent on the convenience of relying on those
who work around the church to satisfy personal needs can
create confusing dual relationships

Taking an excessive interest in another's activities (e-mailing or
phoning too much) and showing unusual kindnesses
toward them (special favors, gifts, making them exceptions
to policies) can be a form of grooming behavior that rede-
fines the pastoral relationship into one with sexual interest

Sexualizing conversations by use of innuendo, "off-color"
humor, or directing the conversation to sexual topics
heightens the sexual interest in the relationship

Getting hooked on cybersex puts us on the ramp to acting out
our sexual fantasies

2. Know our warning signs.

Closely related to recognizing our personal risk factors is knowing the warning signs that tell us we are shifting from having a pastoral
interest to a sexual interest in the other. Some common warning signs
are these:

Intuition or free-floating feelings that "something is not right here"

Somatic feelings, such as muscle tension or sweaty palms

Becoming sexually aroused physically

Using stimulators of sexual arousal, such as intimate touching
(holding hands a little longer in shared prayer, letting an
arm linger a little longer on the shoulder, turning hugs
into embraces, neck and shoulder massages, kissing),
creating a romantic environment, conversing about sexual
experiences, becoming preoccupied with sexual fantasies,
assuming seductive postures and dress

Creating unnecessary dual relationships

Seeking out more private space to meet, and spending more
time together apart from scheduled pastoral meetings

Turning pastoral meetings into luncheon or dinner dates

Rearranging our schedules so as to free up time to be with a
particular person

Feeling excited in anticipation of a meeting with a special person
by spending a little more time with personal grooming to

look and smell attractive, and feeling disappointed when
he or she cancels the appointment

Becoming distracted by our sexual fantasies and entertaining
them to the point that they begin to shape our social
behavior

Becoming more self-disclosing about our interests, needs, or
sexual feelings and moving the conversation away from
what the other needs to talk about so that we can talk
about our self

Exchanging gifts, not those like the conventional gift certificate,
but items more costly and of a more personal nature—
cologne, jewelry, clothes, intimate apparel—that have
"obligation" written all over them

Becoming secretive about our relationships in our other
relationships with peers, support group, supervisor, or
spiritual director

In addition to these warning signs, some others that focus more specifically on our relationship with minors are these:

Going overboard with physical contact, such as tickling,
wrestling, lap sitting, piggyback rides, massaging

Showing favoritism by giving special gifts without parental
permission

Ignoring policies about interacting with minors

Keeping secrets with children about the nature of the relationship and the behaviors that characterize it

3. Understand the dynamics of transference and counter-transference.

Transference and countertransference are Freudian concepts that
help us understand the unconscious emotional connections we are
making with another person.[19] In transference, the person seeking pastoral help will attribute a role to us, such as parent, spouse, or lover, and
then project onto us unmet needs or unresolved conflicts that are
rooted in a prior relationship with some other significant person whose
role we are now regarded as having. Transference occurs more because
of the role substitution than because of any special attractiveness on our

part. For example, a person seeking a lot of touching and hugs can be reviving a childhood need for nurturance from parents. Transference can also change a hug into a sexual advance because of some prior experience with a conflict between seduction and responsible closeness. If we are not aware of the dynamics of transference, we can misperceive the real relationship and end up responding to a false one.

In *countertransference*, we attribute to the person seeking our help a role of which he or she is unaware, such as friend, confidant, or lover. When we relate to that person in a role, rather than as he or she really is, we superimpose onto him or her our unmet needs, feelings, or unresolved personal conflicts that fit that role. This destroys any sense of objectivity about who the person is or what the person's needs really are. For example, if we do not acknowledge that we need to be attractive to others and to be liked and valued, then if we feel sexually aroused in a pastoral relationship we can easily relate to the other as our lover and concede to a request for a lot of physical closeness, or even initiate it ourselves. This can lead to the other's accusing us of professional misconduct or, on the other hand, wanting to get involved with us further. The danger in countertransference is that we use the other person as a way to meet our own needs but at the expense of the true purpose of the pastoral relationship, which is to serve the needs of the other. Some signs of countertransference are thinking overly much about how the other is doing, dreaming about him or her, being overly solicitous and available at any time, cultivating a dependency, developing affectionate, sexual feelings toward the other person, disclosing our fantasies, feelings, and experiences to the one who is the object of them, and creating a dual relationship.

4. *Avoid dual relationships as much as possible.*

As I pointed out in chapter 5, we can create dual relationships by presuming an equality and mutuality that do not exist in the professional relationship. We are confusing a personal relationship with a professional one when we ignore the inequality of power and try to be a "friend" while at the same time remaining in the professional role as a person's minister. This tendency can be aided and abetted by the very nature of the pastoral situation itself. For example, regular meetings, a private room, a caring disposition, and the soul-searching and soul-bearing disclosures of intimate feelings and personal secrets are like a love potion. A pastoral setting charged with such vulnerable intimacy, together with the ordinary sexual attraction of human relationships, and then the assumption that there is no difference of power to mar our friendly mutuality, can quickly make us oblivious to boundaries. What started out as a relationship held in trust turns into a sexual opportunity. Once our personal considerations become the focus of the relationship, it is no longer possible to maintain a professional pastoral relationship. We cancel ourselves out as being an effective minister for that person. Any attempt to sexualize the relationship creates automatically a dual relationship that undermines the pastoral relationship by betraying the trust that is needed to sustain it.

In those situations where dual relationships are unavoidable because of the nature of our role in the institution (some schools and seminaries) or because of our geographic location (rural settings), we need to adhere to the wisdom of boundaries. We must keep the pastoral role as primary, pay attention to how we are satisfying our own needs, and monitor the development of dual relationships lest we harbor a conflict of interest or exploit the dependency of the vulnerable.

5. Maintain appropriate self-care.

Appropriate self-care is the flip side of giving greater preference to the best interest of the other. We will never have the energy to pay attention to another person's needs if we do not first have respect for our own. If we come to a pastoral relationship in a personally vulnerable condition because we have not taken care of ourselves, then we should not be surprised by the countertransference that goes on in that relationship. This only contaminates the relationship and interferes with our being able to meet the goals of the relationship and to serve the interests of others.

Appropriate self-care has multiple dimensions. Here are some of the more important ones to practice:

Maintain a rhythm of spiritual disciplines.

A rhythm of spiritual practices helps to maintain a clearer sense of whose we are. We belong primarily to God and so ought to be able to find direction for our life from our relation to God. Given the link between our spiritual desire to be in union with God and our sexual energy that orients us toward interpersonal communion, we ought to keep in mind the power of prayer and other spiritual disciplines to focus us and to settle our restless hearts. Regular spiritual disciplines such as taking time for personal prayer, common worship, quiet, beauty, reflective reading, and spiritual direction can keep us centered on God and what our ministry is all about in the first place.

Acquire stress management skills.

We are at high risk for inappropriate behavior when we are in crisis or stressed out. Some ways to manage stress begin by monitoring our workload. We need to stay within the limits of our competence and make referrals for hard cases in counseling or for anyone to whom we become sexually attracted. We need to have clear expectations of our job or role and engage in ongoing education to keep our knowledge up to date, our skills sharp, and our self-confidence high as theological resources for the community. We ought to keep reasonable work hours in a week. This means not working longer days than usual, avoiding extending appointments beyond the regular time for meeting, taking days off, and having regular vacations. In addition to monitoring our work, we also need to take time for leisure, to pursue hobbies, and to get regular exercise, enough sleep, and proper nutrition. We ought to cultivate friendships with peers and family lest we overburden our pastoral relationships with dual relationships that try to satisfy our needs for companionship, affirmation, and belonging. We need to maintain a network of friends apart from our pastoral relationships so that we have others with whom we can have fun and feel safe to gripe and complain. As needed, we ought to seek therapy for growth and for keeping perspective.

Make use of supervision.

So many of us work alone and in isolation without anyone monitoring our performance or serving as a consultant or life coach. A good preventative strategy for avoiding boundary violations is to maintain structures of accountability in our lives. Many of us receive no further supervision of our ministerial practice once we complete a formation or internship program. The lack of ongoing supervision is one of the most serious structural features that makes sexual boundary violations likely. Without some structures of accountability that include a space for self-disclosure about one's life and ministerial experiences, counter-transference can run wild. The more we try to make it on our own, the more likely we are to have inappropriate outlets for our sexual energy. Good self-care ought to include having someone to whom we can turn to review our performance on the job and to examine how our ministry fits into our life more generally. This can be done formally with a designated supervisor, or less formally with a friend, mentor, coach, or peer support group with whom we can meet from time to time to make such a review.

Many factors contribute to sexual misconduct. The preceding are only a few suggestions of what we might do to prevent it and to move toward a more just ministry. The model of professional ethics presented here and the suggested strategies for prevention may help us to be more professional and ethical in our ministry. However, there are no sure ways to prevent false allegations of professional misconduct, no matter how professional and ethical we try to be.

7
CONFIDENTIALITY

Sr. Mary is the spiritual director of Jane, a candidate for her community. In the course of direction, Sr. Mary learns that Jane had been sexually abused by her uncle when she was five years old. Sr. Mary knows that the state requires abusive behavior to be reported. Since the confidentiality of spiritual direction is not absolute, as is the seal of confession, she wonders whether she should inform the state. She wonders, too, whether Jane's uncle is still abusing children. Sr. Mary does not want to be responsible for protecting a child abuser, so she considers she ought to report the uncle to the state.

Sr. Mary also learns in the course of direction that Jane has an eating disorder that is related to her being abused as a child. Jane experiences prolonged bouts of depression and sometimes goes for many days without proper nutrition to the point of endangering her health. As far as Sr. Mary knows, the rest of the community thinks only that Jane is a thin woman who is careful about putting on weight. Since Jane meets all of her community responsibilities well, no one really pays attention to her physical and psychological condition. But Sr. Mary knows that Jane is a serious health risk to the community and ought to be under professional supervision for her depression and eating disorder. Sr. Mary wonders whether she can disclose this to the superiors of the community for the sake of protecting the good of the community and make this intervention on Jane's behalf in order to get her the help she needs.

Privacy is a rare privilege these days. Almost daily, we have access to intimate details of the lives of people in politics, sports, or entertainment who are regularly investigated by news agencies. Almost anyone can access private information through electronic data and retrieval systems. We enjoy fewer zones of privacy in which we can feel confident that information about us will be respected. A confidential relationship is one of those places.

The ministry has a long tradition of being a safe haven for confidential information, and we ought to try to keep it that way. As one pastor said to me, "Confidentiality is a gift we can still give to people in a world with few secrets." Keeping a confidence is one of the firmest rules of professional ethics. The sacrament of reconciliation is the prototypical safety zone, with the "seal of confession" being absolute, lasting forever, and defended without compromise. However, not all pastoral conversations, even spiritual direction, come "under the seal," even if some people think that they do, and some priests try to treat anything they are told as a "confession." A loose understanding of confidentiality can instill complacency about ethical responsibilities to and for confidential matters, and in this lays the challenge to keeping secrets.

This chapter explores this core conviction: Ministerial relationships are held together by trust. With the exception of the sacramental forum in which confidentiality is an absolute, trust requires a strong presumption in favor of keeping a confidence unless there is a clear and present danger that harm will come to another unless disclosure is made to appropriate persons.

Being trustworthy is the key to effective pastoral care of another person and of the community as a whole. People want to trust their ministers. For the most part, they still do, as amazing as it may seem in this post-sexual-abuse-scandal era. However, some priests feel that the trust in priests that was once implicit in them has eroded considerably over the past few years. If this is true, then the foundation of pastoral ministry is beginning to crumble, for pastoral ministry depends on trust. But why should we want to give a strong presumption in favor of confidentiality in the first place? The first section of the chapter deals with this issue.

To say that there is a "strong presumption" in favor of confidentiality already implies that confidentiality has limits. The sexual abuse scandal has certainly taught us that, under the cover of confidentiality, we can easily contribute to a conspiracy of silence about violations of professional ethics. Legal demands for testimony from ministers, for example, along with some states making them mandated reporters of child abuse, are breaking into the silence. If confidentiality were absolute, we would be answerable only to God in the privacy of our consciences. However, when confidentiality is not absolute, then we are answerable not only to God but also to society. Sr. Mary of the opening scenario is very aware of this. There may be instances when a disclosure of private information may have to be made for the sake of the well-being of others. For that reason, we need to explore more carefully, from the perspectives of canon law, civil law, and professional ethics, the grounds upon which we can justify disclosing information that we have acquired in confidence. The second section of the chapter discusses the ethical foundations of confidentiality.

We probably abuse confidentiality more than we abuse sexual boundaries. We do so not because we are ill willed, but because we are careless. Because we get involved in people's lives at so many different levels and in different places, we have many opportunities to disclose what ought not to be made public. The third section of this chapter turns to some of the common ways confidentiality is betrayed in ministry. Finally, this chapter closes with a few suggestions for preventing the betrayal of confidentiality.

THE PRESUMPTION OF CONFIDENTIALITY

According to Sissela Bok in her book *Secrets*, a major treatise on this issue, confidentiality concerns both the boundaries protecting from public access any information that we acquire under the assumption that it would not be revealed and the process of guarding those boundaries.[1] Confidentiality is how we exercise good stewardship of the power we have over others who make themselves vulnerable to us by their self-disclosure. It holds in trust what they do not want disclosed further without their permission.

Determining what information must be kept confidential is not always easy. Because pastoral ministers interact with people in so many different settings and over a great variety of personal and human concerns, it is not easy to sort out what is truly a "professional secret" and ought to be kept confidential and what is not. However, we can get some idea of what should be kept secret by reflecting on the following aspects of communication:

What?

Asking the "What?" question disposes us to discover a possible "natural secret." How personal is the information? Are we learning material that is already public knowledge, or are we learning something of a more intimate nature? Is what we are learning something that would bring harm (such as physical injury, social isolation from the loss of reputation, or significant emotional trauma that is more than the red cheeks of embarrassment) to another person if it were revealed? If, in the course of acquiring information, we learn that a person is likely to harm another or is at risk of being harmed, we know that this information needs to be made public because harming another or being harmed is an offense against the dignity of persons and the common good. Justice requires that the community be protected. Confidentiality is limited by what is necessary to do in order to protect public order and safety.

Why?

We must also ask, "Why are you telling me this? What is the purpose of the communication?" Confidential information usually arises when one is seeking advice to resolve a personal conflict, or is sorting out one's values, or is trying to identify what to do in a situation that is new or ambiguous and involves the lives of others. A casual conversation over business or social affairs in which the communicant is not seeking advice is not likely to be confidential.

Way?

The way the information is communicated can indicate its personal significance and intention. Is the person deliberate, whispering, or showing facial expressions and other forms of body language that communicate "This is really special"? Information is confidential that one person intends another to keep secret. Sometimes the intention and personal significance of the communication are underscored by the manner in which it is communicated or by the speaker asking in advance for a promise to keep the information secret.

Context?

Is the communication shared in a public or private setting? If the conversation takes place in the hallway after a meeting while people are milling about and others can easily overhear the conversation, then it is safe to assume that it is not intended to be confidential. However, if the conversation is behind closed doors, in a private room, in a formal meeting, or while we are serving in our professional role as representative of the church to give spiritual or religious advice, aid, or comfort, then this communication implies a greater expectation of confidentiality. Information is confidential that one person intends another to keep secret and that is shared in a context that implies that it ought to be kept secret.

In light of these aspects, the following general principle can govern professional communication: The more formal the process and private the information and context of the communication, the stronger is the presumption of confidentiality.

ETHICAL FOUNDATIONS

Three values support giving the presumption in favor of keeping a confidence: the dignity of the person, the benefit it brings to self and society, and the fidelity needed to sustain a relationship.

THE DIGNITY OF THE PERSON

The key principle of a Catholic social vision is the commitment to protect the dignity of the person. Our theological convictions about God in covenant with us and our being made in the image of God vigorously affirm the sacredness and dignity of every person. These convictions also establish respect for human dignity as the basic criterion for judging the moral quality of a professional relationship. The implication of this foundational claim is that we ought not to treat another as having only instrumental value whereby we manipulate the person for our personal gain.

One of the ways that we show respect for the dignity of persons is by protecting and promoting their ability to give direction to their lives by allowing them to retain control over their personal information, plans, thoughts, actions, and property. If they are to do this, we must allow them the freedom to choose who gets access to their personal information and how much information they get. When they invite others into their inner lives by sharing very personal information, they are not giving away their right to exercise control over that information. Keeping a confidence is the way to ensure that the one who owns the information determines access to it. Without confidentiality, we would not be able to maintain control over how others see us or exercise any choice about the direction we want our lives to take. Sissela Bok maintains that, if we were stripped of our secrets and had no control over what others knew about us, we could not remain either sane or free. We would easily become subject to the abuse of manipulation and be treated as a mere means to someone else's ends.[2]

JUSTICE

A second value supporting the duty of confidentiality is the justice it serves society while benefiting one's self. The very purpose of entering a professional relationship is to have access to the expert knowledge and skills of someone who can be helpful. Confidentiality encourages the full disclosure of all necessary information needed in order to attain professional help without fearing that this private information will become public. We feel freer to share private information if we know that it will remain private. Any suspicion that confidentiality will not be kept is an obstacle to making appropriate use of a professional service. The confidentiality of the pastoral relationship offers the personal benefit of receiving consolation, guidance, and meaning when one freely bears one's soul to someone who can speak in the name of the church and of God. This relationship in turn benefits society by enabling those who need personal help to get it. When people know that their personal needs can be met in a safe place and step forward to satisfy those needs, then they do not turn into social problems or become a negative influence on the public good.

FIDELITY

A third value grounding the presumption in favor of confidentiality is the fidelity that strengthens human relationships and fosters intimacy. Human relationships could not survive without respecting the personal knowledge gained in sharing information. However, we do not relate to everyone to the same degree and with the same depth of sharing. We disclose information about ourselves relative to the degree of commitment we have to the person to whom we are talking. The duty of confidentiality supports the trust we need so that a relationship can be established and sustained.

These three values—dignity of the person, personal and social benefit, and fidelity—establish the presumption in favor of confidentiality as an integral responsibility of the professional pastoral relationship.

THE LIMITS OF CONFIDENTIALITY

Unlike other professionals, we are more likely to be involved with people in casual as well as official ways. As a result, we often have a much wider range of contact with people and so become privy to more personal information about more people than other professionals do. The information we have often creates conflicts for us between our commitments to fidelity and justice. On the one hand, we try to be faithful to another by respecting his or her privacy. On the other hand, we have a commitment to the common good that may conflict with our fidelity. If we disclose any confidential information, we risk being tagged a betrayer of fidelity and damaging the reputation of the ministry as a safe haven for confidential matter. If confidentiality were clearly an absolute obligation, dilemmas would never arise. But it is not, and they do. What reasons might justify overriding the presumption and making a disclosure of confidential information?

In brief, I advocate the following position: The covenantal nature of the pastoral relationship, which is held together by trust, supports a strong presumption in favor of keeping confidences. This means that we should always favor keeping a confidence, act in its favor when in doubt, and not be on the lookout for reasons to breach it. Confidentiality is absolute only in matters pertaining to the sacrament of reconciliation. In all other instances, confidentiality is binding unless it conflicts with an equal or higher value. If disclosure of confidential information must be made, the burden of proof falls on the one making the disclosure. Before disclosing a confidence, we ought to make a reasonable effort to find other ways to get the necessary information into the hands of those who need it. As a general rule, the one who owns the information should be the one who makes it public. If it is not possible to elicit personal disclosure and the well-being of another is seriously at stake without disclosure, we ought to explore as many options as possible to making a direct disclosure. However, if the disclosure has to be made, we ought to tell only those who would benefit from the information and disclose only what they need to know in order to avoid the threat of serious harm.

Given this position, I now examine its limits from the perspectives of canon law, civil law, and professional ethics.

CANON LAW

In the Catholic tradition, a sacramental confession is secret information that must be treated with absolute confidentiality. Simply put, this means that it is to be concealed from others forever. The term "seal of confession" is an apt indicator of the strict confidentiality required of this sacrament. As the *Catechism of the Catholic Church* puts it, "This secret, which admits of no exceptions, is called the 'sacramental seal,' because what the penitent has made known to the priest remains 'sealed' by the sacrament."[3] The priest's obligation to total silence regarding a sacramental confession exists prior to any particular confession. It is part of the priest's moral commitment to the church, and so the faithful can rightfully presume its observance by all priests, who are "bound under very severe penalties to keep absolute secrecy regarding the sins that his penitents have confessed to him."[4]

The absolute confidentiality of a sacramental confession is governed principally by canons 983 and 984. (A related canon, 1388, pertains to the penalties incurred for violating the seal.) Canon 983 reads:

Confidentiality

1. The sacramental seal is inviolable; therefore, it is absolutely forbidden for a confessor to betray in any way a penitent in words or in any manner and for any reason.
2. The interpreter, if there is one, and all others who in any way have knowledge of sins from confession are also obliged to observe secrecy.[5]

In addition to the interpreter, which the canon mentions explicitly, this canon affirms that the obligation of absolute secrecy binds *anyone* who deliberately or accidentally becomes privy to confessional matter. Frederick McManus express the absolute secrecy of confessional matter clearly in his commentary on this canon: "No distinction is made among the matters confessed, whether the sinful action itself or attendant circumstances, or the acts of satisfaction or penances imposed, etc. The secrecy to be maintained concerning the penitent and his or her confession of sins is properly described as total."[6]

Canon 984 focuses on what the confessor can do with the knowledge gained from the confession:

1. A confessor is prohibited completely from using knowledge acquired from confession to the detriment of the penitent even when any danger of revelation is excluded.
2. A person who has been placed in authority cannot use in any manner for external governance the knowledge about sins, which he has received in confession at any time.[7]

McManus explains that the force of this canon is to protect both the identity of the penitent and the secrecy of the confessional matter. So the priest cannot use the information gained in a confession in any way that would be detrimental to the penitent (such as invoking a disciplinary procedure that would affect the penitent) or that would in any way be advantageous to himself (such as revising an administrative procedure or using information about a theft to find the money for himself). McManus underscores the seriousness of the limitation on using knowledge gained in a confession by drawing upon an older instruction from the Holy Office that counsels against preachers using what they learned in confession as an illustration in preaching.

Even though all danger of disclosure or injury might be absent, the broad confidence of penitents in the inviolability of the sacramental secrecy might be lessened. As an example, a preacher might legitimately employ information learned from confession for illustrative purposes, provided there is no possibility that the transgression might be linked to a given individual penitent; even in this case, however, if the preacher does indicate that the source of the information is a confession, he might weaken the confidence of his hearers in the inviolability of the sacramental seal.[8]

These canons and the commentary of Frederick McManus show the full force of keeping the "seal of confession." This seal does not expire upon the death of the penitent or the resignation or retirement of the priest. By keeping the seal, priests can safeguard not only the institution of the sacrament but also everyone's peace of mind about making a sacramental confession.

A controversial issue is whether the penitent can ever release the priest from the obligation of the seal. Canon law does not explicitly and directly address this issue. Canon 1550 touches on it, but this canon pertains only to witnesses of an *ecclesiastical* court. About those who are considered incapable of testifying, section 2.2 of this canon states the following: "2. Priests regarding all matters that they have come to know from sacramental confession even if the penitent seeks their disclosure; moreover, matters heard by anyone and in any way on the occasion of confession cannot be accepted even as an indication of the truth."[9]

The commentary on this canon by Craig Cox underscores the absolute prohibition of using anything the priest has learned in the sacrament of penance as testimony. "Even the penitent's explicit request that the confessor testify does not release him from the obligation to maintain the confessional seal."[10] However, whether the penitent can release the priest from the obligation of the seal of confession in any other context than an ecclesiastical trial remains open. For example, is it ever permissible for the penitent to release a confessor so that he can confer with a penitent's counselor or reveal to civil authorities what he has come to know only in a sacramental confession? Clearly great caution is required here.[11] But even if it were legally permissible for the penitent to release a confessor from the seal, the confessor is still not morally obliged to disclose. The confessor may maintain secrecy in order to honor the good of the integrity of the penitential relationship that depends on the inviolability of the seal of confession.

The seriousness with which the tradition has taken the absolute inviolability of the seal of confession forbids the priest from ever initiating a conversation with a penitent about the content of the confession outside the sacramental context in which it was first introduced. Before the priest can ever address the confessional matter again in another context, the penitent must be the one who takes the initiative to bring it up, as in another celebration of the sacrament or in a spiritual direction session, for instance. Then the priest can address the matter as presented in this new context, but not as prior confessional matter.

Even though the penitent is not obligated to secrecy by the seal of confession, out of respect for the integrity of the penitential relationship and the confidentiality it enshrines, the penitent should keep silent about the confessional communication and not disclose what the priest said during sacramental confession.

Further proof of the seriousness with which church law regards the seal of confession is found in canon 1388, which declares the penalty of automatic excommunication reserved to the Apostolic See for a priest who directly betrays the penitent's trust by violating the seal of confession. Thomas Green's commentary on this canon also notes that since 1988, the Congregation for the Doctrine of the Faith has decreed the same excommunication "for anyone deliberately using technical instruments to record and/or publish in the mass media anything said in sacramental confession by the confessor or the penitent, real or feigned."[12] An indirect violation is subject to a penalty that fits the confessor's indiscretion, such as being prohibited from serving as a confessor in the future.

These canons reiterate the serious concern of the church to preserve the tradition of absolute confidentiality of anything learned within the forum of sacramental confession. This tradition of the absolute secrecy of the seal of confession is well integrated into the pastoral ministry of the church and has thus far been respected by civil law.

CIVIL LAW

Beyond the canonical limits safeguarding the confidentiality of the sacramental forum, pastoral ministers have no other codified guidance. As a result, pastoral ministers tend to adopt the standards of the therapeutic community and/or to look for moral guidance from legal statutes.

In a society and in a church in which following the law is highly valued, what the law requires readily becomes equated with what morality demands, above all when legal liability is attached to an action. This especially applies to confidentiality. Yet law and ethics are not always identical. Generally, the law is a reliable guide to moral behavior, but not always. Good morality can prompt an illegal action, and a legal action may be unethical. Recall acts of civil disobedience that prompted a change in segregation laws.

Certainly, ministers need to be aware of the law as a matter of self-protection. Mary Angela Shaughnessy's little book, *Ministry and the Law*, is a good resource in this regard.[13] However, an overreliance on the law for defining moral responsibility misses the mark of what ethics demands. As a rule, legal standards should not be a substitute for ethical ones. Legal reasoning distorts ethical analysis by giving undue attention to rights and duties. While these are important, there is more required of a morally responsible professional minister than the fulfilling of rights and duties. Moral considerations also include personal character, lifestyle, virtuous sensibilities, vision and commitments informed by religious beliefs, role obligations, and the right use of power. A legally dominated approach to the exercise of ministry can undervalue these elements.

In general, the law recognizes a public interest in holding inviolable the confidentiality of communication between persons in some special relationships, such as lawyer-client, husband-wife, physician/therapist-patient, and clergy-penitent. Thus we have the legal notion of "privileged communications." This refers to information that is immune from being subpoenaed as evidence in a court proceeding. Rendering legal justice depends on gathering facts from witnesses willing to testify to what they know to be true, and yet some communication is "privileged" because it is an exception to the general requirement that all citizens must give testimony when subpoenaed.

The clergy-penitent privilege is more generally called the "religious privilege," or more specifically, "the clergy privilege." Simply put, it ensures that whatever information is given to a "duly ordained minister" by those seeking sacramental absolution, religious guidance, comfort, or aid cannot be used against these people in court. However, the extent of the privilege is not clear or simple. Since the clergy privilege has not been defined by federal law, each state has had to develop its own statutes on the matter. Thus, vast differences exist.[14] Ministers would be wise to understand the extent of the clergy privilege in their state and those instances when it can be invoked.

The difference among statutes, and the complexity of applying these laws, runs along several lines.[15] One complicating difference concerns defining those who count as "clergy" to whom the privilege pertains. The appearance of the word *minister* in one's job description does not necessarily qualify a person for coverage under the privilege. The legal sense seems to be that the privilege applies to those who are duly ordained, licensed, and subject to the laws of their religious body. For Catholics this would include only bishops, priests, and deacons. (The extent to which deacons are covered by this law is limited in some jurisdictions.[16]) Moreover, the privilege covers the ordained only when they serve in a religious capacity and not in some other role, such as a teacher, guidance counselor, or director of a homeless shelter or day care center.

Nonordained ministers, such as religious women and brothers, religious and lay spiritual directors, campus ministers, catechists, and others are on unsteady legal ground when it comes to invoking the religious privilege. For example, a New Jersey court (*In re Murtha*, 1971) ruled that a religious woman serving as a spiritual director for a suspected murderer could not appeal to the protection of religious privilege because she was not authorized by ecclesiastical law with the power to perform such a ministry.[17] Nevertheless, courts differ. Fourteen years after the *Murtha* ruling, the State of Missouri granted the protection of the clergy privilege to Sr. Dominic Rowe in her role as spiritual director.[18]

While everyone recognizes spiritual direction as a valid ministry in the church, canon law does not recognize it as an official ministry and civil law varies in granting the clergy privilege to nonordained ministers. Yet, many spiritual directors treat the confidentiality of spiritual direction as absolutely as the confessional seal, even though these fora are not technically the same. Thus, what is ethical and what is legal for spiritual directors can come into conflict. Canonist Donna Ioppolo's summary statement on this issue is worth heeding:

> In summary, based on state statutes and the cases interpreting them, it is rare that a court will extend the clergy privilege to those outside of ordained ministers. Consequently, non-ordained ministers should be fully aware that communications made to them, regardless of the minister's and the communicant's intent, are probably not privileged under the law.[19]

Sr. Mary, from the scenario at the beginning of this chapter, wonders about the extent of her moral responsibility to disclose because she does not equate spiritual direction with the seal of confession and the clergy privilege.

Another complicating difference is that not every communication made to a minister is considered privileged communication. Richard B. Couser, in his work, *Ministry and the American Legal System*, interprets the boundary of the religious privilege this way:

> The privileged conversation must be one that was made for the purpose of seeking religious advice, comfort, absolution, or other spiritual or pastoral care. The mere fact that a statement is made to a member of the clergy does not bring it within the privilege. The communication must, in fact, be confidential. The presence of third persons or other circumstances indicating that the person did not intend or expect confidentiality is likely to result in the loss of the privilege.[20]

It seems, then, that the communication is less likely to come under the privilege the more public it is and the further it moves from being spiritual advice given by an ordained minister functioning in an official capacity. This still puts the communication with lay ministers beyond the limits of the protection of the religious privilege.

Confidentiality

Canonists recognize that the diversity of civil laws and their interpretations of the religious privilege, together with the absence of provision in the Code of Canon Law to cover the confidentiality of communications made to nonordained ministers, makes it unlikely that the religious privilege will be extended to all pastoral ministers. Nonetheless, James Serritella suggests that

> a well-defined diocesan program for non-ordained ministers, which includes formation, discernment, and certification, followed by a formal mandate to work as a Church professional under the supervision and direction of a clergyman would strengthen an argument that these ministers should be covered by the privilege.[21]

He then goes on to specify further what this would demand:

> It will be much easier to argue for the inclusion of non-ordained ministers under the protections of the privileged communication statute if these ministers are formally mandated in the position they hold following a regular program of formation and certification and are not authorized to act in the diocese without such a mandate. A requirement that such ministers work under supervision and direction of a clergyman is also critical to an effective argument here. Employment contracts, while important, may not be enough to bring these ministers under the provisions of the statute. A well-developed diocesan policy, including personnel guidelines and job descriptions for all ministries, will certainly add weight to an argument on behalf of these ministers.[22]

Other differences in state statutes that complicate the legal boundaries of the religious privilege concern the kind of relationship the minister must have with the one making the communication. Ultimately, the scope of the religious privilege depends on how the language of the statute is drawn. The privilege will be upheld only if the facts surrounding the communication come squarely within the circumstances defined by the statute.

The ordained, and certainly any nonordained, minister cannot easily invoke the religious privilege in matters of civil disputes. The variety of statutes that express the religious privilege and the complexity of interpreting and applying them make it impossible to give a categorical answer to questions of exactly who and what are covered under the privilege and when it applies. In civil disputes, a minister should always consult with an attorney before testifying in court to see whether the laws of privileged communication apply. Simply receiving a subpoena to testify should not end the question of whether to speak or to remain silent. Ethical factors also ought to be considered.

ETHICAL LIMITS

Conflicts over confidentiality are in effect conflicts over power. In pastoral relationships, we receive a great deal of personal information about those who seek our service. Their self-disclosure makes them vulnerable and increases our power over them. To ensure that we conduct ourselves in the pastoral relationship with the highest respect for personal dignity, we must be sensitive to the power that we have and to the way we use it. Giving the presumption in favor of keeping a confidence helps us to ensure that we steward well the power we have over others in the pastoral relationship.

While some people may think that everything they say to a priest, and by extension to other pastoral ministers, is either "under the seal" or is "privileged communication," that is simply not true. Not all pastoral communication is confidential. Apart from the absolute prohibition of disclosing any communication exchanged in the sacrament of reconciliation, confidentiality is, as moralists like to say, "a general rule that applies generally." That means that, as a principle, it cannot articulate every morally relevant difference among cases and so must admit to exceptions. So, while our fundamental stance in a pastoral relationship is to give a presumption in favor of confidentiality, there are some instances, few though they are, in which the duty to disclose may, and sometimes must, override the presumption. Our commitment to the virtues of justice, fidelity, and prudence can help us determine when this is the case.

Justice

Justice is the virtue that recognizes our interdependence with all people. It cultivates sensitivity to fairness that relativizes the bonds of the individual pastoral relationship by protecting the well-being of others. Justice looks beyond the welfare of one individual when the welfare of others, especially the innocent and vulnerable, is at stake. Privacy is protected by the virtue of fidelity but not to the extent that would permit doing harm to others. In such a case, justice trumps fidelity. Sr. Mary faces this dilemma in the scenario at the beginning of the chapter. Does she put the good of the community over her fidelity to Jane?

Whereas fidelity allows disclosure if permission is given, justice requires disclosure even without permission when a serious risk of harm might occur if the information should be suppressed. The greater the likelihood that someone is in clear and present danger of causing harm to self or others changes the moral mandate of confidentiality. Except in cases that fall under the "seal of confession," when serious harm is at stake, there is an overriding obligation to disclose. The strength of this obligation depends on the seriousness of the harm that might be done, on whether the harm is a clear and present danger and not simply a report of some past threat or action, on the degree of vulnerability of the one at risk of being harmed now, and on the reasonable identifiability of the victim. Given these conditions, Sr. Mary in the opening scenario is not obligated to report Jane's abuse of twenty years ago. However, when the risk to harm is a clear and present danger to a vulnerable person, then maintaining confidentiality can become unethical, for it serves to cover up a dangerous practice or to cooperate in an act of violence. The *Catechism* advocates as much:

> *Professional secrets*—for example, those of political office holders, soldiers, physicians, and lawyers—or confidential information given under the seal of secrecy must be kept, save in exceptional cases where keeping the secret is bound to cause very grave harm to the one who confided it, to the one who received it or to a third party, and where the very general harm can be avoided only by divulging the truth.[23]

The *Tarasoff* ruling in California (1976)[24] has brought into public consciousness the professional's conflict between wanting to protect either an individual's well-being or the public safety. The ruling was that the duty of confidentiality in psychotherapy is outweighed by the duty to protect an identifiable victim from life-threatening danger. This duty can be discharged by warning the victim directly, informing others who can warn the victim, or notifying the police. That we had to have such a ruling shows that only with great reluctance should confidentiality be broken and then only in the face of clear and present danger.

Protecting the vulnerable from harm is also the basis for reporting known and suspected incidents of child abuse as well as the abuse of elders and the disabled. Many state laws require such reporting and specify the professionals mandated to make the report. Some states include ministers among those mandated, others do not, and some even clearly exempt us.[25] However, whether the law requires it or not, justice demands disclosing incidents of abuse as a moral imperative. Protecting the vulnerable from harm also follows upon the covenantal nature of the pastoral commitment. The biblical experience of the covenant includes the mandate to protect those who are especially vulnerable to harm. These are symbolized in "the orphan, the widow, the poor, and the stranger" who are vulnerable to exploitation because they do not have the built-in supports of the family or a community. Thus the covenant mandates the entire community to be responsible for protecting them.

Fidelity

The requirements of justice are sometimes in tension with fidelity. Fidelity is the virtue needed to maintain the covenantal bonds that we make with the one seeking our pastoral service. It honors the dignity of the person by giving the presumption in favor of keeping a confidence so as to enable the one seeking the pastoral service to retain a zone of privacy and to control the direction of his or her thoughts, plans, and actions. While holding to a firm absolute for confidentiality in the sacramental forum, fidelity favors maintaining confidence in all other communications, including computerized records, sacramental records, and financial records.

Fidelity is not betrayed, however, if, in a nonsacramental context, the person who has communicated the information gives permission for the disclosure to be made in order to serve his or her well-being. This happens, for instance, when someone asks a pastoral minister to write a letter of recommendation for a job. However, even if permission is granted as a necessary condition for safeguarding fidelity, the permission alone is not a sufficient condition. A disclosure may be allowed, but it is not necessarily obliged. The permission to disclose is not an obligation to disclose. We ought to be mindful of the forum in which we acquired the information and the kind of ministry we are providing when we do. Some come under a stronger commitment to confidentiality than others do. If we serve as a regular confessor to someone or as a spiritual director, for example, then we might refrain from writing the letter of recommendation in order to protect the integrity of these special ministries wherein confidentiality is so strictly observed, even if spiritual direction does not carry the weight of absolute secrecy that belongs to the sacramental forum. By so acting, the confessor or spiritual director strengthens the public image of these special ministries as a guaranteed safe haven for spiritual growth. Such restraint is further justified when other people are available to write the recommendation. But if we had occasional "private" conversations, but have not had prolonged meetings with that person over private matters, then we would be freer to give letters of recommendation without undermining the privilege of pastoral or sacramental communication.

Another case of nonsacramental disclosure is reporting information from financial and sacramental records. This may be done for statistical purposes, for example, if the identity of the individual is concealed. If a governmental agency required a review of records, consultation with a lawyer would be wise before releasing these records.

Fidelity can be easily strained, however, in the case of dual relationships that can make us double agents. When this happens, we confuse our loyalty. For example, if we are on a formation team that sends an assessment to the bishop or to the leadership team about the fitness of a candidate for ordination or incorporation into the community, and if we serve at the same time as the spiritual director for that candidate, then for whom are we working? The candidate? Or the diocese or religious community? For this reason, spiritual directors ought not to be advisors in the public forum of the same person for whom they would have to write an evaluation, nor should spiritual directors speak on behalf of their directees in a public forum of evaluation or vote on their fitness for a call to orders or incorporation into the religious community. Those for whom we work need to know where our loyalty lies and where their personal information is going to go.

Since the effectiveness of pastoral ministry would be undermined if confidences were broken easily, the responsibility of protecting the boundaries of confidential information favors being the agent of one person at a time. If we become known as the kind of person who breaks a confidence or betrays a trust because of our double agency, then we acquire the reputation of being untrustworthy. Such a characteristic would not only damage our own ministry but also undermine the reputation of ministry as a whole as a safe haven for personal matters.

Prudence

Prudence is the virtue of discernment. It enables us to make a discriminating judgment about when justice prevails over fidelity. Since the decision to disclose a confidence is not easy to make, prudence is needed in order to exercise discretion in determining those situations in which the vulnerable are at serious risk and when receiving information is or is not an invasion of rightful privacy. Prudence involves knowledge of all parties involved, where they have come from, what they hope for, and what they are capable of doing. From this vantage point, prudence judges how best to speak the truth in love. Since cases differ in their particulars, honest differences of judgment must be allowed in the exercise of prudence.

In ambiguous situations, when we are not sure just how much confidentiality we owe the other, we ought to favor silence. However, in those special instances in which confidentiality ought not to be kept because the risk of harm is too great, a prudential process of disclosure would meet certain conditions:

> A reasonable effort is made to elicit voluntary disclosure so that the one who owns the information is the one making the disclosure.
> A high probability exists that harm will be done unless a disclosure is made.
> Only those who have a need to know are informed.
> Only information necessary to avert harm is disclosed.

A campus minister, Marsha, followed these guidelines when she learned in the course of doing premarital counseling that John was HIV+ but had refused to tell his fiancé, Jane. The time of the wedding drew near and Marsha had not been able to persuade John to tell Jane about his condition. Marsha informed John that she was going to tell Jane herself if he did not because of the great risk that Jane could contract the infection from John. He still refused to tell. Therefore, Marsha made the disclosure.

That case stands in stark contrast to the catechist who learned that one of her students was HIV+. In fear and panic for the safety of the other students, she announced to the class that Joey was infected. She then proceeded to call the parents of each of her students to warn them of the danger. In this instance, since the risk of harm to others was not great, the disclosure was an unjustified invasion of privacy.

This, in brief, is an ethical assessment of the limits of confidentiality, which is an important professional, pastoral obligation. Confidentiality is justified on the basis of the respect it affords the dignity of the person, and for the contribution it makes to enabling others to have easier access to pastoral services without fearing that their personal concerns will become public. Apart from the sacramental seal of confession, which is absolute, our commitment to fidelity gives a strong but not absolute presumption in favor of confidentiality. Justice can override this presumption when there is a high risk that serious harm will be done, and prudence will help us to judge the case.

BETRAYALS OF CONFIDENTIALITY

By now I hope the presumption in favor of confidentiality is clear. The subject matter, context, and implicit and explicit expectations of confidentiality make it easy to know what we are to keep in confidence. However, when these indicators of what to keep confidential are not so clear, we may not be so careful. Common betrayals of confidentiality occur in casual encounters. These are due, I would like to think, more to our carelessness than cruelty. We do not intend to betray a loyalty and cause harm, and we are generally unaware that we have. Pointing out some common ways that we betray a confidence may help us be more vigilant in the ways we protect the dignity, identity, reputation, and freedom of those who entrust themselves to us in our pastoral ministry.

INVASIONS OF PRIVACY

We are in a much more ambiguous role regarding confidentiality than are most other professionals. Doctors, lawyers, or therapists, for instance, acquire knowledge of their clients in well-defined, formal settings. They rarely have to work side by side with these same clients in other institutional or social settings, and, as a general rule, they do not socialize with them. These boundaries, however, do not hold firm in pastoral ministry. We meet with our people in a great variety of places, not just the office; and we work along with them on diverse projects, not just religious ones. It is not always clear when people are relating to us in our religious role and when they are not. So, expectations of confidentiality get confusing.

Moreover, people share private matters with us in very public contexts, such as social gatherings, recreational events, and civic gatherings. I believe this has a lot to do with our bearing the authority of representing God, the church, or matters religious wherever we are. People perceive us as bringing the safety zone of the sacramental forum into every area of life, even when sacramental confession is not in question. When people project the sacramental seal into settings far beyond its canonical limits, we find ourselves in a real dilemma over invasions of privacy. What appears to be general public information on the basis of the context and manner in which it is shared may actually be expected to be private information that the person wants kept confidential. If we let the secret out, then we are perceived to be invading privacy and betraying trust.

Here are some common ways we can invade privacy, intentionally or unintentionally, and risk betraying trust.

PASTORAL VISITS

Deacon John had gone to make his regular hospital visitations on Friday afternoon. In the hospital corridor, he was surprised to meet Dolly, a prominent parishioner, whom he did not know had been admitted to the hospital. That Sunday, he met Dolly's sister, Peg, coming out of Mass. He told her that he saw Dolly at the hospital on Friday. He asked Peg to wish her well for him until he himself was able to get back to see her on Monday. Peg was astonished, for she did not know that Dolly was in the hospital. She phoned immediately to see what the matter was. Dolly was very upset that anyone had found out that she had admitted herself to the hospital for personal reasons and a private surgical procedure. She especially felt betrayed when she learned that the news got out through the deacon.

At first glance, this scenario seems innocent enough, and no one would fault Deacon John for his actions. His mentioning to Peg that he had seen Dolly in the hospital seems to be sharing information of a common interest. It did not seem to be saying anything about Dolly that would be objectionable to a family member with reasonable sensibilities for people, especially one's own sister. Deacon John did not think that Dolly's admission to the hospital was so private that it had to remain concealed. But that is certainly not how Dolly saw it. Her expectations of what anyone could do with the information about her hospital admission were different from what Deacon John presumed. While this incident may not be sustained in court as an invasion of privacy, its moral character is less clear. It shows how much pastoral ministers are at risk of a moral invasion of privacy when expectations are not clear and the setting from which the information comes is ambiguous. In matters of uncertain boundaries, the safer course is to favor keeping silent.

ILLUSTRATIONS IN PREACHING AND TEACHING

Every preacher wants to connect the gospel message with the grit of human experience. What better source to use than one's own experiences within the community to which one is preaching? Yet using one's ministerial experiences within the community can jeopardize the safety zone of confidentiality. Other members of the community can too easily recognize the event and identify the people involved.

I remember hearing one preacher, who was also a therapist, using examples taken from his therapy with people in the community. He may have changed the names, but the examples were all too vividly from life in this community. That was clearly a boundary violation. Another one would read excerpts from letters he had received in the mail to illustrate his homiletic points. That, too, is a violation. However, what if we get permission to use our experience? Even if permission is granted, we still risk compromising our ministry as a safety zone in which people realize that nothing is sacred with us.

Marilyn Peterson illustrates in her book, *At Personal Risk*, how confidentiality and privacy can be violated in preaching:

> I was having major sexual and financial problems with my husband and was worried about the delinquent behavior of my children. I had been to see my minister several times for his advice. I remember I always felt scared when he gave his sermons. He always started by saying, "A woman walked into my office. She was such and such an age and she had these problems." I always feel this pit in my stomach and thought that maybe he was going to talk about me. He never began his sermons with stories about men. The details that he shared about these women didn't even seem related to the main point of his talk.
>
> Anyway, I remember one Sunday he began talking about this woman who was my age and described the specific sexual and financial concerns she had with her husband. I felt really embarrassed but also really special because he had chosen a story about me for his sermon. I remember sitting with my friend and having her say to me, "You know, that sounds like you." That's when I really started to feel unsafe. It started to feel real messy because he had so much personal information about me.[26]

Peterson explains how this preacher assumed the right to use as subject matter in his sermon this woman's personal material, which he acquired from offering her pastoral service. He undermined the fidelity of the pastoral relationship by giving himself permission to invade her privacy and to violate her confidence.

PRAYERS OF THE FAITHFUL

Another common way to invade privacy is through the way we formulate our public intercessions, or prayers of the faithful. While the liturgical instructions are to make these "general" intercessions, many times we hear some very detailed accounts of a person's domestic life, health, or business practices. These sound more like an announcement or news bulletin than a petition of prayer. The solidarity we want to express through this prayer and our commitment to be a prayerfully supportive community of faith is well intentioned, but the formulation of these prayers can disclose details that ought to remain private in order to allow people to retain some control over their reputation and life plans.

RECORDS AND RECORDINGS

Documents such as personnel files, sacramental records, and financial records are not to be open to the public. Nor are personal journals from spiritual direction. Records like these are to be respected as private property and not objects of curiosity. They ought to be properly stored, or kept in a safe place, and not lying around on a desk or coffee table for easy perusal.

Recordings, such as photographs, or sound or videotapes of anyone other than the author, should not be used without permission of the person whose image or voice is being used.

ENVIRONMENT

We can also invade privacy by not securing the environment in which we do ministry. Appropriate soundproofing so that our conversations do not become public ones is a way of respecting privacy. This can be as simple as closing the door or window, or as elaborate as making architectural changes that divide private space from easy public access. Confidentiality is endangered if several people share the same room at the same time so that there are multiple desks in the room, with each one having clients, but there is no physical space to create privacy.

A private environment also includes keeping one's desk free of confidential documents when others come to meet with us while at our desk. Computer screens, too, ought to be shut down when we are working on personal material that is of no business to the person meeting with us.

GOSSIP

"Gossip," says Sissela Bok, is "informal personal communication about other people who are absent or treated as absent."[27] Defined as such, not all gossip is harmful.[28] Bok says that we can hardly condemn on moral grounds talk about "who might marry, have a baby, move to another town, be in need of work or too ill to ask for help."[29] Gossip is a moral problem, however, when it is the occasion for lowering one's esteem for another.

Somehow, we like to think that we are above all of that. However, as one pastor said to me, "The stories we swap about parishioners and church leaders rival anything found in the supermarket tabloids!" Perhaps this quip attributed to Oscar Wilde says more about our interest in prurient gossip than we care to admit: "If you can't say something good about someone, come over here and sit next to me."[30] The lure of a titillating tidbit of information that reaches behind someone else's public façade is hard to resist, but resist it we must if we are to preserve ourselves and the pastoral ministry as a zone of safety for private concerns. If we make gossip our habitual way of speaking and learning about others, then we have moved beyond gossiping as an occasional offensive behavior to becoming a gossip, an offensive kind of person. When we become known as a gossip, or even as the occasional means or source of gossip, then the whole institution of confidentiality in the ministry could be threatened and the trust that sustains the pastoral relationship tarnished.

PASTORAL PUBLICATIONS

More formal than gossip and more easily subject to civil lawsuits are various forms of publications. Newsletters, fliers, parish bulletins, posters, even remarks at parish council or board meetings are all opportunities by which we can give public exposure to private facts about people that anyone with reasonable sensibilities would find objectionable if made public.

Saying something about another that damages the person's reputation or ruins his or her professional life is a form of defamation. Accusing another of willful deceit, gross incompetence, or immorality can be deemed defamatory. Historically in civil law, if this publication were made orally, it would be called slander; if in writing, it would be libel. Today, the more general term *defamation* covers these distinctions.[31] In the moral tradition, we spoke of "calumny" when remarks about another were false and gave rise to false judgments concerning them. We used "detraction" when we spoke the truth about another's faults but without a valid reason. All statements made in the context of evaluating candidates for ministry, or in the context of disciplinary actions in which negative remarks are made about a person, should be well founded and not based on rumor or guesswork. These discussions should remain in house and discussed only with those who need to know the information for official reasons. These discussions are privileged discussions and not generally the subject of civil suits for defamation.[32]

Since we acquire so much information about people in the course of our pastoral ministry, we must be especially vigilant in protecting people's reputations. However, it is easy to forget that. It is so much easier and tempting to pass on an interesting, shocking, or depressing piece of information to our friends, staffs, or families about people whom we have met in our ministry. In their own ways, these various distinctions all point to the wrong of making statements about others that grossly damage their reputation. These are the kinds of invasions of privacy that call our character into question and undermine public trust in the ministry.

STRATEGIES FOR PREVENTION

As a conclusion to this chapter, I offer a few suggestions for maintaining ethical behavior in pastoral ministry in the matter of confidentiality:

The presumption is always in favor of keeping the confidence of a pastoral relationship.

The more formal the context in which communication is exchanged, the weightier is the obligation to confidentiality.

We should take necessary steps to ensure confidentiality by seeing that offices are properly soundproof, records are secure, and staff members are informed of their duty in matters of confidentiality.

We should communicate our understanding of the limits of confidentiality early in the pastoral relationship, so that the other will know whose agent we are, how much we can share with others, and under what circumstances we will make disclosures.

Outside the sacramental forum, we should not offer a blanket promise of confidentiality since there are some things we might have to disclose for the sake of protecting the well-being of others, such as child abuse.

Before promising confidentiality, it is better to hear what we are being asked to keep secret.

Confidential information should not be shared without the permission of the one who has disclosed the information.

If we must override the presumption in favor of keeping a confidence, we should make a reasonable effort to elicit voluntary disclosure. If we must disclose, we should tell only those who need to know and then only what they need to know to protect another from serious harm.

We should know the laws covering mandated reporters and the religious privilege in our jurisdiction.

If we are in doubt about whether a matter ought to be confidential or not, we ought to resolve the doubt in favor of silence.

Confidentiality

We should not participate in gossip or presume any negative
   facts about someone without establishing their foundations.
We should avoid any form of publication, oral or written, that
   could injure another's reputation and that is not necessary
   for the general public to know.
We should always get permission to use another person's name,
   image, or statements in any of our official publications.

We live in a world where so much is intrusive—cell phones,
video phones, electronic surveillance, tabloid disclosures, and so on.
So little remains private, yet privacy has been highly prized in ministry.
Our people count on it, and we should continue to do what we can to
remain guardians of their privacy.

8

PASTORAL CARE

Fr. Ray, ordained for only two years, is now in his fourth month as pastor of St. John's, an inner-city parish. He is beginning to feel a bit overwhelmed by the multiple demands made on him for pastoral care. He came to St. John's with the reputation of being a good preacher and spiritual director. In his previous parish, parishioners would frequently ask him for copies of his homilies, but now he has little time to pray over the texts and has reduced his preparation time to a few hours on Saturday afternoon. He feels that his homilies are becoming trivial and unrelated to the life of the people in his new parish. He knows that he has the skills to become a good preacher, but he does not yet know his parishioners well enough to preach to them effectively. He is confident that his preaching will improve when he builds into the rhythm of his week more time to reflect on the biblical text and as he gets to know his parishioners better.

Fr. Ray is also having a hard time sorting out financial matters. Personally he is running a large debt on his credit card and so welcomes any opportunity to take advantage of a clerical discount. But when people give him money, he isn't quite sure whether he is to use it as a personal gift or if it ought to go to the general parish fund. He is working with the parish finance council to establish some guidelines in order to sort out the various uses of the money coming in.

While people are still coming to him for spiritual direction, he finds that what they really need is moral guidance or, most often, pastoral counseling. But he doesn't feel prepared to do either. He thinks many people are saying that they want spiritual direction because that is what he says that he can offer and he doesn't charge any fee for it. Trying to be clear with them about the kind of individual pastoral care he is competent to offer has become a real challenge for him.

Offering pastoral care is at the heart of the pastoral ministry. It is what ministers do. Pastoral care is the basic ministry we extend to everyone. However, to do it in a professional way that respects the ethical integrity of the different forms of pastoral care is the persistent challenge to a just ministry. This is precisely the challenge Fr. Ray is facing as a new pastor. He is not alone; there are many like him.

What we call pastoral care today was once known as "the care of souls" (*cura animarum*). Such a way of talking about this ministry clearly focuses on the religious or spiritual dimension of the community's or a person's life so that the care that was offered was seen within the context of a relationship with God. This chapter examines ethical aspects of two forms of pastoral care directed toward the community—preaching and managing finances—and one form of pastoral care offered to an individual—moral guidance.

PREACHING

Preaching is hard. In fact, it may be the most demanding ministry any of us will ever undertake. The Second Vatican Council gave a very special place to the ministry of preaching when it focused its understanding of the priesthood on the proclamation of the Word. It declared preaching as the primary duty of the parish priest.[1] Preaching is an awesome responsibility that cannot be taken lightly. Preaching can be the ministry that draws people into the life and mission of the church, or it can turn them away, perhaps forever. Preaching is the most common teaching role in the church, and it is the point of greatest contact with people. It is where we interpret the tradition and apply it. To this end, it requires learning in scripture and theology, spiritual maturity, a discipline of prayer, a breadth of personal experience, familiarity with the local community, communication skills, imagination, and time to prepare. Through preaching we reveal our character and spirituality, whether we want to be transparent about these things or not. If you really want to know a minister, listen to him or her preach.

Preaching, as an expression of pastoral care, can take many forms. It can be as straightforward as the personal witness of one's life. In this form, we do not even need to use words! Preaching can also be the primary catechetical opportunity to teach doctrine or the forum for inspiring and guiding behavior through moral exhortation. It can take the form of explaining a biblical text, giving an interpretation of experience in the light of faith, providing sacramental preparation, or even giving a tip on healthy living. Preaching can be as elaborate as a retreat conference and a mission talk, or as simple as a story of devotional inspiration. Preaching can occur within or outside a liturgical setting. I suspect that there are probably as many ideas about what preaching is or should be as there are preachers and people who listen to them. For my purposes here, I restrict preaching to the ministry we provide at Mass Sunday after Sunday, where most people most of the time hear the Word of God.

One of the best understandings of liturgical preaching is found in the document published by the Committee on Priestly Life and Ministry of the National Council of Catholic Bishops (NCCB) entitled *Fulfilled in Your Hearing*.[2] It understands the Sunday homily to be more interpretive than instructive. It is "a scriptural interpretation of human existence which enables a community to recognize God's active presence, to respond to that presence in faith through liturgical word and gesture, and beyond the liturgical assembly, through a life lived in conformity with the Gospel."[3]

Interpreting human experience in light of the scripture text for the day, the preacher represents both the assembly in its diversity of experiences and the God revealed in Jesus and now present in the power of the Spirit. Good preaching draws upon the biblical narrative to provide believers with an interpretive framework within which to understand their lives in the light of God's continuing presence and action in the world. If we preach well, people will be able to name God's action in their lives and so respond to God's saving presence not only through participating in the Eucharist but also by being drawn into following Jesus more faithfully.

Given this understanding of the Sunday homily, my model of an ethics of preaching involves a threefold fidelity: to the *text*, which is the medium for identifying the presence and action of God; to the *experience* of the preacher as a participant, with the people, in a broad cultural context; and to the *community* for whom the text is being interpreted.

FIDELITY TO THE TEXT

To say that fidelity to the biblical text used in the liturgy is the first ethical obligation of preaching ought to be obvious enough, since the homily is "a part of the liturgy itself"[4] and "flows from the Scriptures which are read at that liturgical celebration, or, more broadly, from the Scriptures which undergird its prayers and actions."[5] But to say that preaching should be faithful to the text does not mean that preaching ought to be teaching the text in the way one might interpret a biblical text in a class on the Bible. About such use of the Bible in preaching, biblical scholar Donald Senior once said, "Nothing is deadlier than a sermon or homily that turns out to be simply an analysis of the biblical text."[6] *Fulfilled in Your Hearing* better expresses what fidelity to the text means when it says, "The homily is not so much *on* the Scriptures as *from* and *through* them....The preacher does not so much attempt to explain the Scriptures as to interpret the human situation through the Scriptures."[7] In other words, texts need interpreting. Preaching as interpretation is not only concerned with what the text meant, but also with what it means now for those who hear it: What are we to do with what the text says?

Fidelity to the text begins with the preacher's attentive listening to the text. We have to listen to the biblical story as a story about ourselves. We have to imagine our way into the story and imagine our way out. This takes time and the spiritual discipline of quiet prayer and some form of *lectio divina*. This ancient spiritual practice approaches the biblical text with an imagination of faith. It seeks not so much to be informed by the text as to be transformed by it through an imaginative entry into the text so that we can see and feel how it opens us to the presence of God in our personal and communal history. The preacher must first be a hearer of the Word: What does this text say to me?

Through *lectio*, the story begins as a window into an unfamiliar world and into the lives of people we do not know. However, the more we look through this window, the more likely will it become a mirror in which we see ourselves in the characters of the story and we see our own lives unfolding in the events of another world. Our task for preaching is first to welcome the wisdom of the story into our own lives and then to make it accessible to others. As homiletician Robert Waznak once put it, "I suspect that the reason we often fail to preach in a way that has to do with people's real lives is that we preachers have not first encountered God's word prayerfully and creatively in our own lives."[8] This is what Fr. Ray of the opening scenario was unable to do because he let other pastoral duties take priority over preparing his homilies. He did not give himself enough quiet time to let the window of the text become a mirror that reflected his own life. Fidelity to the text includes praying with the text as part of faithful preparation for preaching. According to *Fulfilled in Your Hearing*, "A week of daily meditation on the readings of the following Sunday is not too much time to spend on preparation."[9]

In addition to listening to the text speak to our own life, we can fill in the background of the text by turning to the work of biblical scholars. Even though being faithful to the text does not imply giving a scholarly exposition of it, a moral responsibility of the preacher is to make use of the labors of biblical scholars in order to have an accurate grasp of the text in its literal and applied senses. The scriptures come out of a time and culture different from our own. Because of this difference, we can easily miss the historical and cultural cues that help us catch its meaning. For this reason, preachers ought to have ready access to the tools of biblical scholarship. Minimally, this would include biblical and theological dictionaries and standard biblical commentaries on the texts of the lectionary. These tools help us to take the biblical text on its own terms so that it can challenge us to see our own lives by analogy in a new light. For the purpose of preaching, we should respect both the strengths and the limits of biblical scholarship for interpreting the meaning of the text for today.[10]

Fidelity to the text includes at least the discipline of listening prayerfully as the text speaks to our own life and of carefully studying the text so that it will ground the homily in the Word of God. But to catch the meaning of the text for today, we must also be in touch with the experiences of the people of today.

FIDELITY TO EXPERIENCE

Fidelity to the text leads to fidelity to experience, the second requirement of an ethics of preaching. Preaching is not just a matter of creatively retelling the biblical story; it is a seeing through the biblical story to the experiences of the present. What makes fidelity to experience an ethical requirement of preaching is the theological conviction that the same Spirit that was active in the history of Israel, in the life of Jesus, and in the church that gave us the Bible is still present and active in our own day.[11] Preaching is to make the connections between the God who has acted and spoken in the past to the God who is acting and speaking to us today.

One of the moral tasks of the preacher is to reflect on human experience to discover the work of God there. So not only must we have knowledge of the scriptures and theology, but we must also engage a sustained reflection on experience—personal experience, parish happenings, world events, cultural developments. This moral responsibility for preaching lines up clearly with the professional competence of theological reflection that I singled out in chapter 2 as the distinctive competence of the pastoral minister. Preaching employs the skill of theological reflection to interpret the life situations of the congregation in light of the faith convictions, stories, people, and images of the biblical text.

To do theological reflection of this sort, fidelity to experience requires that the preacher engage in a critical dialogue with contemporary culture. Part of our professional responsibility as preachers is to be familiar with the politics, economics, literature, music, art, theater, and cinema that express the culture of our time and that provide material for critical reflection on what concerns people today. As *Fulfilled in Your Hearing* affirms, reading novels, going to the movies, visiting a museum, reading the paper, watching the evening news, and conversing with people involved in the social, political, and economic issues of our day are not just leisure-time activities for a preacher. They are moral responsibilities that are an integral part of preparing to preach Sunday after Sunday.[12] Not to be attentive to experience can become spiritual neglect on our part. Neglect leads to our being absent from the community both morally and spiritually.

FIDELITY TO THE COMMUNITY

Fidelity to the community, the third ethical responsibility of preaching, flows from fidelity to experience. To preach, we must attend to the religious experience and condition of the people who will hear our words. Whenever I have heard positive comments about a homily, the focus of attention has not been on the preacher's theatrical performance but on the relevance of the homily to a current event or to the meaning it had for the life of the people who heard it. Theologically speaking, the preacher named the graces found in their lives. But this can only happen if we are being faithful to the community by listening to their experience.

Ethical preaching means that we are able to speak to the people who are present. Even basic communications theory asserts that effective communication is audience driven. The speaker needs an audience to complete the communication. This requires that the speaker know the audience—what they need and are able to hear. To this end, if we are to preach in a responsible way, we are morally required to get to know the people to whom we preach. Not to do so is spiritual neglect.[13] Part of Fr. Ray's frustration in our opening scenario is that he did not yet know his new community in all its diversity. If we are unaware of the interests that occupy most of the people's time, it will be virtually impossible for us to show how the Word sheds light on their situation. There are many ways that we can get to know the local community. The normal course of pastoral service provides many of them—parish organizations, sacramental preparation, social events, and opportunities to offer individual pastoral care, to name a few. These can be supplemented by following the developments in the news and by conversations with people who have political, social, religious, and economic influence in the area.

Attending to these means of getting to know the community is a moral responsibility for us, not just a social curiosity. However, even with all this effort at listening to the people, the very nature of the diversity of cultures, ages, and lifestyles in a parish makes it virtually impossible for any of us to preach effectively to everyone. Inevitably, we will be morally and spiritually absent from some of them. But this absence need not become spiritual neglect if we are trying to get to know the community and can provide other means, such as other preachers, who will be able to help the community recognize in the Word of God a word that responds to their lives. We already have a model for this in the way some parishes have a special Liturgy of the Word for children.[14]

This, then, is a brief sketch of an ethics of preaching based on the threefold fidelity that is integral to the nature of homiletic preaching: fidelity to the biblical text of the day, fidelity to the experience of the preacher and of those who will hear the Word, and fidelity to the community for whom the homily is intended. Being faithful in these ways meets the professional responsibility for liturgical preaching and avoids the unethical professional conduct of spiritual neglect of the congregation in this important expression of pastoral care.

PREACHING ON MORAL ISSUES

However, focusing on the homily as a model of preaching is rather narrow. It cannot carry the full weight of the pastoral care of preaching. Some people want preaching to contain more doctrinal instruction, others want social or political analysis, some want to hear moral exhortations, and still others want something more devotionally inspiring. How do we serve them all? Ultimately, we have to make a judgment as to what form of preaching will serve the community best at any particular time and with our given talents.

I offer the following points to keep in mind when we move beyond the confines of the homily that interprets experience in the light of faith and move into preaching as instruction and exhortation, especially on moral issues.[15]

1. *Recognize the inherent temptations and limitations of the forum of the pulpit.*

The pulpit is not a classroom lectern. From the pulpit, we do not engage the congregation and invite immediate feedback, such as through questions or rebuttal the way we might in the classroom. The pulpit puts us in a position of great power. It is tempting to abuse it, especially when a moral issue is at stake. Because we do not have to contend with immediate questions or criticism while in the pulpit, we can easily be lured into moralizing in a heavy-handed, judgmental way that pushes us to the edge of spiritual abuse.[16] That preachers have crossed the line and become abusive has given preaching a bad name and spawned some negative connotations, such as in the defensive remarks, "Don't go preaching to me!" or "Now you're getting preachy."

Moreover, a presentation by a single person without a chance for mutual interaction the way a classroom allows, for example, is not the best way to instruct or to bring about a change of attitude or behavior. As *Fulfilled in Your Hearing* affirms, an oral presentation by a single person is more effective in reinforcing an attitude or knowledge previously held. That is what makes the homily more appropriate for the pulpit, because it draws out implications of a faith the people already have.[17]

2. Respect the parish's regular rhythm of social involvement and social preaching.

Preaching on a moral issue, as well as social or political ones, ought to have a context in the life and rhythm of the parish. One of the key responsibilities of preaching on moral issues is to create a context in the parish in which this sort of preaching can take place. For example, a parish that has an active social ministry witnessing to the social mission of the church affords a better context for hearing someone preaching on a social issue than does the parish that does not have a clear commitment to social ministries, or has not already established the practice of drawing out social implications of the gospel in its regular rhythm of preaching. Suddenly to preach on a moral issue, or to present the official teaching of the church on an issue, when there is no context for it in the life of the parish, may be heard more as an indictment than as a call to conversion or an effort to inform conscience.

3. Be modest when proposing prudential judgments.

Sometimes we are very vague about a call to justice or to moral conversion and then leave it up to the people to decide what shape that might take. At other times, we may move from a general principle to specific application. In those instances, we ought to present the application as a prudential judgment, acknowledging that others may disagree. The congregation should experience us not only as someone who is willing to state a position to stimulate thinking but also as someone who is still seeking the right course of action in light of the gospel, but who does not have it all figured out. The U.S. Bishops did as much in their pastoral letters *The Challenge of Peace* (1983) and *Economic Justice for All* (1986). Such a strategy made their letters morally challenging without being dogmatic. They were able to show that the gospel does have implications while at the same time stimulating dialogue on crucial issues of peace and human dignity. We could do well to model such pastoral leadership in our preaching.

4. *Respect the experience and competence of the congregation.*

The congregation is made up of diverse people with a wealth of knowledge and expertise that no one preacher can ever match in scope and depth. We ought to speak to the people with a respect for their ability to address their own struggles and make prudential decisions in a thoughtful way. Encouraging and supporting them to draw upon their own experience and competence is a way to promote moral maturity in the congregation and it is a way to witness to the respect due to conscience.

When we realize that the Sunday homily remains for many people their only contact with the interpretation of the Bible, preaching becomes an awesome pastoral responsibility. Preaching is a just ministry when it is faithful to the text, to experience, and to the community. Being faithful in these ways gives the preached word a greater chance of naming the movements of grace stirring in the lives of the people, and it avoids creating the impression that the preacher is morally absent or neglecting the pastoral care that engages life's experiences from convictions of faith and values.

MANAGING FINANCES

The practical matter of administration, especially of managing money, is a way of doing justice to the community. Yet, if we can rely on anecdotal evidence, many of us find this aspect of pastoral care to be the most disagreeable part of ministry, not only because it is so time consuming, but also because so many of us are not good at doing it. Fr. Ray in our opening scenario represents those who have not yet developed an ability to manage money. Yet managing finances is integral to ethical pastoral care. It can be off-putting because it has a ring of being secular, worldly, and materialistic. However, what if we approached it as a spiritual discipline and tried to see it as a practice that supports the faith life of the community?

Managing money is a spiritual discipline that not only expresses our relationship to God but also reflects our commitment to the community. In relation to God, managing money well is our way of thanking God for the gifts we have received through the work of human hands and the sacrifice people are making to support the mission of the church. Managing money well witnesses to a grateful heart. In relation to the community, managing money well reflects our interdependence and commitment to the common good. But if we misuse credit and accumulate debt personally and corporately, we can harm the community by generating a reputation of being unreliable, selfish, a poor risk, and unfit for pastoral leadership. We can become known as one who uses others to get out of debt or as someone who withdraws from the community in order to avoid the embarrassment of our recklessness. Managing money responsibly, however, is not only a good accounting skill but also a commitment to stewardship—a way of managing wisely what has been entrusted to us by others. Good stewardship will manifest itself in the way we develop a savings plan, spend within our limits, avoid conspicuous consumerism, and refuse to insist on professional discounts before making a purchase.

A just ministry opposes any financial arrangements that mismanage funds or curry favors through financial privileges. How money is raised and used reflects the just character of ministers. Catholics are already familiar with the precepts of the church that include the financial support of the church's mission. According to the *Catechism*, "The faithful also have the duty of providing for the material needs of the Church, each according to his abilities" (no. 2043). The footnote to this precept refers to canon 222, in which we learn that the laity, religious, and clerics are to provide financial support for the mission of the church. Robert Kaslyn's commentary on this canon reminds us of the church's right to ask the faithful to give financial support, and the bishops are to remind the faithful of this obligation.[18] Notice, however, that this precept and its corresponding canonical regulation focus our attention on what we owe the church. We also need to ask what the church, through its ministers, owes everyone else regarding our ways of obtaining and using money.

One of the byproducts of the sexual abuse scandal has been a focus on the way the church manages money. In light of the church's long-standing social teaching on labor, those employed by the church ought to be able to earn appropriate wages and benefits that support a decent way of living. More recently, in the shadow of the Enron and

Arthur Andersen scandals of fraudulent financial reporting, we ought to model social justice in the way we manage finances. A poor system of internal controls is often behind incidents of fraud.

The Committee on Budget and Finance of the NCCB has identified the minimal requirements for internal controls governing finances.[19] I summarize them here in order to show what a just ministry looks like in matters of managing money.

1. Honest and capable employees

This requirement affirms that character matters in managing money. While we certainly need good policies and appropriate structures, we also need honest and capable employees to implement them. For that reason, employees ought to be screened for their positions, educated on policies, and supervised in their performance.

2. Separation of duties

One of the key features of internal control is to keep financial duties separate. As a general rule, involving more people in the accounting system lessens the chances for fraud unless, of course, there is collusion. The separation of duties should prevent any one person from performing all aspects of a financial function. For example, the person who keeps the financial records should be separate from the person who authorizes funds; the person who prepares the checks should be separate from the person who signs them or who mails them; the person who has access to payroll records should be separate from the one who has access to personnel files; the person who counts the Sunday collection should be separate from the person who makes out the deposit slip, who is also separate from the one who records amounts to parishioner records, who is separate from the one who brings the money to the bank.

3. Authorization

Closely related to the separation of duties is the structural feature that requires daily financial operations to be carried out by the one authorized for the task. Their operations should be subject to specific guidelines for borrowing or disbursing funds.

4. Documentation

Maintaining good records is the key to transparency and to fair audits. Financial transactions should correspond with financial records.

Making checks payable to "cash" with no documentation for the expense is an example of abuse. Except for petty cash, all cash disbursement should be made by check corresponding with a receipt to ensure proper authorization of the expense and to have a record of receipts for audit.

5. *Physical control over assets and records*

Physical control of records means using barriers to access— locked rooms or drawers accessible only to those who are delegated to use them; computer files backed up and stored off site; storing important documents in fireproof safes. Control over assets involves an inventory of furniture and equipment as well as providing documentation for moving financial assets in and out of the organization.

6. *Verification of performance*

Verification occurs by periodically taking an inventory of furniture and equipment and by reconciling bank accounts with the general ledger. Annual audits by an independent accounting firm are also standard ways of verification. Audits should be the standard of practice when there is a change of leadership in any institution.

These elements of internal control help to establish the boundaries that distinguish "thine from mine." To keep the church's money clearly separate from one's own, church bank accounts should never be opened in the name of an individual but only of the institution. The pastor, who is canonically responsible for parish finances, should not mingle parish funds with his own account, nor should he ever borrow from the parish account.

Distinguishing "thine from mine" also means that money that was raised for or given to the church ought to be used by and for the church, whereas money that comes from salary or personal gifts belongs to us for our personal use. Everyone in the church needs to be able to tell the difference between money that is for personal use and money that belongs to the church. Fr. Ray, from the opening scenario, was having a hard time with this. A general rule in law and in ethics is that the intention of the donor ought to govern the use of the funds.[20] This means that monies given to the church should be used on the projects for which it was specified. If no conditions are placed on the contributions, then the church is free to use the money as it chooses. When a gift is given for a specific purpose, and the pastor sees that circumstances may change that would make this specification an imprudent use of the money, then the pastor, or the one responsible for these institutional funds, may want to ask the donor to be more flexible in designating its purpose.

The Bishops' Committee on Budget and Finance offers the following warning signs of fraudulent behavior:

Changes in an employee's lifestyle, spending habits, or behavior
Inventory shortages
Ignoring of internal and external policies or audit recommendations
Unusual banking activities
Decline in employee morale or attendance
Exceedingly high expenses or purchases
Unexplained budget variances

In summary, an ecclesial culture that forbids oversight is the breeding ground for fraud. Implementing structures of internal control, along with transparency, clarity, and honesty in accounting and vigilance in detecting fraud, can go a long way toward restoring trust in the church and in the integrity of ministers. The parish should know where the money comes from and where it goes. The people should be assured that their money is being spent on the purposes for which it was raised. Full financial reports should be made available on a regular basis, and there should be checks and balances in place to monitor the collection and expenditure of money.

PASTORAL MORAL GUIDANCE

Pastoral moral guidance is the art of the possible. That is to say, it focuses on the person and what that person can do based on his or her capacity of knowledge, freedom, and emotion to appreciate and choose moral values enshrined in moral standards. Pastoral moral guidance seeks the best possible expression of those values that the person can make at this time to satisfy what love demands. "Love one another as I have loved you" is our norm for living and must be followed continuously. However, there is a limit to what can be done by each person at each time in order to live truthfully, compassionately, and respectfully of self and others. To refuse to accept that we must try to do the best we can within our limits, and to demand perfect love from imperfect people, would be unwise and unhelpful. But to face the reality of our human sinfulness and to accept our limited ability to love is not to dissolve the gospel demand to be loving. Rather, it recognizes that we are still in need of conversion while we continue on the way to the full flowering of love.

Pastoral moral guidance assesses a person's capacity by asking, "To what extent are you able to appreciate and choose (that is, have the knowledge, freedom, and emotional stability for) a way of life that fulfills what love demands?" And, "Given where you are, what is the next step you can take toward the ultimate good of living according to God's call to love?" In this way, pastoral moral guidance is directed toward the best possible moral achievement of the person for now, while encouraging and supporting the person's openness and growth toward living the fullness of love. The attitude of the one seeking moral guidance should be one of openness to conversion and moral growth. The pastoral guide must first nurture that growth by helping the other see where he or she still needs to go, identify the obstacles that lie between here and there, and then assist the person in overcoming these obstacles.

Traditionally, pastoral guidance followed the principle of gradualism. This means that a person progresses one step at a time toward a deeper integration of what morality demands. For example, we may not always be able to fulfill immediately what justice, compassion, or fidelity demand of us. The pastoral moral guide must pay attention to what limits a person's ability to fulfill moral standards because of the state of his or her moral development or because of the impediments to his or her freedom. Each person moves toward the fullness of love only at the pace and to the extent that he or she can. The sensitive moral guide needs to respect the dynamic of conversion at work in a person's moral growth. The principle of gradualism is the basis for treating with compassion those who are not yet able to realize all that love may require of them. The pastoral guide is concerned with the next step in goodness the person can take for now.

In this understanding, pastoral moral guidance does not abandon moral standards when a person is not able to measure up to them and so give way to a softhearted sentiment that anything goes. Nevertheless, neither does the pastoral guide use those standards to beat a person into submission and berate the person for not measuring up. That would border on spiritual abuse. Pastoral guidance always holds in tension the standards of morality (such as those we find in the official teaching of the church) and the particular person's capacity for responsibility. In this way, the pastoral judgment of what to do will always be related to moral standards and subject to them, but the pastoral guide does not expect the standard to measure the limited achievement of the one seeking guidance. By helping a person reflect on where he or she is now in light of where he or she ought to be, the pastoral guide uses the standard to show where there is room for moral growth.

Holding in tension both moral standards and a person's capacity for action addresses the common dilemma of offering moral guidance: "How can I fulfill my professional responsibility as a formal representative of the church to uphold its moral teaching while, at the same time, honoring the struggle of those who sincerely try to live up to that teaching but are not yet able to integrate it fully?"

Pope John Paul II sets the direction for the responsible exercise of this pastoral task in his encyclical, *Veritatis Splendor*, especially in the section on conscience (chapter II, part II) and on obedience to God's law (chapter III, nos. 102–5). About striving to adhere to the objective norms of morality, he says, "Even in the most difficult situations, man must respect the norm of morality so that he can be obedient to God's holy commandment and consistent with his own dignity as a person" (no. 102).

To assist another in striving toward this goal, we must be able to represent as clearly as possible the objective norms of morality as reflected in the law of God, natural law, and the teaching of the church while also encouraging the full appropriation of the moral truth that these norms express.

However, in actual practice, we know that not everyone is able to make such a full appropriation. In his teaching on erroneous conscience and invincible ignorance, Pope John Paul II recognizes as much. Even the sincere conscience striving to know moral truth may not be able to internalize a commandment of God, a teaching of the church, or a valid precept of natural law disclosing an objective demand of the moral order (no. 62). He says, "It is possible that the evil done as the result of invincible ignorance or a non-culpable error of judgment may not be imputable to the agent; but even in this case it does not cease to be an evil, a disorder in relation to the truth about the good" (no. 63).

While a wrong judgment does not make something that is evil into something good, neither does it forfeit the dignity of conscience or render the person morally guilty. Conscience compromises its dignity only when it is culpably erroneous, that is, when it shows insufficient concern for what is true and good.

Pope John Paul II's position on the relation of conscience to objective morality and the respect we must have for the person while still presenting moral truth in a clear way reflects the long-standing Catholic moral and pastoral tradition.[21] This tradition realizes that *ought* implies *can*. This means that we are not to require a particular obligation in practice, however justifiable it may be theoretically, if the person, for good reason, cannot perform it. While everyone is required to do what he or she can, no one is ever required to do what is beyond his or her reach. The preeminent Catholic moral theologian of the past century, Bernard Haring, reflects the wisdom of Saint Alphonsus Liguori, the patron of moral theologians, in giving this pastoral advice: "One should never try to impose what the other person cannot sincerely internalize, except the case of preventing grave injustice toward a third person."[22] The implication of this wisdom is that we are accountable for doing what is within our capacity, and we are morally culpable for failing to do what we are capable of doing. So, two people facing the same situation (for example, a debilitating illness) can have different degrees of moral responsibility toward it.

It would be an offense against the dignity of conscience and a person's authentic freedom to force him or her to act against his or her sincere judgment of conscience, or to impose behavior prescribed by a norm that he or she cannot sincerely internalize. Pope John Paul II gives these instructions on the relation of presenting the official teaching of the church and respecting a person's capacity to appropriate it:

> Still, a clear and forceful presentation of moral truth can never be separated from a profound and heartfelt respect, born of that patient and trusting love which man always needs along his moral journey, a journey frequently weari-

some on account of difficulties, weakness and painful situations. (no. 95)

What may look to an outsider like an erring conscience may actually be the best possible appropriation of the truth that a person can make for now. A proper pastoral procedure, then, attempts both to expand a person's moral capacity by presenting objective moral truth and to maximize a person's strength by encouraging him or her to take the next step in love toward the full appropriation of the objective norms of morality. Such a perspective and procedure affirm that we can fulfill our duty to represent the church in its moral teachings and still be an understanding guide of persons striving to do what is right. An index of maturing in one's role as a pastoral moral guide is the ability to hold in tension what the moral standards say we ought to strive for and what a person is able to achieve for now because of limited moral capacities. Holding the tension does not dismiss the standard as irrelevant or demand that others be more capable than their growth allows.

In light of this understanding of the fundamental responsibility of pastoral moral guidance, I sketch a model of moral guidance based on three creative imperatives: Let there be understanding, let there be encouragement, and let there be challenge.[23]

1. Let there be understanding!

Our ultimate goal in providing moral guidance is to enable others to act in good conscience, that is, to live authentically according to what they believe is morally true so that they stand in right relationship with God. The Catholic moral tradition has been outstanding in the way it has upheld the primacy of conscience. Granted this teaching has been misused when it is taken as giving a license to do whatever one wants. However, the primacy of conscience does not mean that. It means that each person is responsible to form and follow conscience by answering the call of God as he or she discerns it in the depth of his or her being.

One way we can let understanding be is to listen without blame or judgment. What do we listen for? We listen for what others are asking of us. What they expect can often reflect their attitude toward authority. Some come wounded by the abuses of authority in the past and so have felt shame for not measuring up to moral standards. They may be defensive, suspicious, or feel that anyone who represents authority will be heavy-handed, if not downright abusive. Yet there is something that brings them back to seek guidance. We must be understanding and gentle.

Others may come to us with little or no respect for their own authority so they have unreal expectations of us. These are the ones who expect us to have all the answers, to be all knowing, always to be there when they need us, and ultimately to tell them what to do. We must resist the temptation and the invitation to be paternalistic with them.

Still others have learned to trust their own authority. They do not need to be told what to do, but they want to draw on us for clarity and for a broader vision so that they can take charge and give direction to their life in a more informed way. We must respect their freedom and dignity.

When we hear clearly what others expect of us, then we can be clear about what we can offer them. Perhaps it is information that they need, or someone to clarify their conflict, or to see further down the road than they can and identify some consequences that need to be considered, or someone to offer a religious interpretation to their experience. But if we don't listen with understanding, we won't be able to serve them in a way that enhances their knowledge, freedom, and emotional stability with regard to their issue. Without these, there is little likelihood that they will be able to act in conscience.

When we have given others a safe space to tell their story and the dilemma they face, they may uncover what they truly believe and care about with heartfelt commitment. For those seeking guidance, the present moral conflict is of a piece with other experiences, pressures, and choices. By helping them to see this situation within the context of the larger story of their lives, they can come to a more critical understanding of the sort of persons they have become, the moral strength and limitations with which they must work, and the direction in which their lives have been moving.

2. Let there be encouragement!

Since the primary responsibility of a decision belongs to the one making it, we ought to be concerned that he or she is making as honest a decision as possible. We can encourage this to the extent that we help others to recognize their values and to accept their moral character and the direction they want their lives to take. We can also help them to see patterns that have emerged in their lives as a result of prior choices. As chapter 3 on ministerial character showed, well-established patterns are a sign that we hold to certain convictions, that we have been building a certain character, and that we have established a basic commitment to a certain way of life. People take time to think through a moral decision and seek counsel in doing so because they want to set a clear and purposeful direction for themselves. This direction is generally a further development of the basic moral identity they have already achieved.

One way to let there be encouragement is by helping people set goals. From the earlier chapters on the virtues, we can draw some goal-setting questions in the language of virtue: Who do you want to become? What kind of life are you trying to create for yourself? How do you want to get there? By helping people understand themselves better and to set goals, we encourage them to discern more carefully whom they want to become and what they want to do. Remember that moral growth only happens when we take our own steps in our own way. Others may point out a direction for us, but if we don't ultimately choose that way for ourselves, then we are not making any moral progress. Not until we acknowledge and accept our limitations and our strengths will we possess our own moral capacity and be able to take the next step toward God's call to be loving.

3. Let there be challenge!

We can't stop with simply encouraging others to be conscientious, since sometimes a sincere judgment of conscience can bring great harm to others. If one is about to do harm to others, we need to use all the moral persuasion we can to prevent that from happening. Sometimes we might even have to intervene directly, or appeal to lawful authorities to intervene, in order to prevent others from inflicting harm on innocent parties.

More often than not, our challenge will come in the form of calling the other to conversion by raising larger questions (Whose interest is being served here? What kind of community will this make?), appealing to another set of values or principles (the common good over radical autonomy), invoking moral absolutes (murder, stealing), reframing the situation by means of another image (covenant over contract), or holding up as examples the lives of morally virtuous people (Thomas More or Mother Teresa) so that the one seeking guidance can become more self-critical and self-directing.

Another way that we can be challenging is by making distinctions where there are true differences. We all like to argue from analogy by comparing cases. However, not all aspects of our comparative cases are analogous. We need to recognize the differences. Moreover, too many times people want a simple answer to a complex question. Passing over the complexities of the case with a simple rule is not helpful. It avoids the challenge of critical reflection and too easily settles for pat answers in a morally complex world filled with shades of gray.

We can challenge critical thinking, too, by unearthing more of the "What if?" and "What else?" involved in every possible choice. These are simple questions, yet they make one think more deeply about the course of action one might want to pursue. I believe that more often than not we make the wrong choice not because we are unthinking but because we are just too unimaginative.

This, then, is my model of pastoral moral guidance. In this ministry of pastoral care, we can guide the process of making a moral decision by making a sincere effort to understand those seeking guidance, encourage them to make a sincere effort to discern what is morally fitting in light of moral standards and their capacity in the situation, and then challenge them by raising larger questions and a broader vision. If those seeking our guidance decide in a way other than we would, we must be able to honor their freedom of conscience, unless serious harm would come to themselves or others. Upholding the dignity of conscience demands no less. In the end, each of us is bound to live according to our own discernment of what God is asking of us.

Throughout this book I have tried to highlight the professional aspects of the vocation to pastoral ministry. My aim has been to stimulate a new attitude among pastoral ministers to view themselves as professionals and to take seriously the responsibilities that come with this identity. Viewing pastoral ministry professionally emphasizes the centrality of a person of good moral character who acquires theological competence and pastoral skills to serve the religious needs of the people in a trustworthy manner. It recognizes the inequality of power between the pastoral minister and the people and that their relationship must be managed so as to provide a safe haven for people to get their religious needs met without fear of being exploited.

This vision of professional ethics for ministry looks to Jesus as the model of pastoral service in his ministry of healing, reconciling, and liberating. But if we are to practice ministry in the spirit of Jesus, then we need to be part of the community of faith that tries to model its life on Jesus and to help one another be faithful and creative in the ways we witness to discipleship today. As a community with a shared mission, we can hold one another accountable to the ways we carry out our role and with the quality of service we provide. We need the church to be a true fellowship of support, challenge, and correction. It is not always, but it should teach us that ministry is a cooperative adventure through which we come to be a clearer sign and agent of God's love transforming the world.

Appendix

STATEMENTS OF MINISTERIAL COMMITMENT

This appendix brings together the main themes of this book and highlights some specific professional responsibilities in the form of two Statements of Ministerial Commitment. These statements were developed by two of my students who were introduced to the material in this book in their required course, "Professional Ethics in Ministry." The major project for this course was to develop a personal "Statement of Ministerial Commitment." The aim of this project was to synthesize the course in the form of a tailor-made set of guidelines that could be used as an instrument of accountability when serving in their ministries upon completing their theological training. These personal statements illustrate how others have incorporated this material into their vision of what developing a habit of mind as a professional minister would look like. The students have given me permission to use their statements here. Perhaps these student projects can serve as a model and inspiration for you to develop something similar in relation to your own ministry.

These statements are structured according to the fivefold set of responsibilities that are used in the document of the Canadian Conference of Catholic Bishops, *Responsibility in Ministry: A Statement of Commitment.*[1] The first is the statement of Mrs. Pat Morgan, who serves as a pastoral minister in a parish. The second is the statement of Br. Jeff Shackleton, OFM, who serves the disenfranchised in society through his Franciscan community.

STATEMENT OF MINISTERIAL COMMITMENT

MRS. PAT MORGAN

Introduction

My commitment to pastoral ministry in the parish springs from my baptismal promises. I believe that God revealed in Jesus is the ultimate source and sustainer of my life. I also believe that all life is sacred as it comes from the hand of God, especially everyone made in the image of God. I believe that God is always present in creation, in each human person, and in the relationships we form to make up our parish community. My commitment to ministry is a commitment to care not only for each person as an individual in this parish but also to care for individuals *in community*. Since the details of parish life, like the juggling of room assignments and managing egos, can sometimes be overwhelming and obscure the fundamental purpose of being a parish, I make this statement of commitment to remind myself that amidst the stressful realities of the parish God is calling me to regard this community as sacred ground.

As a Catholic Christian minister, I root myself in Christ who models for me the qualities of the minister as a servant-leader (John 13:14–15). I know that holding a ministerial position in the parish necessarily contains elements of power. But in imitating Christ's style of servant leader, this power need not be domineering or oppressive. Just as Christ shunned the power of domination for the loving power of service, so too do I commit myself to rejecting any use of power that will not serve to build up the life of this parish community.

My commitment to the sacredness of the ministerial relationship and to being a servant-leader demands that, among all the virtues that an effective and ethical pastoral ministry requires, I approach ministry above all with reverence and humility. Reverence disposes me to respect the other and to honor our relationship. Since this attitude will not always be easy to maintain, I make this statement of commitment to challenge myself to respect each person, especially in those instances when a parishioner is being difficult or confrontational. Likewise,

241

humility disposes me to recognize my own gifts honestly and to be grateful for them and for the gift of others. To imbue my pastoral ministry with the ideals of servant leadership and the sacredness of life, I must distance myself from any arrogance or pride.

A. Responsibilities to Those to Whom I Minister

Desiring to model my ministry after Jesus and to exercise leadership that is about service, not power, and that calls and enables others to serve, I will:

Address the spiritual needs of those I serve in light of their total human experience (the intrapersonal, interpersonal, structural and environmental aspects of life)

Encourage parishioners to develop their gifts through the process of theological reflection

Ensure the proper care of those for whom I am responsible by recognizing the limits of my expertise and referring parishioners to appropriate professionals when necessary

Develop and maintain a network of those community services and resources that could benefit parishioners

Continue to develop knowledge and skills needed for ministry through a regular plan of ongoing education

Respect those who have entrusted me with their private thoughts by maintaining strict confidentiality unless a clear danger exists for them or for others

Evaluate on a regular basis how I am managing the differences of power in my pastoral relationships in order to ensure that I am not abusing my power by becoming manipulative or exploitative

Maintain primarily professional relationships with parishioners by not encouraging dual relationships

Endeavor to lead an exemplary life in order that I may never be a source of scandal for those to whom I minister

Be clear and unambiguous in my words and actions so that the care and concern I show in ministering to parishioners is not misinterpreted

B. Responsibilities to Colleagues

Acknowledging that many gifts are present in the community and that effective ministry calls for a collaborative style, I will:

Value my colleagues as coworkers in our common ministry to the parish by drawing on their gifts rather than jockeying for power in our work situations

Encourage my colleagues to engage in the process of theological reflection in order to serve better the needs of the parish in which we minister

Confront colleagues if patterns of spiritual abuse or neglect are evident in their ministries and be willing to be personally open to the scrutiny of my colleagues in this regard

Hold in confidence any private information about colleagues (except in instances of unethical or illegal professional behavior and in cases of sexual abuse)

Maintain the integrity of the workplace by refraining from gossip

Maintain clear sexual boundaries with my coworkers to ensure that they cannot reasonably infer romantic interest

C. Responsibilities to the Diocesan and Universal Church

Recognizing that ministry is a function of the mission of the church, I will:

Practice the servant leadership modeled by Christ

Abide by all diocesan employment policies for staff members and all diocesan policies regarding volunteers and those for whom I am responsible

Abide by all diocesan guidelines and procedures for sexually ethical behavior in ministry and report all violations

Abide by diocesan and parish policies regarding the management of finances

D. Responsibilities to the Wider Community

Knowing that members of other faiths also seek God and mindful that social justice is an integral dimension of the Gospel, I will:

Be open to offering pastoral care to nonparishioners

Show my respect for the larger community by refraining from gossip and hurtful speech about community leaders

Ensure that my interactions with members of the wider community are not tarnished by exploitative or manipulative power plays

Remain connected with and show my support for the wider community by participating in community events

Recognize my responsibility to the community at large by working toward a more just and safer environment for all in our neighborhood

Encourage parish involvement in the surrounding neighborhood by supporting local initiatives

Foster dialogue with leaders of the neighboring centers of worship (churches, synagogues, and mosques) in order to create a positive and unified partnership within the community

E. Responsibilities to Self

Knowing that effective ministry calls for physical, emotional, and spiritual well-being, I will:

Take regular opportunities to nurture my personal relationships with my husband, family, and friends in order that I can have my own physical and emotional needs met apart from my pastoral relationships

Make spiritual direction and theological reflection an essential component of my life

Cultivate my personal relationship with God through daily prayer and meditation and through twice-yearly scheduled retreats

Obtain clearly stated expectations in any position for which I am hired

Recognize my limitations and be open to seeking the assistance
and expertise of others

STATEMENT OF MINISTERIAL COMMITMENT

BR. JEFF SHACKLETON, OFM

Introduction

As a Christian and a practicing Roman Catholic, I acknowledge
that my role as a disciple of Christ is inextricably intertwined with the
world in which I live. Echoing the ministerial theology of Vatican II,
John Paul II observes in the apostolic exhortation *Christifideles Laici*
that the threefold mission of Christ—that of priest, prophet, and
king—is a mission shared by all who are baptized (no. 14). Moreover,
Gaudium et Spes calls us to exercise our ministry within the context of
lived experience, amid the "the joy and hope, the grief and anguish" of
all humanity, "especially of those who are poor or afflicted in any way"
(no. 1). These ecclesial statements about mission and context shape
and inform the theological basis of my own commitment to ministry.
As a vowed religious in the Franciscan tradition, I envision participating in my own baptismal mission through direct service to the disenfranchised of our society, either in a parish setting or within the context
of a nonprofit organization.

My Statement of Commitment to Ministry is designed to support
and nurture my aspirations to be a minister of good moral character
who exercises the ministry in a skilled, competent manner. Among the
virtues I hope to express in ministry, I want to single out three that will
be especially significant to serving as a minister to the marginalized:
justice, fidelity, and generosity. Justice will dispose me to attend to the
social dynamics affecting the lives of the disenfranchised; fidelity disposes me to be trustworthy with my responsibilities; and generosity
disposes me to put the needs of others before the gratification of my
own. In my ministry to the disadvantaged, I will also give priority to
acquiring certain skills and knowledge related to my area of ministry,

245

especially language skills in Spanish and cultural customs of the Hispanic community.

A. Responsibilities to Those to Whom I Minister

Desiring to model my ministry after Jesus and to exercise leadership that is about service, not power, and that calls and enables others to serve, I will:

Provide those whom I serve with a level of ministry that reflects theological competency in my faith tradition and incorporates appropriate professional standards of practice. To this end, I will continue to expand my education through taking appropriate academic/school courses, reading journal articles and ministry-related materials, and participating in professional seminars and workshops

Acknowledge and claim the greater power I have in my relationships with those who receive my ministerial care, and regularly examine my exercise of authority to ensure that I empower the people I serve

Establish and maintain clear boundaries between myself and those to whom I minister

Examine my pastoral relationships on a regular basis for signs of boundary violations

Support the dignity of all persons to whom I minister by using and promoting inclusive, nondiscriminatory language

Refer those seeking my pastoral care to a qualified person if I do not have adequate expertise or time to address their needs

Refrain from physically intimate or personally exclusive relationships with the people I serve in my ministry

Refrain from sexually charged and sexually explicit language, and from sexual innuendo and sexualized humor

Monitor my use of touch in ministry, and familiarize myself with customs pertaining to physical contact held by the various cultures I serve in my ministry

Respect the privacy and dignity of those whom I serve by keeping the information they share with me confidential, unless I am given permission to share the information or I

perceive that maintaining confidentiality poses serious
threat of harm

Describe my "ground rules" of confidentiality to those seeking
my confidence, informing such persons that I will make
every effort to hold their information confidential except
in cases of threat to life, safety, or health

Make reasonable efforts to elicit voluntary disclosure in those
cases in which I must override the duty of confidentiality,
and then limit my disclosure to those who need to know,
and to what they need to know to prevent harm

Presume a duty of confidentiality in situations or instances
where an actual expectation of confidentiality is unclear

B. Responsibilities to Colleagues

Acknowledging that many gifts are present in the community and that effective ministry calls for a collaborative style, I will:

Hold myself accountable to both customary and explicitly artic-
ulated professional standards of conduct in my interaction
with my colleagues in ministry

Hold my ministerial colleagues accountable to maintaining
appropriate boundaries with those seeking pastoral care

Bring to the attention of those violating boundaries the inappropriate behavior that I see in their pastoral relationships

Report any reasonable suspicion of sexual boundary violations
with a minor to the police/child protective services, and to
the provincial minister of my religious community if the violation involves another member of my religious community

Acquaint myself with any policies in my place of work that refer
to neglectful and abusive behavior

Introduce the topics of spiritual neglect and spiritual abuse at
meetings with my ministerial colleagues in order to raise
awareness of these issues in our work environment

Bring to the attention of the offenders any instances of spiritual
abuse or neglect I detect in my place of ministry

Refrain from engaging in physically intimate or sexual relationships with my colleagues

Refrain from gossiping about my colleagues

Refrain from divulging personal information about my colleagues unless they have given me permission to do so or I
perceive there is a serious threat of harm in keeping the
information confidential

C. Responsibilities to Diocesan and Universal Church

Recognizing that ministry is a function of the mission of the church, I
will:

Seek out and hold myself accountable to applicable ministerial
guidelines or standards of practice issued by my diocese
and religious province, as well as appropriate guidelines or
ministerial formation materials offered by the Church

Familiarize myself with and hold myself accountable to guidelines established by my diocese and religious province
regarding managing finances

Familiarize myself with any expectations my diocese or religious
province may have regarding my ministry in order to be
trustworthy in fulfilling the duties that are part of my
ministry

Seek out and hold myself accountable to any applicable guidelines established by my diocese and religious province
regarding sexual boundary issues

Acquaint myself with and hold myself accountable to any applicable guidelines established by my diocese and religious
province regarding issues of confidentiality in ministry

D. Responsibilities to the Wider Community

Knowing that members of other faiths also seek God and mindful that
social justice is an integral dimension of the Gospel, I will:

Establish and maintain appropriate personal and professional
boundaries between myself and members of other faith
traditions, mindful of the fact that as a Catholic minister I
am a symbolic representation of my parish faith community, my religious order, and the Roman Catholic Church

Participate in workshops and forums with ministers of other
denominations and faith traditions to share wisdom and
information related to issues of justice and abuse

Take part in seminars and ongoing education opportunities with
ministers of other denominations and faith traditions to
share information and collective wisdom about sexual
boundary issues

Carefully monitor my place of ministry and my own ministerial
activity for manifestations of sexism, including sexist language, and make changes where possible

Participate in seminars and continuing education workshops with
ministers of other denominations and faith traditions to discuss and share information about legal issues in ministry

Familiarize myself with those areas of civil law, including
employment law, that pertain to my area of ministry

E. Responsibilities to Self

Knowing that effective ministry calls for physical, emotional, and spiritual well-being, I will:

Develop professional relationships with other ministers and
participate in professional or ministerial associations

Engage in regular self-care and renewal practices, setting aside
time for prayer, rest, exercise, proper nutrition, and, when
necessary, professional counseling

Nurture relationships with family and friends so that my needs
for companionship, intimacy, and confidentiality are met
outside of pastoral care relationships

Evaluate my pastoral and ministerial relationships on a regular
basis, especially any dual relationships, to identify signs of
impending or current boundary violations

Monitor my own personal and emotional well-being, giving
particular attention to boundary issues during those times
when I feel most needy

Evaluate my own behavior, setting aside a few minutes each day
to review my actions and to look for any signs of spiritual
neglect or spiritual abuse in my actions

JUST MINISTRY

Commit to maintaining a reasonable workload to reduce the
   danger of (a) acting out of anger, (b) neglecting ministerial
   duties, or (c) committing boundary violations
Identify those conditions and situations that tempt me to act in
   neglectful, abusive, or professionally inappropriate manners
Engage in spiritual direction on a monthly basis in order to
   have a place to share information about my spiritual
   journey in a safe, confidential environment
Seek the sacrament of reconciliation on a quarterly basis,
   availing myself of the sacramental healing of the Church
   and the gift of absolute confidentiality

NOTES

CHAPTER 1:
MINISTRY AS VOCATION

1. This sociological view is well represented by Patricia M. Y. Chang, "An Ethical Church Culture," in Jean M. Bartunek, Mary Ann Hinsdale, and James F. Keenan, eds., *Church Ethics and Its Organizational Context* (Lanham, MD: Rowman & Littlefield, 2006), 187–94.

2. This theological attitude is reflected in Thomas J. Reese, *Archbishop: Inside the Power Structure of the American Catholic Church* (San Francisco: Harper & Row, 1989), see 251.

3. A helpful resource for understanding vocation is a significant work on the classic Protestant doctrine of vocation by Douglas J. Schurman, *Vocation: Discerning Our Callings in Life* (Grand Rapids: Eerdmans, 2004); from the Catholic tradition with insights from contemporary psychology, see John Neafsey, *A Sacred Voice Is Calling* (Maryknoll: Orbis, 2006); and with a Quaker influence, see Parker J. Palmer, *Let Your Life Speak* (San Francisco: Jossey-Bass, 2000).

4. Secretariat for the Laity, National Conference of Catholic Bishops, *Called and Gifted: The American Catholic Laity*, Reflections of the American Bishops commemorating the fifteenth anniversary of the issuance of the *Decree on the Apostolate of the Laity* (Washington, DC: United States Catholic Conference, 1995).

5. Secretariat for the Laity, National Conference of Catholic Bishops, *Called and Gifted for the Third Millennium*, Reflections of the U.S. Catholic Bishops on the thirtieth anniversary of the *Decree on the*

Apostolate of the Laity and the fifteenth anniversary of *Called and Gifted* (Washington, DC: United States Catholic Conference, 1995).

6. Committee on the Laity, United States Catholic Conference of Catholic Bishops, *Co-workers in the Vineyard of the Lord: A Resource for Guiding the Development of Lay Ecclesial Ministry* (Washington, DC: United States Catholic Conference, 1995).

7. Brid Long, "Lay Ecclesial Ministry in the Parish," *New Theology Review* 19 (May 2006): 5–13.

8. National Conference of Catholic Bishops Committee on the Laity, *A Report of the Subcommittee on Lay Ministry. Lay Ecclesial Ministry: The State of the Question* (Washington, DC: United States Catholic Conference, 1999), 16.

9. I am indebted to a conversation with Michael Guinan for this interpretation of the call of Samuel as being more like the general experience of hearing the call of God. He has treated this story briefly in his segment of the essay, "Call/Vocation," in *The Collegeville Pastoral Dictionary of Biblical Theology*, edited by Carroll Stuhlmueller (Collegeville: Liturgical Press, 1996), 113–15.

10. These questions are inspired by the reflection on discernment by Michael J. Himes, *Doing the Truth in Love: Conversations about God, Relationships, and Service* (Mahwah: Paulist Press, 1995), 55–58.

11. Palmer, *Let Your Life Speak*, 19–20.

12. Ibid., 16. The full quote from Buechner is, "The place God calls you to is the place where your deep gladness and the world's deep hunger meet." Frederick Buechner, *Wishful Thinking: A Seeker's ABC* (San Francisco: HarperSanFrancisco, 1993), 119.

13. Edward P. Hahnenberg has written consistently of the communal role of a vocation to lay ecclesial ministry. See his "Wondering about Wineskins: Rethinking Vocation in Light of Lay Ecclesial Ministry," *Listening: Journal of Religion and Culture* 40 (2005): 7–22; "When the Church Calls," *America* 195 (October 9, 2006): 10–14; and "The Vocation to Lay Ecclesial Ministry," *Origins* 37 (August 30, 2007): 176, 178–82. For some good examples of how some men have heard the call to priesthood come through other people, see the vignettes of vocation provided by Paul Stanosz, *The Struggle for Celibacy* (New York: Crossroad, 2006), 106–13.

14. Hahnenberg, "When the Church Calls," 14.

CHAPTER 2:
MINISTRY AS PROFESSION

1. For this background of the term *professional*, see Dennis Campbell, *Doctors, Lawyers, Ministers: Christian Ethics in Professional Practice* (Nashville: Abingdon, 1982), 17–20.

2. John P. Beal, "Turning Pro: Theologico-Canonical Hurdles on the Way to a Professional Ethic for Church Leaders," in Jean M. Bartunek, Mary Ann Hinsdale, and James F. Kennan, eds., *Church Ethics and Its Organizational Context* (Lanham, MD: Rowman & Littlefield, 2006), 170–71.

3. Ibid., 171.

4. Ibid., 171–75.

5. For contrasting features of contract and covenant, see William F. May, *The Physician's Covenant* (Philadelphia: Westminster, 1990), esp. 73–103.

6. For a covenantal model of the moral life where these features are developed, see Joseph L. Allen, *Love and Conflict* (Nashville: Abingdon, 1984), 15–81.

7. On these qualities of God in the covenant and their related actions, I am drawing on Bruce C. Birch, *Let Justice Roll Down* (Louisville: Westminster/John Knox, 1991), 146–57.

8. The National Association for Lay Ministry, the National Federation for Catholic Youth Ministry, and the National Conference for Catechetical Leadership, *National Certification Standards for Lay Ecclesial Ministers* (Washington, DC: NALM, NCCL, NFCYM, 2003).

9. May, *Physician's Covenant*, 134.

10. The Episcopal Conference of Australia was the first conference to issue a code of ethics for ministers, but it was designed for clergy and religious. It did not include lay ecclesial ministers in its scope. See *Integrity in Ministry* (1999). Dioceses in this country have also begun to issue codes of ethics.

11. For a more detailed analysis of codes of ethics, see Joe E. Trull and James E. Carter, *Ministerial Ethics*, 2nd ed. (Grand Rapids: Baker Academic, 2004), 185–214.

CHAPTER 3:
THE MINISTER'S CHARACTER

1. This tripartite structure of a teleological virtue ethics is developed by Joseph J. Kotva Jr. in *The Christian Case for Virtue Ethics* (Washington, DC: Georgetown University Press, 1996), 17–20. This structure is used again by James Keenan in his essay "Virtue Ethics" in Bernard Hoose, ed., *Christian Ethics: An Introduction* (London: Cassell, 1998), 84–94. Keenan also uses this structure in his work coauthored with Daniel Harrington, *Jesus and Virtue Ethics: Building Bridges between New Testament Studies and Moral Theology* (Lanham, MD: Sheed & Ward, 2002).

2. Austin Fagothey, *Right and Reason*, 4th ed. (St. Louis: Mosby, 1967), was republished by Tan Books, New York, in 2001.

3. Antonio Damasio, *Descartes' Error* (New York: G. P. Putnam's Sons, 1994). Timothy O'Connell has made good use of Damasio's research to explain the place of feelings in acquiring and transmitting moral values. See *Making Disciples* (New York: Crossroad, 1998), 65–74.

4. Daniel Goleman, *Emotional Intelligence* (New York: Bantam, 1995).

5. Ibid., 195.

6. Ibid., 226.

7. Sydney Callahan, *In Good Conscience* (New York: Harper-Collins, 1991), 95–113; Charles Shelton, *Morality of the Heart: A Psychology of the Christian Moral Life* (New York: Crossroad, 1990), and his *Achieving Moral Health* (New York: Crossroad, 2000); Goleman, *Emotional Intelligence*.

8. For a survey of literature on emotions in the moral life among philosophers and psychologists, see William C. Spohn, "Passions and Principles," *Theological Studies* 52 (1991): 69–87. For a philosophical account of emotion based on Aristotle and in line with modern theories, see Nancy Sherman, The *Fabric of Character: Aristotle's Theory of Virtue* (Oxford: Clarendon Press, 1989), 44–50; also, Rosalind Hursthouse, "Virtue and the Emotions," in *On Virtue Ethics* (New York: Oxford University Press, 1999), 108–20; and Martha C. Nussbaum, *Upheavals of Thought: The Intelligence of Emotions* (New York: Cambridge University Press, 2001), esp. chap. 1, "Emotions as Judgments of Value," 19–88.

9. Daniel C. Maguire has contributed significantly to understanding the affective dimension of morality. See especially his *Moral Choice* (Garden City: Doubleday, 1978), 71–75, 84–86, 263–67, 281–305.

10. Callahan, *In Good Conscience*, 128.

11. Ibid., 101.

12. Saint Thomas called these the affective and spirited emotions *ST* I-II, q. 23., aa. 2, 4.

13. Sherman, *Fabric of Character*, 47.

14. Sidney Callahan, "The Role of Emotion in Ethical Decisionmaking," *Hastings Center Report* 18 (June/July 1988): 14.

15. Aristotle, *Nichomachean Ethics*, Book II at 1106b 20 and 1109a 25.

16. Ibid., Book III at 1114b; Iris Murdoch, *The Sovereignty of Good* (New York: Schocken, 1971); Lawrence A. Blum, *Moral Perception and Particularity* (New York: Cambridge University Press, 1994), 30–61.

17. Iris Murdoch, "The Idea of Perfection," in *Sovereignty of Good*, 37.

18. H. Richard Niebuhr, *The Responsible Self* (New York: Harper & Row, 1963), 63.

19. Alice Walker, *The Color Purple* (New York: Washington Square Press, 1982); for the whole scene, see 175–79.

20. As quoted in Charles R. Foster, et al., *Educating Clergy* (San Francisco: Jossey-Bass, 2006), 22.

21. Charles E. Curran, "The Stance of Moral Theology," in *New Perspectives in Moral Theology* (Notre Dame: Fides, 1974), 47–86. More recently Jack Mahoney has proposed creation, sin, salvation, and fulfillment as the four beliefs about God that ought to be the ultimate moral resource for living our faith. See his "Christian Doctrines, Ethical Issues, and Human Genetics," *Theological Studies* 64 (December 2003): 719–49.

22. For a review of this research, see Callahan, *In Good Conscience*, 186–90; see also Shelton, *Morality of the Heart*, 33–59, and *Achieving Moral Health*, 124–39.

23. John Shea, *Starlight* (New York: Crossroad, 1992), 102–3.

24. Ibid., 103.

25. *Nicomachean Ethics*, Book II, 1106a 15.

26. This theme has been explored to great effect in the popular book by Malcolm Gladwell, *Blink* (New York: Little, Brown, 2005).

27. *ST* I, q. 6, ad. 3; *ST* I-II, q. 58, a. 5.

28. *Nicomachean Ethics*, Book VI, 1143b 14.

29. Ibid., Book II, 1103b.

30. Ibid., Book II, 1105a 30.

31. Ibid., Book II, 1103b 25.

32. Frederic Maples and Katarina Schuth, "Character and Assessment of Learning for Religious Vocation: Interview Study of Roman Catholic Students and Faculty," *Theological Education* 40 (2005): 1–45.

33. William F. May, "Professional Ethics: Setting, Terrain, and Teacher," in Daniel Callahan and Sissela Bok, eds., *Ethics Teaching in Higher Education* (New York: Plenum, 1980), 231.

34. *Nicomachean Ethics*, Book II, 1103b 14–21.

35. On appealing to the paradigmatic individual, see Harold Alderman, "By Virtue of a Virtue," in Daniel Statman, *Virtue Ethics: A Critical Reader* (Washington, DC: Georgetown University Press, 1997), 145–64.

36. On this notion of moving imaginatively from the story of Jesus to the present situation by analogical reasoning, see William C. Spohn, *Go and Do Likewise* (New York: Continuum, 1999), 50–71.

37. For this interpretation of the foot-washing scene, see Sandra Schneiders, "The Foot Washing (John 13: 1–20): An Experiment in Hermeneutics," *Catholic Biblical Quarterly* 43 (January 1981): 76–92; see esp. 80–88.

38. Information about Fr. Raymond Carey's workshops is available from National Religious Vocation Conference in Chicago, Illinois (773-363-5454).

39. Spohn, *Go and Do Likewise*, 14.

40. Joseph Kotva Jr., "Transformed in Prayer," in James F. Keenan and Joseph Kotva Jr., eds., *Practice What You Preach* (Franklin, WI: Sheed & Ward, 1999), 147–56.

41. Paul J. Wadell, "What Do All Those Masses Do for Us?" in Kathleen Hughes and Mark R. Francis, eds. *Living No Longer for Ourselves* (Collegeville: Liturgical Press, 1991), 153–69.

42. On the link between virtue and community, see Lawrence A. Blum, "Virtue and Community," in *Moral Perception and Particularity* (New York: Cambridge University Press, 1994), 144–69.

43. Paul J. Wadell has given an extensive analysis of friendship for moral formation in *Friendship and the Moral Life* (Notre Dame: University of Notre Dame Press, 1989) and in *Becoming Friends* (Grand Rapids: Brazos, 2002). See also the short essay by Joseph Kotva Jr., "Seeking Out Good Friends," in Keenan and Kotva, *Practice What You Preach*, 71–80.

44. Timothy O'Connell has provided a helpful analysis of the role of mentors and models in moral formation in *Making Disciples* (New York: Crossroad, 1998), 87–94.

45. For this understanding of culture, see Robert Bellah et al., *Habits of the Heart* (Berkeley: University of California Press, 1985), 333.

46. James Davidson Hunter, *The Death of Character* (New York: Basic Books, 2000), 163.

CHAPTER 4:
THE VIRTUOUS MINISTER

1. James F. Keenan, "Proposing Cardinal Virtues," *Theological Studies* 56 (December 1995): 709–29. In this proposal, Keenan does not elaborate on the virtue of charity. In a later rendition of his cardinal virtues, Keenan replaces "self-care" with "self-esteem." See his *Virtues for Ordinary Christians* (Kansas City: Sheed & Ward, 1996), 70–75.

2. A helpful interpretation of charity as friendship with God is in Paul J. Wadell, *Friendship and the Moral Life* (Notre Dame: University of Notre Dame Press, 1989), 120–41; and also in his *The Primacy of Love* (New York: Paulist Press, 1992), 63–78.

3. *ST* II-II, q. 23, a. 1, ad. 2.

4. *Lumen Gentium*, V.

5. For an excellent analysis of self-love, see Edward C. Vacek, *Love, Human and Divine: The Heart of Christian Ethics* (Washington, DC: Georgetown University Press, 1994), esp. chaps. 6 and 7.

6. *ST* I-II, q. 51.

7. This pattern of the "imitation of God" for the moral life is drawn out more completely by James M. Gustafson, *Can Ethics Be Christian?* (Chicago: University of Chicago Press, 1975), 114–16.

8. Robert Emmons, *Thanks!* (Boston: Houghton Mifflin, 2007), 6.

9. John Shea, *Starlight* (New York: Crossroad, 1993), 83.

10. Gustafson, *Can Ethics Be Christian?*, 100.

11. Emmons, *Thanks!*, 9.

12. Ibid., 185–209 for ten suggestions on practicing gratitude.

13. Elizabeth A. Johnson, *She Who Is* (New York: Crossroad, 1992), see esp. 179–85, 266–69.

14. Eric J. Cassell, *The Nature of Suffering* (New York: Oxford University Press, 1991), 30–47.

15. James F. Keenan, *Moral Wisdom* (Lanham, MD: Rowman & Littlefield, 2004), 68–69.

16. Stanley Hauerwas, *Naming the Silences* (Grand Rapids: Eerdmans, 1990), 53.

17. Daniel Callahan, *The Troubled Dream of Life* (Washington, DC: Georgetown University Press, 2002), 96–97.

18. The link of humility to self-esteem is developed by James Keenan, *Virtues for Ordinary Christians* (Kansas City: Sheed & Ward, 1996), 71.

19. On this interpretation of humility as the practice of seeking self-knowledge, see Lisa Fullam, "Humility: A Pilgrim's Virtue," *New Theology Review* 19 (May 2006): 46–53.

20. Ernest Hemingway, *The Old Man and the Sea* (New York: Simon & Schuster, Scribner Paperback Fiction, 1995), 110.

21. Viktor Frankl, *Man's Search for Meaning*, trans. Ilse Lasch, rev. ed. (New York: Simon and Schuster, 1962), 65.

22. On piety as a virtue, see James Gustafson, "Say Something Theological," 1981 Ryerson Lecture at the University of Chicago, 5–7; see also Mark Allan Powell, *Loving Jesus* (Minneapolis: Fortress, 2004), 18–22.

23. *Nicomachean Ethics*, Book III, 1115a 30.

24. *ST*, II-II, q. 124, aa. 2, 3.

25. These are the three elements of courage that Rushworth M. Kidder uses to structure his book, *Moral Courage* (New York: Morrow, 2005).

26. As adapted from the John Wayne reference in Kidder, *Moral Courage*, 9.

CHAPTER 5: THE DYNAMICS OF POWER

1. On the implications for ministry of a baptismal spirituality, see Michael Downey, "Ministerial Identity: A Question of Common Foundations," in Susan K. Wood, ed., *Ordering the Baptismal Priesthood* (Collegeville: Liturgical Press, 2003), 3–25. See also Edward Hahnenberg, *Ministry: A Relational Approach* (New York: Crossroad, 2003).

2. See the essays in Richard Miller, ed., *Lay Ministry in the Catholic Church: Visioning Church Ministry through the Wisdom of the Past* (Liguori: Liguori Publications, 2005).

3. The theme of the risk of ethical misconduct by minimizing or ignoring our power runs through the book of Marilyn R. Peterson, *At Personal Risk: Boundary Violations in Professional-Client Relationships* (New York: Norton, 1992).

4. James D. Whitehead and Evelyn Eaton Whitehead, *The Promise of Partnership: A Model for Collaborative Ministry* (San Francisco: HarperCollins, 1993), 63–86.

5. Taken from the videotape *Choosing the Light: Victims of Clergy Sexual Misconduct Share Their Stories* (Milwaukee: Greater Milwaukee Synod of the ELCA, May 22, 1990).

6. Ibid.

7. Whitehead and Whitehead, *Promise of Partnership*, 81.

8. The image of "chalk on our shoes" to convey a boundary violation is the image of Raymon E. Mason as found in William J. Byron, *The Power of Principles* (Maryknoll: Orbis, 2007), 37.

9. Such a view is advocated by Carter Heyward, *When Boundaries Betray Us* (New York: HarperCollins, 1993).

10. A "friendship" model for ministry is advocated by Lynn N. Rhodes, *Co-Creating: A Feminist Vision of Ministry* (Philadelphia: Westminster, 1987).

11. See, for example, the perspectives advocated by Marie Fortune, "The Joy of Boundaries," and Karen Lebacqz and Ronald G. Barton, "Boundaries, Mutuality, and Professional Ethics," in *Boundary Wars*, ed. Katherine Hancock Ragsdale (Cleveland: Pilgrim, 1996), 78–95 and 96–110.

12. *Choosing the Light.*

13. Martha Ellen Stortz, *PastorPower* (Nashville: Abingdon, 1993), 111–17.

14. Peterson, *At Personal Risk*, 64.

15. Ibid., 117–19.

16. The interview with Fr. John Madigan was conducted by Terry McGuire, associate editor of the *Progress*, newspaper of the Archdiocese of Seattle, and reprinted with permission in *Touchstone*, a publication of the National Federation of Priests' Councils, Vol. 9 (Spring 1994): 1.

17. Peterson, *At Personal Risk*, 154.

18. Ibid., 155.

19. For this I am relying on the analysis of power as found in James D. and Evelyn Eaton Whitehead, *The Emerging Laity* (New York: Doubleday, 1988), 35–49.

20. Edgar H. Schein, *Organizational Culture and Leadership* (San Francisco: Jossey-Bass, 1986), 6.

21. On four different cultures influencing the U.S. Bishops' response to the sexual abuse crisis, see Chester Gillis, "Cultures, Codes and Publics," *America* 187 (July 29–August 5, 2002): 8–11.

22. Schein, *Organizational Culture and Leadership*, 13–20.

23. Whitehead and Whitehead, *Emerging Laity*, 42–44.

24. On the clerical culture, see Donald Cozzens, *Sacred Silence* (Collegeville: Liturgical Press, 2002), 112–23; also Michael L. Papesh, "Farewell to the 'Club,'" *America* 186 (May 13, 2002): 7–11; and his *Clerical Culture, Contradiction and Transformation* (Collegeville: Liturgical Press, 2004).

25. I have taken this key insight for professional ethics on the limits of virtue in light of the influence of social power in institutional structures from Karen Lebacqz, *Professional Ethics: Paradox and Power* (Nashville: Abingdon, 1985), esp. chap. 9, 137–51. This same theme on the limit of virtue and the influence of the social setting on behavior is developed at great length in John M. Doris, *Lack of Character* (New York: Cambridge University Press, 2002).

26. Lebacqz, *Professional Ethics*, 128–29.

27. Darrell Reeck, *Ethics for the Professions: A Christian Perspective* (Minneapolis: Augsburg, 1982).

28. Rollo May, *Power and Innocence* (New York: Norton, 1972); see esp. chap. 5, "The Meaning of Power," 99–119.

29. For this interpretation of liberating power in the ministry of Jesus, see John Shea, "Jesus' Response to God as Abba: Prayer and Service," in Francis A. Eigo, ed., *Contemporary Spirituality: Responding to the Divine Initiative* (Villanova: Villanova University Press, 1983), 54.

30. For this interpretation, I am following Shea, "Jesus' Response to God as Abba," 53.

31. For this interpretation, see Mary Daniel Turner, "Woman and Power," *The Way Supplement* 53 (Summer 1985): 113–14.

32. For this interpretation of the passion from the perspective of power, see Donald Senior, "Passion and Resurrection in the Gospel of Mark," *Chicago Studies* 25 (April 1986): 21–34, esp. 25–27.

CHAPTER 6: SEXUALITY

1. Two helpful sources for understanding the "promise and peril" of sexuality are Evelyn Eaton and James D. Whitehead, *A Sense of Sexuality* (New York: Doubleday, 1994), and Karen Lebacqz and Ronald G. Barton, *Sex in the Parish* (Louisville: Westminster/John Knox, 1991), esp. chaps. 1 and 2.

2. On the connections between sexuality and spirituality, see James B. Nelson, *Between Two Gardens: Reflections on Sexuality and Religious Experience* (New York: Pilgrim, 1983), 3–15.

3. Peter Rutter, *Sex in the Forbidden Zone* (New York: Ballentine Fawcett Crest, 1989).

4. Michael Crichton, *Disclosure* (New York: Knopf, 1993).

5. Rutter, *Sex in the Forbidden Zone*, 22.

6. These two documents are available on the USCCB Web site at http://www.usccb.org/ocyp/charter.shtml and http://www.usccb.org. ocyp/norms.schtml.

7. On judging the experience of others through feedback loops and putting on notice, see Peter Rutter, *Sex, Power and Boundaries* (New York: Bantam, 1996), 19–22. Rutter explains here that it is unusual for a person to be charged for harassment on a one-time behavior (unless it is an egregious physical or verbal act), but there must be a pattern of crossing boundaries by failing to read the feedback of the recipient.

8. David Mamet, *Oleanna* (New York: Vintage Books, 1992), 70.

9. For a brief treatment of the substance of the manualist teaching, see Bernard Haring, *The Law of Christ*, Vol. III, *Special Moral Theology*, trans. Edwin G. Kaiser (Westminster: Newman Press, 1966), 296–98.

10. Rutter, *Sex, Power and Boundaries*. Managing fantasy is the theme of chap. 4.

11. Ibid., 92–98.

12. Jennifer Schneider and Robert Weiss, *Cybersex Exposed* (Center City, MN: Hazelden, 2001), 7.

13. Patrick Carnes, David L. Delmonico, and Elizabeth Griffin, *In the Shadows of the Net: Breaking Free of Compulsive Online Sexual Behavior* (Center City, MN: Hazelden, 2001), 10–12.

14. Ibid, 14.

15. David Delmonico and Elizabeth Griffin, "In the Shadows of the Net: Understanding Cybersex in the Seminary," *Seminary Journal* 9 (Winter 2003): 42.

16. Carnes et al., *In the Shadows of the Net*, 32–38. See also ibid.

17. Carnes et al., *In the Shadows of the Net*, 26–27.

18. Although Margaret Farley does not use the virtues of justice and fidelity in quite this way, her work on sexual ethics has highly influenced my interpretation of what justice and fidelity demand. See her *Just Love* (New York: Continuum, 2006), esp. 215–32.

19. Melvin Blanchette, "Transference and Countertransference," in Barry Estadt, John Compton, and Melvin C. Blanchette, eds., *The Art of Clinical Supervision: A Pastoral Counseling Perspective* (New York: Paulist Press, 1987), 83–96; and Robert J. Wicks, "Countertransference and Burnout in Pastoral Counseling," in Robert J. Wicks, Richard D. Parsons, and Donald Capps, eds., *Clinical Handbook of Pastoral Counseling*, Vol. I, exp. ed. (New York: Paulist Press, 1993), 76–96.

CHAPTER 7: CONFIDENTIALITY

1. Sissela Bok, *Secrets* (New York: Vantage Books, 1983), 119.
2. Ibid., 24.

3. *Catechism of the Catholic Church*, no. 1467.

4. Ibid.

5. All translations of the canons are taken from John P. Beal, James A. Coriden, and Thomas Green, eds., *New Commentary on the Code of Canon Law* (New York: Paulist Press, 2000), 1163.

6. Ibid., 1164.

7. Ibid., 1163.

8. Ibid., 1165.

9. Ibid., 1681.

10. Ibid.

11. On the need for caution in this question of a possible release of the confessor from the obligation of the seal, see Dexter S. Brewer, "The Right of a Penitent to Release the Confessor from the Seal: Considerations in Canon Law and American Law," *The Jurist* 54 (1994): 424–76. After reviewing arguments for and against the right of the penitent to release a confessor from the seal, Brewer concludes that the prevailing canonical and theological view is that there are times when a penitent can do so, but the confessor must be certain of the penitent's free and explicit consent, and the priest must take every precaution to guard against scandal resulting from a misunderstanding by the community.

12. Thomas Green's commentary on this canon notes the incident of a prisoner's confession being taped without the confessor's knowledge. See Beal et al., *New Commentary*, 1592–93. See also "A Prisoner's Secretly Taped Sacramental Confession," *Origins* 26/3 (June 6, 1996): 33, 35–36; "Recording of Prisoner's Sacramental Confession Violated Rights," *Origins* 26/33 (February 6, 1997): 537, 539–45.

13. Mary Angela Shaughnessy, *Ministry and the Law* (New York: Paulist Press, 1998).

14. For a summary of all fifty state statutes on the clergy privilege, see Donna Krier Ioppolo, "Statutes and Court Decisions of the Fifty States," in *Confidentiality in the United States: A Legal and Canonical Study* (Washington, DC: Canon Law Society of America, 1988), 49–92; see also Ronald K. Bullis and Cynthia S. Mazur, *Legal Issues and Religious Counseling* (Louisville: Westminster/John Knox, 1993), 82–89. Since changes are made to these statutes with some frequency, these statements ought not to be substitutes for direct legal advice.

15. These differences and complexities are well delineated in the following: Jacob M. Yellin, "The History and Current Status of the Clergy-Penitent Privilege," *Santa Clara Law Review* 23 (1983): 95–156; Donna Ioppolo, "Civil Law and Confidentiality: Implications for the Church," in *Confidentiality in the United States*, 3–47; and Bullis and Mazur, *Legal Issues and Religious Counseling*, 68–80.

16. See Ioppolo, "Civil Law and Confidentiality," 8.

17. Ibid., 9–10; also, Ronald P. Stake, "Professionalism and Confidentiality in the Practice of Spiritual Direction," *The Jurist* 43 (1983): 214–32; also, Bullis and Mazur, *Legal Issues and Religious Counseling*, 71–72.

18. Iopollo, "Civil Law and Confidentiality," 10–11.

19. Ibid., 12.

20. Richard B. Couser, *Ministry and the American Legal System* (Minneapolis: Fortress, 1993), 267.

21. James A. Serritella, "Confidentiality, the Church, and the Clergy," *Proceedings of the Forty-Eighth Annual Convention of the Canon Law Society of America* (1986): 88. A similar proposal was made earlier by Stake, "Professionalism and Confidentiality in the Practice of Spiritual Direction," 229–30; for his model statute, see 231–32.

22. Seritella, "Confidentiality," 92.

23. *The Catechism of the Catholic Church*, no. 2491. Even though "pastoral ministers" is not explicitly mentioned in this listing of "professions" in this article, they, too, would fall under the obligation of keeping a professional secret.

24. For a summary of this case, see John C. Bush and William Harold Tiemann, *The Right to Silence*, 3rd ed. (Nashville: Abingdon, 1989), 172–73.

25. Donna Ioppolo, "Civil Law and Confidentiality," 35–37; also, Ronald K. Bullis, "Child Abuse Reporting Requirements: Liabilities and Immunities for Clergy," *Journal of Pastoral Care* 44 (Fall 1990): 244–48; also, Alexander D. Hill and Chi-Dooh Li, "A Current Church-State Battleground: Requiring Clergy to Report Child Abuse," *Journal of Church and State* 32 (Autumn 1990): 795–811.

26. Marilyn Peterson, *At Personal Risk* (New York: Norton, 1992), 91.

27. Bok, *Secrets*, 91.

28. William H. Willimon makes a case for the positive role of gossip in "Heard about the Pastor Who…?" Gossip as an Ethical Activity," *Christian Century* 107 (October 31, 1990): 994–96.

29. Bok, *Secrets*, 93.

30. Cited in Willimon, "Heard about the Pastor Who…?" 994.

31. Thomas F. Taylor, *Seven Deadly Lawsuits* (Nashville: Abingdon, 1996), 41.

32. Ibid., 53.

CHAPTER 8: PASTORAL CARE

1. Decree on the Ministry and Life of Priests, no. 4.

2. The Bishops' Committee on Priestly Life and Ministry, *Fulfilled in Your Hearing* (Washington, DC: USCC, 1982).

3. Ibid, 29.

4. *Constitution on the Sacred Liturgy*, no. 52.

5. *Fulfilled in Your Hearing*, 17.

6. Donald Senior, "Not by Exegesis Alone: From Scholarship to Preaching," Church 2 (Fall 1986): 16.

7. *Fulfilled in Your Hearing*, 20.

8. Robert Waznak, "The Preacher and the Poet," *Worship* 60 (January 1986): 51.

9. *Fulfilled in Your Hearing*, 10.

10. On the role of biblical scholarship in preparing a homily, see Senior, "Not by Exegesis Alone," 16–17.

11. This incarnational theme of God's continuing to act is the core argument of the theology of preaching developed by Mary Catherine Hilkert, "Naming Grace: A Theology of Proclamation," *Worship* 60 (September 1986): 434–49.

12. *Fulfilled in Your Hearing*, 13–14.

13. Karen Lebacqz and Joseph Driskill have introduced the notion of spiritual neglect as a category of unethical professional conduct in ministers. Neglect involves failing to help someone thrive spiritually by violating the professional duty to act in the best interest of the other. As Lebacqz and Driskill claim, "To the extent that this [spiritual] growth and well-being [of churches and parishioners] is neglected, clergy are not providing good spiritual care, and are not

undertaking a central mandate of their calling. Spiritual neglect is therefore a serious matter for clergy." *Ethics and Spiritual Care* (Nashville: Abingdon, 2000), 103.

14. Lay preaching in Masses with children give us a hermeneutical principle that can be more broadly interpreted to apply to adult communities, too. William Skudlarek has appealed to such a broader interpretation to make his case for allowing lay preaching of homilies. See his "Lay Preaching and the Liturgy," *Worship* 58 (1984): 500–506.

15. My vision shares in many ways the model of pastoral leadership in social issues proposed by David Hollenbach, *Justice, Peace and Human Rights* (New York: Crossroad, 1988), see esp. chap. 13, "Preaching and Politics," at 209–11.

16. "Spiritual abuse" is a strong term. It is rather new in the literature on the professional conduct of ministers. Lebacqz and Driskill have surveyed its use to show that one of its primary characteristics is that spiritual abuse comes from a place of power. Often this power is expressed through a strong, control-oriented style of pastoral leadership that is not subject to accountability and so is beyond confrontation and correction. See *Ethics and Spiritual Care*, 129–37.

17. *Fulfilled in Your Hearing*, 26.

18. John P. Beal, James A. Coriden, and Thomas A. Green, eds., *New Commentary on the Code of Canon Law* (New York: Paulist Press, 2000), 282.

19. Committee on Budget and Finance, NCCB, "Diocesan Internal Controls" (Washington, DC: USCCB, 1995).

20. Cynthia S. Mazur and Ronald K. Bullis, *Legal Guide for Day-to-Day Matters* (Cleveland: United Press, 1994), 105.

21. Bernard Haring, *Free and Faithful in Christ*, Vol. 1, *General Moral Theology* (New York: Seabury Press, 1978), see esp. 239–43 on the erring conscience and culpability. See also a brief summary of the tradition on this theme in Linda Hogan, *Confronting the Truth: Conscience in the Catholic Tradition* (New York: Paulist Press, 2000), 81–85.

22. Haring, *Free and Faithful in Christ*, 289.

23. James Keenan has offered another approach to offering moral guidance that includes much of what I include here plus more. See his "On Giving Moral Advice" in *Commandments of Compassion* (Franklin, WI: Sheed & Ward, 1999), 109–17.

APPENDIX: STATEMENTS OF MINISTERIAL COMMITMENT

1. Canadian Conference of Catholic Bishops' Ad Hoc Committee on Responsibility in Ministry, *Responsibility in Ministry: A Statement of Commitment, Origins* 25 (March 14, 1996): 633, 635–36.

INDEX

Index

Power: assessing use of, 151–54; nature of, 123–43; personal, 123; social, 143; sources of, 123–25

Preaching: ethics of, 221–24; on moral issues, 225–27

Prudence: as a virtue, 93–95

Seal of confession, 196–99

Self-esteem: as a virtue, 89–93

Sexuality: definition, 159; peril of, 160; promise of, 159; sexual abuse, 161–63; sexual exploitation, 163–64; sexual fantasy, 166–68; sexual harassment, 164–66; sexualized behavior, 160–78

Spiritual abuse, 225, 233, 247, 250, 253n16

Spiritual neglect, 224, 247, 250, 253n13

Spiritual practices: and forming character, 77, 80; and holiness, 109–10; and preaching, 221; and self-care, 187

Symbolic representative, 30, 36; as source of power, 126–28, 158; and touch, 174

Theological reflection, 31–34, 124, 223, 242, 243, 244

Touch: as sexualized behavior, 172–78, 246

Transference and counter-transference, 184–85

Trust: and boundaries, 129–33; and code of ethics, 39–40; and confidentiality, 190ff.; and covenant, 27–28

Virtue, 60–65; cardinal, 83–95; everyday, 96–115; and virtue ethics, 44ff.

Vocation, 3–5